D1649364

IN THE FULLNESS OF LIFE:
A BIOGRAPHY
OF
DOROTHY KAZEL, O.S.U.

April 20, 2012

Dear Maggie,

May you continue to live the spirit of Dorothy, and like her, promote justice and spread joy wherever you go; may you always live life fully! Congratulations on this honorable award.

God bless you always,

Cynthia Glavac, OSU

IN THE FULLNESS OF LIFE:
A BIOGRAPHY
OF
DOROTHY KAZEL, O.S.U.

Cynthia Glavac, O.S.U.

DIMENSION BOOKS
Denville, New Jersey 07834

Excerpts from '"Fight Sexism, Paternalism in Church' — Kane" by Mary Badar Papa reprinted with permission of the *National Catholic Reporter*, 115 East Armour Boulevard, Kansas City, Missouri 64111.

Excerpts from *Gifts from the Poor* by John F. Loya, 1990, used with permission by Winston-Derek Publishers Group, Inc., P.O. Box 90883, Nashville, Tennessee 37205.

Excerpts from "The Peace Progress in El Salvador (A Hermeneutic of Suspicion)" reprinted with permission of America Press Inc., 106 West 56th Street, New York, NY 10019. In the absence of Daniel Santiago, O.Carm. ©1995 All Rights Reserved.

Excerpts from *Salvador Witness: The Life and Calling of Jean Donovan* reprinted by permission of the William Morris Agency, Inc. on behalf of the author. Copyright ©1984 by Ana Carrigan.

The map of El Salvador, which appears in *The Same Fate as the Poor*, 1995, by Judith Noone, M.M., used with the permission of Orbis Books, P.O. Box 308, Maryknoll, New York 10545-0308.

The poem "Adelante" reprinted with permission of Renny Golden, Northeastern Illinois University, 5500 N. St. Louis, Chicago, Illinois 60625.

The poem "I Want New Saints" by Mary A. Bowen, which appears in *Women Psalms*, 1992, used with the permission of Saint Mary's Press, 702 Terrace Heights, Winona, Minnesota 55987-1320.

Copyright ©1996 Cynthia Glavac, O.S.U.
ISBN 0-87193-289-X
All rights reserved.

For my parents, Mary and Robert,
my Cleveland Ursuline Congregation,
and Ursulines everywhere who incarnate
the voice and vision of
Angela Merici and Dorothy Kazel

"If one must live, let it be done so fully; if one must die, let it be for something worthwhile."

Rev. Alfred Winters,
funeral homily for Dorothy Kazel, O.S.U.,
Cathedral of St. John the Evangelist,
Cleveland, Ohio, December 10, 1980

Cover: Dorothy is sitting on a stone formation in Machu Picchu, Peru, where according to legend, centuries ago the Incas sacrificed young virgins in thanksgiving to Mother Earth, or "Pacha Mama." The sacrificial blood flowed through the crevices of the stone slabs, shaped like a condor, to the ground below. The photograph was taken by Martha Owen, O.S.U., in February 1978.

I Want New Saints

I want new saints
saints with birch-tree souls
whose leaves turn color and fall
whose cruel winters freeze their
naked branches.

I want saints with sunrise eyes
whose Springs awaken sweat-sweet fertility,
musk lusty,
played out on sodden sheets,
whose golden Summers bake
their bodies brown.

I want angry saints
with molten wills
who squeeze their carbon hearts
in rage and
bring forth diamonds,
weary saints,
torn by countless beatings.

Saints who make
extravagant mistakes
and laugh,
certain that, more than perfection,
God desires truth.

Mary A. Bowen

Contents

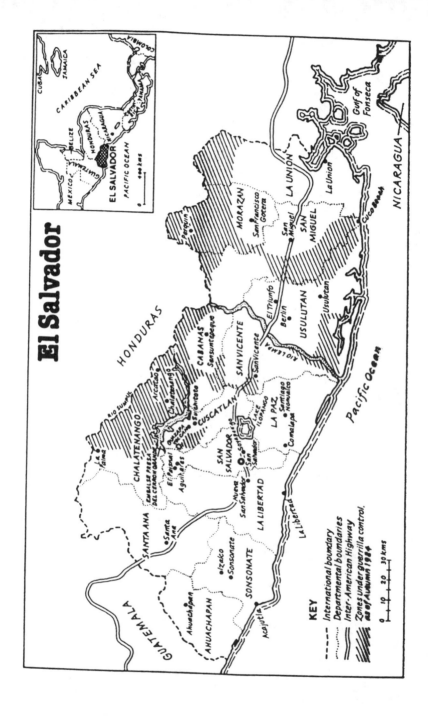

El Salvador

KEY
--- International boundary
···· Departmental boundaries
—— Inter-American Highway
////// Zones under guerrilla control.
as of Autumn 1984.

0 10 20 30 kms

Chronology

June 30, 1939	Born to Lithuanian-American parents, Joseph and Malvina Kazel, in Cleveland, Ohio; has an older brother, James who was born on November 10, 1936.
August 6, 1939	Baptized "Dorothea Lu."
1944-1953	Attends St. George Elementary School, Cleveland.
May 23, 1948	Receives her First Communion at St. George Church.
1953-1957	Attends Notre Dame Academy, Cleveland.
July 1955	Kazel family moves to Euclid, a suburb of Cleveland.
June 2, 1957	Graduates from Notre Dame Academy.
Summer 1957	Works as a medical secretary at Doctors' Hospital in Cleveland Heights and enrolls in St. John College, Cleveland.
1957-1959	Is a student in the "Cadet Program," an elementary teacher training program, at St. John College; works various part-time jobs in the Cleveland area.
Spring 1959	Is engaged to Donald Kollenborn.
Sept. 1959-June 1960	Teaches the third grade at St. Robert Bellarmine School in Euclid.
March 1960	Decides to break her engagement to enter the religious congregation of the Ursuline Sisters of Cleveland.
June 29, 1960	Formally applies to the Ursuline Sisters of Cleveland.
July 1960	Formally breaks her engagement to Donald Kollenborn.
September 8, 1960	Enters the novitiate of the Ursuline Sisters of Cleveland.

August 12, 1961	Receives the religious habit of the Ursulines and the religious name "Sister Mary Laurentine."
August 13, 1963	Professes vows for three years as an Ursuline Sister of Cleveland.
June 1, 1965	Graduates from Ursuline College, Cleveland.
1965-1972	Teaches typing, business, and religion courses at Sacred Heart Academy.
August 13, 1966	Renews vows for an additional two years.
November 1967	Volunteers to go to El Salvador to do missionary work.
August 13, 1968	Pronounces final vows as an Ursuline Sister of Cleveland.
Summer 1969	Teaches Catholic doctrine to Native Americans of the Papago Tribe in Topawa, Arizona.
Summer 1970	Begins graduate studies in guidance and counseling at John Carroll University, Cleveland.
June 1972	Is assigned to Beaumont School in Cleveland Heights when Sacred Heart Academy closes.
1972-1974	Teaches typing and serves as a counselor at Beaumont School.
Spring 1974	Is assigned to serve on the Cleveland Latin American Mission Team in El Salvador.
1974-1975	Ministers in the parish of Nuestra Senora de Guadalupe in Chirilagua.
1975-1977	Ministers in the parish of San Carlos Borromeo in La Union.
1977-1980	Ministers in the parish of the Immaculate Concepción in La Libertad.
December 2, 1980	Is raped and murdered with lay worker Jean Donovan and Maryknoll Sisters Maura Clarke and Ita Ford by five Salvadoran National Guardsmen.

Preface

Since I began researching Dorothy Kazel's life six years ago, the question I am most frequently asked is "Did you know her?" Before she died on December 2, 1980, in El Salvador my association with Dorothy had been minimal, even though we had lived six houses apart on the same street in Euclid, a suburb of Cleveland, Ohio, for a few years. However, when Dorothy moved to our street in 1955 as a sixteen-year-old teenager, I was only a year old. Five years later she joined the religious congregation of the Ursuline Sisters of Cleveland.

My first recollection of actually meeting Dorothy dates back to late spring 1973, several months after I joined the same congregation. At that time, she was ministering as a typing teacher and guidance counselor at Beaumont School, one of my congregation's high schools, and I was a postulant[1] who had been sent from our motherhouse[2] to the convent there to experience religious life in a smaller community setting, as well as to help out in the school until the end of the semester. So for about five weeks, Dorothy and I lived and worked together as any members of the same local religious community would.

A year later, in July 1974, Dorothy left to begin her missionary ministry in El Salvador. During the next few years, I saw Dorothy on several occasions, mainly because in 1977 I had been assigned to teach at Beaumont School and to live at Beaumont Convent, Dorothy's home base when she came to Cleveland for her yearly vacation. The last time I saw Dorothy was when she came home during the summer of 1980.

Some months later when I received word of Dorothy's murder and its violent circumstances, I reacted in shock and disbelief along with the rest of the world. And secretly I mourned that I had not taken the time to get to know Dorothy better, never imagining that a decade later I *would* begin to get to know her — very intimately, in fact — and that the opportunity to do so would be initiated by Dorothy herself in a few short years.

At some point during the 1983-84 academic year (I do not remember the date) while I was teaching at Beaumont School, I had a dream in which Dorothy appeared. I was the only other character in the dream, and when it began, Dorothy and I were standing a distance apart from each other in an open area of undetermined setting and time. From where I stood, I could see that Dorothy was dressed in the modified Ursuline habit[3] and was holding an object in her hand. She then began to walk toward me, and I stood still, watching her approach. When she joined me, Dorothy smiled and without a word gave me what she had been carrying: a large manila folder. The dream abruptly ended as I stretched out my hand and accepted the folder.

I then woke up and for a few seconds wondered if the dream had really been a dream or if the dream's events had actually happened because I strongly sensed Dorothy's presence in my bedroom. I did not feel frightened, as her presence was a gentle, non-threatening one, but I did feel puzzled: what was in the folder I so willingly took from Dorothy?

Later that morning I related my experience of the dream to a friend, Joanne Gross, O.S.U., who was also living at Beaumont at the time. After mulling over the dream for several days and guessing at its significance, I mentally laid it aside and did not give it another thought until six years later.

In late 1989, as I was nearing completion of the coursework and preliminary exams for my doctorate in literature from Bowling Green State University, Ohio, a friend in my congregation, Eileen Collins, suggested I investigate the possibility of writing Dorothy's biography for my dissertation. When I told Joanne about Eileen's idea, however, Joanne remembered my dream and exclaimed, "The dream! Dorothy was giving you the dissertation in that folder!"

I truly believe Joanne did interpret the significance of my dream, for a year later my proposal to write a biography of Dorothy was approved by my dissertation committee. For the next two years, besides reading biographies and information about El Salvador, I intensely researched Dorothy's life. I began by interviewing her family members, friends, and acquaintances and by closely examining her personal belongings which date back to her elementary school years (certificates of awards, photograph albums, autograph book, etc.) through the six years she spent in El Salvador (mementos, books, and 13 photo albums). I have also read the large bulk of Dorothy's personal writing that survives: 11 bound journals, approximately 75 unbound pages containing journal entries, prayers, and spiritual-reading notes, four diaries, eight notebooks, and 180 letters to family and friends which include 43 lengthy ones Dorothy recorded onto cassette tapes. When time permitted, I traveled to the areas in Cleveland where Dorothy grew up and later ministered as an Ursuline Sister.

In May of 1992, I completed my dissertation. With the goal in mind of someday publishing an expanded version of my biography of Dorothy, I continued my research for the next four years. I spent two weeks in El Salvador where I interviewed people who knew Dorothy, and I visited all the areas where she lived and worked. And, of course, I made a pilgrimage to the field where she and her companions, Jean Donovan, Maura Clarke, M.M., and Ita Ford, M.M., had been murdered and buried. My other ventures included trips to Washington, D.C. and Maryknoll, New York, to conduct more interviews and to do research in the Maryknoll Mission Archives. I also completed my interviews in Cleveland which brought the total to 85.

The capstone of my research, though, was listening to the 43 surviving cassette taped letters that Dorothy sent to her family and friends throughout the six years she spent in El Salvador.[4] From beginning to end of this rich narrative spectrum, Dorothy relates in a detailed but engaging fashion her varied experiences from those of a novice missionary struggling with language and cultural differences, to those of a seasoned one so committed to her vocation that she accompanied the Salvadoran people on a road that ultimately led to her own death. Besides the information Dorothy discloses on her tapes, she also unknowingly reveals much of her character through her manner of description and voice inflection. Surely these tapes told me more about Dorothy than any other person could, for through them *she* tells her own story — an all at once enlightening but ironically poignant one.

*   *   *   *   *   *   *   *   *

My approach to Dorothy's life is not strictly chronological but a *combination* of both the chronological or traditional and the thematic, a non-traditional approach. The bulk of the first half of the biography is chronological. "A Record of a Life" sets Dorothy's story in time and place as well as supplies background information for the sociological and religious trends that impacted her life. This chapter also provides some insights into Dorothy's character but in no way yields a complete representation of it. The following chapter, "A Record of a Death," chronicles in great detail Dorothy's final year and a half in El Salvador. In this chapter I incorporate as many of her letters into the text as possible to reveal her voice speaking out against government-induced violence and terrorism.

Because I wished to highlight certain aspects of Dorothy's life and character that a purely chronological approach would not enable me to do, the second half of the biography consists of a trio of *thematic* chapters. In the first of these chapters, "A Woman of Dimensions: Dorothy's Personality," I describe her multi-faceted personality. I continue to dig deeper into the depths of Dorothy's life to her spirituality in the next chapter, "A Woman of Depth: Dorothy's Spirituality." In the third chapter, "A Woman of Dedication: Dorothy's Missionary Ministry," I examine her motivations for working with the poor, oppressed, and the marginalized, as well as the nature of her missionary work in El Salvador.

By taking a thematic approach to Dorothy's life in these three chapters, I have constructed a circular plot for them. In each of these chapters there is some overlapping of time as I move among past, present, and even future events in Dorothy's life. I also make references to, and in some cases, expand the telling of events in these chapters which I had only mentioned in the previous chronological chapters. And in an effort to reveal what Virginia Woolf called the "granite-like solidity" of truth and the "rainbow-like intangibility" of personality,[5] I have incorporated into these three chapters as much of Dorothy's personal writing as I could.

I complete my biography of Dorothy with an opening and closing essay. In the first, "Introduction: The Significance of a Life," I discuss Dorothy's place in the history of American religious women and reasons why it is important and necessary at this point in time to record her story. The second essay, "Epilogue: The Significance of a Death," is a summary of an update of the events regarding Dorothy's murder since its occurrence sixteen years ago. With the help of various people who personally knew Dorothy, I conclude this essay with descriptions of the witness value of her death.

*   *   *   *   *   *   *   *   *

Many times during the past six years, I have contemplated my dream of Dorothy, and for some known and as yet unknown reasons, I do feel that she had commissioned me to write her life. Another friend of mine, Jean Marie Konyesni, O.C.D., has frequently confirmed my feelings: "Dorothy entrusted her life story — every dimension of it — to you to interpret and pass on." As a result of such a serious charge, I have produced what I believe is an accurate, multi-dimensional portrait of Dorothy. But in the process of doing so, I have also come to realize the profound effect that Dorothy's life has had on *my* own life. And although I have spent countless hours and immeasurable amounts of energy preparing my biography of Dorothy, I have received much more from her than I could ever have imagined — or have given to her — certainly when I began what for me was a purely academic project.

Something of great significance Dorothy has given me is a global perspective. Very early in my research she ushered me out of the sheltered world of academia into many other worlds. The most important world was actually the "worlds" of the lives of all the people I encountered through my interviewing. These wonderful people not only shared bits and pieces of Dorothy's life with me but parts of their own lives. The experience was indeed a great privilege — and a gift, as some of Dorothy's friends have now become my friends. Through Dorothy I have also traveled to the worlds of El Salvador and Maryknoll, New York, ones I otherwise would not have had the opportunity to visit. Needless to say, what I learned from these journeys I could not learn from any amount of library research. Finally, Dorothy's introduction of the Salvadoran culture to me has given me an interest in learning about and teaching cultures other than those of North America and Europe. As a result, several years ago I designed and taught a course on African literature, and last year, I developed a course on Latin American women's literature.

Dorothy has also raised my consciousness regarding the political and economic issues of El Salvador as well as those of other Latin American countries and our government's role in them. Because of my interest in these areas, I have become a member of several peace and justice organizations, including Pax Christi and the InterReligious Task Force on Central America and Mexico, and have thus learned information which has enabled me to put Dorothy's experiences and those of El Salvador into a larger context. After reading Dorothy's descriptions in her letters of mass murders and other atrocities committed by Salvadoran soldiers using weapons and other military equipment supplied by our government, I wonder about the aims of our foreign aid programs. And as a result of my research of the murders of Dorothy, Jean, Maura, and Ita, and consequently, my discovery of our government's knowledge of the cover-up of the crime in El Salvador and failure to prosecute those truly responsible for it, Salvadoran military officers, I now question not only our government's policies regarding the promotion of human rights but its very integrity.

Besides all I have learned about and through Dorothy, though, most importantly, she has become a great source of inspiration and personal growth for me. I look to her mainly as a courageous woman whose particular brand of courage included risk-taking. When I fear taking risks, I contemplate the many risks Dorothy took, in particular the one which led to her death, and I am encouraged to travel beyond the familiar into unknown territory. During my times of complacency and passivity, I am bolstered by Dorothy's independence and spirit of adventure. And her positive attitude — an attainable one because it was tempered by a firm grasp of reality — reminds me to seek the hidden goodnesses of everyday living. For me, too, Dorothy is an example of a faith-filled religious woman who strove to make central what she felt was most important in her life: her spirituality. Dorothy's daily focus on her spiritual life has prompted me to examine my own efforts toward my spiritual growth.

Although I have found much to admire about Dorothy, her struggles and insecurities, though, endeared her to me even more and brought her down a few notches on that pedestal that she had been slowly ascending since her death. In her I discovered a human, ordinary person, certainly, but one to whom I could especially relate because while I was researching and writing Dorothy's life, I happened to be the same age she was during the final six years of her life, those I consider her most significant years of growth. Consequently, I better understand my own life-transitional struggles by recognizing them in Dorothy's. In her, too, I saw mirrored my own vulnerabilities and heard echoes of my own anger. But I have also found comfort and reassurance in her quiet strength as well as the courage to question structures, however long-standing or revered they may be. Ironically, by enabling Dorothy to express her voice, I found my own in some ways.

*   *   *   *   *   *   *   *   *

Throughout the past six years, as in my dream of so long ago, I have also felt Dorothy's presence. It has been an encouraging, caring one, and at times a helpful one, as I have repeatedly invoked her aid in directing me to persons who played important roles in her life and information that would make her story more complete. And although my work on Dorothy's life is now finished, at least in one sense, I will continue to feel her presence as I verbally tell her story and thus learn anew how her life is intertwined with the story of my own life.

Introduction: The Significance of a Life

You cannot understand . . . how hard it is for one to be severe and profound who believes herself to be living a story that is glorious and true. Others can be impersonal but not one who believes that she is on an eminently personal adventure . . . others can be sober and restrained but not one who is mad with the loveliness of life and almost blind with its beauty. . . .

Found in Dorothy's Christian Prayer Book,[1]
Author Unknown

For most of her forty-one years, Dorothea Lu[2] Kazel, who later became Sister Mary Laurentine[3] O.S.U.,[4] and then Madre Dorotea,[5] lived what her friends and acquaintances would call the ordinary life of a contemporary American woman. She was born and raised in a large city and enjoyed all the comforts of middle-class American life: attendance at fine schools, music and skating lessons, family vacations, and various cultural opportunities. As a high-school student, Dorothy was a leader in her class, had an active social life, and held several part-time jobs. When she graduated from high school, she worked her way through college, got engaged, and taught elementary school. At the age of twenty-one, Dorothy broke her engagement to join the congregation of the Ursuline Sisters of Cleveland, Ohio. For the next twenty years, she unobtrusively lived a life of service as a high school teacher, counselor, and foreign missionary.

On December 2, 1980, however, Dorothy's life came to an abrupt halt in an isolated cow pasture on the outskirts of a small town in El Salvador, Central America. The brutal manner and untimeliness of her death brought her world-wide attention. But do the tragic circumstances of Dorothy's death *only* warrant the writing of her biography? Those unfamiliar with her life might ask, was there anything extraordinary about her *life*? or what was *significant* about her life? In short, why write a biography of Dorothy Kazel?

*   *   *   *   *   *   *   *   *

If a function of biography is to interpret history, then the significance of Dorothy's life can first be viewed in relationship to the history of American religious women, specifically that of the years 1945-65. During this time an average of 6,000 women annually entered religious congregations of the Roman Catholic Church. An increase occurred from 1958 to 1962 when 8,000 women entered religious congregations per year.[6] Thus, the total number of women who joined religious congregations between 1945 and 1965 was 128,000. This was the peak number of women in religious congregations in the history of the Catholic Church in the United States.[7] Dorothy Kazel joined the Ursuline Sisters of Cleveland in 1960 and was part of this history. Her experience of religious life exemplified that of 128,000 American women. Dorothy's life is in many ways, therefore, the story of the commonalities shared by these women that has not been adequately *or* accurately told.

Dorothy's life also relates to those women who lived most of their religious life in the post-Vatican II Roman Catholic Church that stresses that "all Christians have ministerial and missionary roles to play."[8] For Dorothy and many others this decree meant reaching out to worlds different from their own: to students in racially integrated schools, to physically challenged children, to inmates of city and state correctional institutions, to the aged and chronically ill, and to the materially poor in surrounding areas, in other parts of the country, or in foreign countries. The Ursuline Sisters of Cleveland, as well as other American religious congregations in the 1960s, sent members to Latin America in response to Pope John XXIII's request for help for these countries. As an Ursuline Sister who spent more than six years in El Salvador, Dorothy was part of *this* historic movement within religious congregations of American women which began in the 1960s. Again, hers is the untold story of countless post-Vatican II religious women.

The significance of Dorothy's life for American religious women, though, also reaches beyond that of the past — and even the present — to the future. That is, her ministry and motivations point to various transformative elements for religious life in the future. The first of these is serving a prophetic role in church and society by witnessing the example of Jesus and the values of the Gospel.[9] For Dorothy this prophetic role took the form of ministering to the poor, the oppressed, and the marginalized."[10] And Dorothy's accompaniment of and listening to the poor transformed all aspects of her life. Maria Augusta Neal, S.N.D. de Namur, in her *From Nuns to Sisters: An Expanding Vocation*, further explains the prophetic witness of Dorothy and her companions, lay volunteer Jean Donovan and Maryknoll Sisters Maura Clarke and Ita Ford:

> In their mode of presence and in their ministry, these women identified more closely with the people among whom they served than with the policies of the government of either El Salvador or of the United States, the latter their country of origin. They were helping the poor exercise their claim to the land they had tilled for centuries. They were teaching religion, witnessing to a simple lifestyle, celebrating Eucharist with the local clergy and people, praying in Christian communities, helping to feed, clothe, shelter, and heal the poorest. But they were also reflecting with them on their rights to the land.[11]

For these acts the women were ultimately raped and murdered, underscoring the reality that participation in a prophetic ministry also involves risk.

Despite the risks Dorothy took, though, or actually, because of them, she has motivated religious men and women, particularly her own Ursuline Sisters, to take a stand for justice in the name of the poor. For example, on November 16, 1995, Claire O'Mara, an Ursuline Sister from New Rochelle, New York, was arrested with twelve others for her participation in a protest to close the School of the Americas (SOA) at Fort Benning, Georgia, where members of the Latin America military are trained. Graduates of the SOA were responsible for the murders of Dorothy and her companions, Archbishop Oscar Arnulfo Romero, six Jesuit priests, their housekeeper and her daughter, as well as thousands of innocent Salvadorans. Claire, 74, who accepted a two-month prison sentence rather than a deferential one of three years' probation, said that she took the risk she did in honor of Dorothy's memory.

More recently, another Ursuline Sister took a stand for truth and justice. On March 31, 1996, Dianna Ortiz, who had been abducted, raped, and tortured in Guatemala six years ago while doing missionary work there, began a silent vigil directly across from the White House in an effort to pressure the U.S. government to declassify all documents related to her case *and* all human rights abuses in Guatemala since

1954. After four weeks of waiting without receiving any information, Dianna began a bread and water fast on April 25.

With hopes of bringing serious and effective attention to Dianna and her search for the truth, supporters from her own Ursuline Congregation in Maple Mount, Kentucky, and members of other religious congregations and justice groups joined her during the week of April 28 to participate in non-violent acts of civil disobedience. On the morning of May 3, thirty-one persons were arrested, including three Ursuline Sisters from Cleveland, Beverly LoGrasso, Diane Therese Pinchot, and Paulette Snyder. As these sisters were being handcuffed, the crowd called out Dorothy's name. Later in the day the State Department released to Dianna several thousand pages of documents, the first given to her in six years. However, these documents did not contain the information most sought by Dianna: U.S. involvement in her case and other cases of human rights abuses in Guatemala.[12] Consequently, Dianna will continue her search for the truth.

> *   *   *   *   *   *   *   *   *

In *Life into Art: Conversations with Seven Contemporary Biographers,* Elisabeth Young-Bruehl states her belief that writing a biography is a very important task: "People need examples — stories of how people live their lives — particularly in difficult times but also in ordinary times"[13] That Dorothy Kazel lived a very ordinary life with many ordinary times will be obvious to any readers of her life. I have found, however, threads of extraordinariness that run through the very ordinary fabric of her life.

Dorothy was extraordinary, first of all, because she was able to leave behind the sheltered environment in which she grew up, a predominantly Lithuanian neighborhood on Cleveland's east side, and ultimately extend herself to a distant third-world country. As a child, Dorothy had socialized primarily with family members and neighbors and attended elementary and high school with the same classmates. At some point, however, even before she considered religious life at twenty years of age, Dorothy thought about working with people whose cultures and life experiences were different from her own.

As a young woman, Dorothy challenged the prescribed roles of women who grew up in the 1950s, and to a certain extent, those of women who joined religious congregations at that time and in the early 1960s. She did not, as her family expected, get a job as a secretary after graduating from high school, but rather, took college courses and earned an elementary school teaching certificate. And later, much to the surprise of most who knew her, Dorothy did not adopt the accepted role of mother and homemaker, but instead, joined the congregation of the Ursuline Sisters of Cleveland. As an Ursuline, Dorothy became a high school teacher and taught business and typing courses for nine years at two different all-girls' academies. However, she eventually left the narrow confines of the schools to minister to the city's poor and marginalized, and eventually, to those in a foreign country.

Because of her inner freedom and solid sense of self, Dorothy was able to challenge stereotypes that either society or various individuals had of her, and simply, be herself. Consequently, she also defied the image of "nun" that is so often depicted in the media: an immature, incompetent, asexual being that floats around in medieval dress and has little knowledge of life in the real world. As any reader of Dorothy's life will discover, Dorothy was never a Sister who fit this stereotype of a simple-minded woman living in another world. And for some, this fact alone may contribute much to the extraordinary quality of Dorothy's life.

*   *   *   *   *   *   *   *   *

More than fifty years ago, in her essay, "The Art of Biography," Virginia Woolf asked, "What is greatness?"[14] Today, we deem people great for accomplishments which may have furthered our knowledge; for their artistic products which remain as reminders of their talent; or simply for their wealth and prestige which stand as monuments of successful endeavors. But how many do we consider great for the way in which they lived their lives, the everyday, ordinary living as Dorothy did: someone who lived life as an adventure; who wholeheartedly embraced it in all its uncertainties; and who loved it to the extent that she poured herself into the lives of so many other people? Greatness, I believe, consists in living life so fully — and leaving behind such heartfelt memories.

For even now, sixteen years after her death, Dorothy's memory is still very much alive. In a matter of seconds, those who knew her in Cleveland can vividly recall times they shared with her—even as far back as elementary school — and qualities of hers they hold most precious: "She valued friendships and did care about the people who were in her life";[15] "She had a unique sense of seeing something that needed to be done and then just doing it very gently";[16] "Dorothy was very wholesome";[17] "She thought for herself, argued things out with herself and with others, seeking for truth and God's will";[18] and "She was just a very human person, and this is something I will always hang on to."[19]

Those who knew Dorothy in El Salvador during the final years of her life also remember her with much fondness: "The experience of living with Dorothy for three years awakened in me a little more the love that God has for each one of us";[20] "She was extraordinarily sensitive to other people";[21] "Dorothy left many things, but she truly gave her heart";[22] "She was never critical or hyper, or she was never down on the people";[23] and "We have a picture of Dorothy that hangs in our church. When we celebrate The Word every Wednesday, we point to that picture because Dorothy is an example of life."[24]

*   *   *   *   *   *   *   *   *

Without the values and convictions that Dorothy chose as her motivations, she could not have made the sacrifice she did. In our society which is filled with so much materialism, selfishness, and so many broken promises, Dorothy's life and the total gift of it to others offer pause for reflection, and hopefully, admiration. And although she lived a counter-cultural lifestyle, she may, at least, cause readers to ponder *the significance* of their own lives. But beyond these and other purposes Dorothy's life serves, I do hope that in a broad sense readers will view her life as a reflection of the *human* spirit, one "that inspires by example and fires the imagination to life's possibilities."[25]

1

A Record of a Life

Life is a vibrant stream. . . .
Through all its twists and
turns and straight ways,
it is always onward plunging —
never turning back — happily splashing
and sparkling over the many
rocky boulders it encounters —
never fearful that such
a one might stop it on its way —
but facing it head on —
as it continues on in its
journey for unity. . . .

Journal, February 9, 1971

Dorothy Kazel's family background was similar to that of many persons who grew up in post World War II America. Both her maternal and paternal grandparents were European immigrants. They came to America from Lithuania in the early twentieth century. Like others who emigrated to America at this time, Dorothy's grandparents sought a better life for themselves and for their children; like many others, too, they settled in small towns and landed blue-collar jobs.

Malvina Kazlauskas, Dorothy's mother, was born on May 28, 1911, in Scranton, Pennsylvania, and lived there until she was eight years old. Her family then moved to a predominantly Lithuanian neighborhood on the east side of Cleveland, Ohio.[1] Malvina attended Saint George's parish school and various public schools in the area, and when she was sixteen, got a full-time job doing clerical work at the Mayer-Marks Furniture Store. It was at this time that she also adopted the abbreviated form of her surname that her brother Stanley had assumed several years earlier: Kastley.[2]

Dorothy's father, Joseph Kazlauskas,[3] was born on February 20, 1911, in Rumford, Maine. When he was five years old, Joseph and his family moved to Bentleyville, Pennsylvania, where they lived for the next ten years. The family then took up residence in Pittsburgh. Desiring to live in a larger, less-crowded city and to be closer to relatives, they left for Cleveland in 1926 and for a short while rented an apartment on the East Side. The Kazlauskas family eventually bought a home in the same Lithuanian neighborhood in which Malvina and her family lived. In the meantime Joseph got a job driving a truck for the Minnehaha Spring Water Company until he was hired by the Standard Products Company as a shipping clerk. Early in his career with Standard Products, Joseph legally changed his family name to "Kazel" at the suggestion of a supervisor who noticed how much time it took Joseph to write "Kazlauskas" on the many invoices he signed each day.[4]

"Joe" and "Mal" met at St. George Catholic Church[5] where they were both parishioners and members of the choir. After a courtship of several years, they were married at St. George's on June 1, 1935. Following the practice of many ethnic groups in Cleveland at this time, Joe and Mal remained in their parents' neighborhood. They moved in with Joe's parents, who lived in a two-family home at 1240 Addison Road. On November 10, 1936, James, Joe and Mal's first child, was born. Their second child and only daughter, Dorothy, was born on June 30, 1939. At her baptism on August 6, 1939, Dorothy was christened "Dorothea Lu" because Malvina just liked the name Dorothea and thought it was something different.[6] The middle name "Lu" was given in honor of Joe's younger sister Lucy Marie Kazlauskas, O.S.F.[7]

As children, "Jim" and "Dottie"[8] experienced a close-knit family life that included extended family members. Joe's parents and Mal's father[9] were always present at holiday and birthday celebrations. Get-togethers with relatives who lived nearby were frequent. Every Sunday the Kazels visited Joe's cousin Chuck and his family on their fifteen-acre farm in Fowler's Mill, Ohio. Aside from providing them with time to exchange family news, these weekly gatherings gave the Kazels the opportunity, as Malvina recalls, "to get out of the city for awhile and enjoy the quiet beauty of the country."[10] The three generations of Kazels also observed the Lithuanian national customs and religious devotions. Each Christmas Eve, for example, they ate the "Kucias," a Lithuanian dinner prepared especially for this occasion. At nearby St. George's the entire family attended Mass regularly and participated in various church functions that included bazaars, dances, and Lithuanian feastday celebrations.

Summer vacations and cross-country trips were a part of the Kazel family life. For at least one week each summer, they rented a cottage in Vermilion, Ohio. Here Jim and Dot would fish and swim during the day and attend movies with their parents in the evening. Some summer days were spent taking short sight seeing trips to places such as Niagara Falls. The Kazel family also kept in touch with extended family members who lived at opposite ends of the country. At least once a year, Malvina traveled by train to Scranton, Pennsylvania to visit her Aunt Anne and some of her cousins. She always took Jim and Dot with her. Several times during their childhood, Jim and Dot journeyed to California with their parents to visit their father's sister Natalie Radauskas and her husband George. One such trip by car was a particularly memorable one for the family. In July of 1951, they visited cities such as St. Louis, Missouri, and Wichita, Kansas, and tourist attractions such as the Painted Desert and the Grand Canyon before reaching their destination of Los Angeles.[11] Three summers before, Dorothy had also traveled by car to visit her Aunt Natalie and Uncle George with George's sister and her husband and daughter.

Another aspect of the Kazel family life consisted of socializing with friends and neighbors. Sometimes on weekends the Kazels and their friends gathered for casual visits at each other's homes or at nearby taverns.[12] During the summer they and several families from the neighborhood picnicked at nearby Metroparks and visited amusement parks such as Euclid Beach and Chippewa Lake. Photographs of these events show the Kazels with groups of people sitting around picnic tables or standing in front of scenic areas in the parks. Good conversation, laughter, and games as well as home-cooked food and drink were in abundance at these get-togethers. Such times, too, afforded Dorothy the opportunity to play with the children who would become her classmates at St. George School.

*   *   *   *   *   *   *   *   *

Beginning with kindergarten in 1944, Dorothy spent the years of her elementary education at St. George's parish school. Staffed by the Sisters of St. Francis of the Providence of God, Pittsburgh, Pennsylvania, the school taught the traditional academic subjects. St. George's also focused on the religious formation of its students by teaching courses in Catholic doctrine, encouraging frequent reception of the sacraments and requiring attendance at daily Mass, as well as other religious functions.

The students' parents approved such a program, for it ultimately underscored the religious values taught in the home.

Because St. George School was not large — it usually had only one class of each grade — practically all of the teachers and students knew each other and each other's families. The bonds of friendship formed between the families of the neighborhood who also belonged to the parish further fostered the school's genial atmosphere. It was within this religious, familial environment that Dorothy spent nine pleasant, carefree years, dividing her time between friends, studies, and various extra-curricular activities.

Fellow classmates remember Dottie as bright and energetic, someone who "never sat still but was always bouncing around."[13] With her wavy golden blonde hair, dancing blue eyes, and well-proportioned features, she was considered the prettiest girl in her class at St. George's. Quick with a smile, Dot made friends easily with the neighborhood children. An autograph book of hers, dated May 16, 1950, contains rhymes and messages from both boys and girls: "Roses are red, violets are blue. Stink weeds stink, and so do you"; "First comes love, then comes marriage, then comes Dorothea with a baby carriage"; "Roses are red, violets are blue. Sugar is sweet, and so — well, maybe!"; and "Firemen, firemen, be on your duty. Here comes Dorothy, the American beauty."[14] Also in the book are words of endearment written by several girlfriends who remained close to Dorothy until her death.

Dorothy spent much of her free time socializing with friends from school and from the neighborhood. A popular girl, she was often invited to birthday and pajama parties. With several of her classmates, Dot formed a "girls' only" club that met each month at the home of a different member who was responsible for providing entertainment and refreshments. She also rode her bike, jumped rope, and played other children's games with three or four close girlfriends. An avid athlete, Dorothy excelled in swimming and roller skating. Baseball was her favorite sport, however, and she played the game with the neighborhood children because St. George School, like other schools at that time, did not have an organized sports program. Sometimes she just "played catch" with her brother Jim. Possessing musical talent, Dottie also took formal accordion lessons.

As a student she earned above-average grades for academic subjects as well as for religious spirit, behavior, health, interest in work, and effort.[15] Several of Dorothy's former teachers agree that for her learning was easy and enjoyable.[16]   In the classroom during the school day, she was cooperative and "always very helpful,"[17] performing small tasks for her teacher. She also got along very well with her classmates.[18]

When she was not studying or playing with her friends, Dorothy participated in school-sponsored extra-curricular activities. While in the intermediate grades, Dot played her accordion for the operettas and plays the school sponsored every spring. She played in the school band, composed primarily of boys, because at this time, it was unusual for a girl to play the accordion. At St. George School, the children learned traditional Lithuanian dances. Dottie, along with the other girls in her class, dressed in Lithuanian costumes,[19] which were decorated in the national colors of red, yellow, and green, and performed at school assemblies and parish activities. She was also a member of the sodality,[20] a parish-sponsored organization.

Dorothy graduated from St. George School on June 7, 1953, an event that formally ended the first stage of her academic and social education. It began another, however, that for her would be filled with even more friends and extra-curricular and social activities: high school.

*   *   *   *   *   *   *   *   *

Like many of her classmates at St. George's, Dorothy attended Notre Dame Academy, a Catholic, all-girls' comprehensive high school conducted by the Sisters of Notre Dame. The school was then located on Ansel Road,[21] about twenty-five blocks east of Dorothy's street. Everyday for four years she rode the bus to the Academy, "the castle on Ansel"[22] as it was then called, where she benefitted from a college-preparatory program of study, as well as from many enjoyable times spent with both old and new friends.

As a high-school student, Dorothy retained the naturally blonde hair and engaging smile of her childhood. Her slender five-foot-six-inch frame, fresh, clear complexion, and pageboy hairdo that softly framed her heart-shaped face, made her appearance even more striking, however. Teachers and students alike agreed that Dorothy had a certain glow[23] that set her apart, even though, like everyone else, she daily wore the Notre Dame uniform: a light blue cotton shirtwaist-style dress worn in early fall and spring and a navy blue gabardine jumper and dacron blouse worn in late fall and winter. Dorothy also maintained the high energy level she had had as a child, for in high school she was in the middle of whatever was going on.[24]

Dorothy's high school permanent record reveals the extent of her involvement in school activities. For four years she was a member of the Student Council, the Athletic Association (AA), and the sodality.[25] On the Student Council, Dorothy served as a homeroom representative for her freshman and sophomore years and as class president for both her junior and senior years. As a member of the AA, she participated in special sports activities and played on the varsity softball, basketball, and baseball teams for three years and on the varsity volleyball team for two years. During her years as a sodalist, she took part in events such as the Living Rosary[26] and the Summer School of Catholic Action (SSCA).[27] Dorothy also belonged to the Mission[28] and Dramatic Clubs for two years each and to the Speech League for a year. While in the Dramatic Club during her junior year, Dorothy performed in a one-act play as part of the Christmas program that year. In her senior year she was accepted into the National Thespian Society and earned the role of Anne Gilbreth in the senior class play *Cheaper by the Dozen*. At the end of her senior year, Dorothy won the award for "Most Cheerful." During all her years at Notre Dame, Dorothy also volunteered at concerts and dinners, and she frequently worked on decorating committees for dances and proms and on the planning committee for "Notre Dame Day."[29]

During Dorothy's four years at the Academy, her extra-curricular activities were often reported in *The Tower*, Notre Dame's school newspaper. Photographs of her with groups of fellow classmates in *The Tower* also served to remind friends and teachers of the many events in which she took part. But what Dorothy's friends recall even more vividly are the numerous social activities in which she participated.

When Dorothy began Notre Dame as a freshman, she continued her friendships with girls from St. George who attended the Academy. Because she was a member of the St. George Sodality for high school students, she also frequently saw her grade school friends at sodality-sponsored religious and social activities. Dorothy got to know other girls in her class at Notre Dame, however, mainly as a result of her involvement in so many extra-curricular activities. By the end of her freshman year, her circle of friends had expanded to include about thirty girls. Throughout her high school years, Dorothy frequently socialized with this group both during and after school hours.

Parties were the most popular means of getting together for Dorothy and her friends. About once a month she hosted "pajama" parties at her home.[30] Here, twenty to thirty girls would stay up all night and gossip and talk about school and their plans for the future while they drank Coke and ate potato chips. At one memorable pajama party, a main activity was smoking, as some of the girls already smoked, and Dorothy had tried it occasionally.[31] However, at this particular party the girls also smoked cigars. Photograph albums Dorothy kept contain pictures of this "cigar-smoking" pajama party as well as of several other pajama parties.[32] Every year someone in Dorothy's group threw a surprise party for her birthday which Dorothy carefully chronicled in her photograph albums. Dorothy and her friends from St. George who attended the Academy would occasionally attend parties with some of the boys who graduated with them from St. George. Pictures of these events are also contained in Dorothy's albums.

By the time she was a sophomore, Dorothy's circle of friends expanded again to include her brother Jim and his friends, who by this time were dating some of Dorothy's friends from Notre Dame. On February 13, 1955, Dorothy began dating Russell Smith, a friend of Jim's from the neighborhood. Russ had actually known Dorothy for a long time, but to him she had just always been Jim's kid sister.[33] Their casual association, however, gradually developed into a more serious relationship when they started socializing within their group of mutual friends.

Dorothy and Russ, along with Dorothy's brother Jim and his girlfriend Dorothy Chapon and couples Jerry Friga and Marilyn Chapas and Vic Tekanic and Inge Decker, gathered for parties at each other's homes and get-togethers around the holiday times. Every weekend during the summer, they went swimming and on picnics at nearby Metroparks. Russ and Dorothy also attended all the dances and proms at both Notre Dame and St. Joseph High School, Cleveland, where Russ was a student. Prom pictures show Russ, tall, lean, his wavy blonde hair combed neatly back, with his arms around Dorothy, who was frequently dressed in a blue formal.[34]

After they dated steadily for a year, Russ gave Dorothy his class ring. At school she wore the ring on a chain around her neck so the nuns could not see it because the girls were discouraged from "going steady" and were not permitted to wear boys' rings during school hours.[35] When Russ graduated from high school in 1956, he enlisted in the Marines. He and Dorothy continued their relationship during this time by writing to each other and by seeing each other when he came home on leave.

Also in 1956, the second-half of her junior year and the first-half of her senior year, Dorothy kept a diary. In it she often wrote about the times she shared with Russ, such as her Junior-Senior Prom on Friday, January 6:

> The big day finally arrived! We went to Mass at school and got out at 12 noon. Mare [Marilyn Friga] and I went down to get our hair done. Mare's hair was parted in the middle like I usually get and I got wavy bangs. It wasn't too bad. That night I got a beautiful corsage of pink roses from Russ. He looked real sharp. I wore Mare's long blue formal. He told me I looked beautiful. The Statler [Hotel] was sharp and everybody looked real nice. Afterwards we went to Morocco's.... It was a nice little place. We ate by candlelight. We had a good time. I'll never forget it![36]

She described other dates, like the following, with Russ: "We went to Nelson Ledges.... We climbed all over the ledges and then ate near some rocks. It was real nice! Then we messed around and played ball.... I still love him!!!"[37] When Russ left for the Marines, Dorothy wrote, "Russ and Jer [Friga] left. It was terrible. We cried so hard. They looked like they were going to their doom."[38]

In her diary Dorothy frequently mentioned her many social events and extra-curricular activities. She referred to academics, however, only when worried about an upcoming exam: "What a dull day at school. Exams tomorrow! Ugh! ...Oh! I found out that they're only taking one point off an error in our typing exam, so maybe I didn't flunk![39] When Dorothy did not fail an exam, she expressed joy and relief: "The shorthand test wasn't too bad, but we have more tomorrow. Today I actually typed thirty words per minute. All year I've been in the hole. I think I should celebrate![40] On another occasion she wrote, "Had our English test. I think I got about a C (I hope)."[41]

Dorothy was not an extraordinary student.[42] Former teachers and classmates at Notre Dame considered her average, and Dorothy herself always said that she was not a "brain."[43] She was a responsible student, however, who regularly did her homework while maintaining a busy social calendar throughout her high school years. During her junior year, she also held a part-time job as a sales clerk at the Higbee Company in Downtown Cleveland.

Another activity that took up much of Dorothy's free time on weekends was roller skating. When she was a child, Dorothy considered skating an enjoyable group sport. By the time she started high school, however, Dorothy began to take a more serious interest in it, even to the point of considering a career in professional skating.

When Dorothy lived on Addison Road, she took roller skating lessons every Sunday morning at Skateland on Euclid Avenue, Cleveland, and then spent the afternoon practicing. She was also a member of Skateland's Figure Club, and with this group of skaters, performed dance routines in skating shows called "Rolla-Revels." In the Rolla-Revels of 1955, Dorothy was featured in the dances, "Hawaii Calls," "Mask Waltz," and "The Mombo Dancers."[44] On the last night of Rolla-Revels, she won first place in a beauty queen contest in the Junior Division. When Dorothy and her family moved to Euclid in July 1955, she skated at the Rollerdrome on Shore Center Drive. On March 20, 1956, Dorothy won second place in a beauty contest held for all Rollerdrome skaters. While skating at both Skateland and the Rollerdrome, Dorothy also participated in the annual State Meets which were held in various cities in northern Ohio.

Dorothy skated for the first three years of high school, making new friends once again, as her fellow skaters were not members of her high school crowd. In her diary of 1956, Dorothy occasionally writes about her skating friends and experiences: "I went skating tonight. Marilyn [Felice] told me she's skating fours with Bill [Kepler], Bonnie [Fox], and Joe [Vero]! The lucky stiff!"[45] "What a Friday the 13th! I ripped [the] big heel off the skate and therefore I get new boots. Going to get Betty Lytets."[46] We had our show again!"[47] and "Today too! Had a party after! Lots of fun and lots of food!!!"[48] The diary entries about skating end, however, with the close of summer 1956, just before the beginning of Dorothy's senior year of high school.

* * * * * * * * *

Although Dorothy was in the college preparatory track at Notre Dame Academy, she really was not thinking of going to college.[49] And while she had seriously considered a career in professional skating, she abandoned this idea in her junior year. So by the time Dorothy's senior year arrived, she was still undecided as to what she wanted to do after graduation.

Partly because of her indecision about a career, Dorothy chose to take business courses during her junior and senior years. Her mother had also suggested that she take such courses, particularly shorthand, because then she would be qualified to get a job anywhere.[50] So, Dorothy took typing and shorthand in her junior year and office practices in her senior year. Apparently deciding that she wanted to pursue a career in business, Dorothy applied to the Carnegie Institute[51] in Cleveland and had her high school transcript sent there on April 25, 1957.[52] She graduated from Notre Dame Academy on June 2, 1957.

* * * * * * * * *

Using her business skills, Dorothy worked as a medical secretary at Doctors' Hospital in Cleveland Heights. Around this time or shortly before, Dorothy purchased the books[53] for the courses she planned to take at the Carnegie Institute. She did not, however, officially enroll in the courses.[54] In the meantime Dorothy continued to live at home with her parents and to correspond with Russ who by this time was overseas with the Marine Corps.

While working at Doctors' Hospital, Dorothy came across a pamphlet advertising a new teacher training program at St. John College, Cleveland, called the "Cadet Program." The program's main objective was to prepare teachers as quickly as possible for Catholic elementary schools, which by the late 1950s, were suffering from a teacher shortage. Cadets took an intensive two-year course of study including two six-week summer sessions. At the end of the program, graduates received an elementary school teaching certificate but no baccalaureate degree.

The Cadet Program caught Dorothy's interest, and she quickly decided to enroll. Her high-school transcript was sent to the Division of Education of St. John College on July 12, 1957.[55] By the end of the summer, she quit her job at Doctors' Hospital.

* * * * * * * * *

It is obvious that at some point during the summer after she graduated from Notre Dame, Dorothy had decided that she was best suited to teach and direct children's lives.[56] What or who prompted her to reach such a decision which ultimately changed the direction of her life is not clear, for during that summer Dorothy talked to nobody about her interest in teaching. Some years later, however, she revealed that she just could not see herself in a commercial position.[57]

* * * * * * * * *

Dorothy's sudden decision to make a career change did not please her parents. They could not afford to pay for a college education and believed that with her training in business, Dorothy could get a good job without a college degree. Like many other parents at that time, Joe and Malvina Kazel also believed that a college education was unnecessary for girls because they would eventually get married, have children, and would not have to find a job.

Yet despite her parents' inability to contribute financially to her college education and their misgivings about her desire to become a teacher, Dorothy proceeded with her plans to attend St. John College. She paid for her education by working a series of part-time jobs. In her first year in the program, she worked as a sales clerk at the Bailey Department Store in Euclid; in her second year she did clerical work at The Retail Credit Men's Association in Downtown Cleveland. During the summers Dorothy worked as a counselor at Camp Isaac Jogues in Madison, Ohio.

Because of her financial situation, Dorothy's choice of the Cadet Program over a more expensive four-year college program was a compromise of sorts. But it was also a compromise because she did not want to be far from home.[58]

*   *   *   *   *   *   *   *   *

During her first semester at St. John's, Dorothy constantly juggled school and work responsibilities. She carried a full course load of eighteen hours and worked at Bailey's whenever she could. In spite of all of this activity, however, Dorothy still managed to fit in extra-curricular activities at St. John's and to maintain an active social life. She was often instrumental in gathering her group of high school friends together on weekends. And at St. John's Dorothy also made new friends with whom she began to socialize.

As a result of her involvement in activities at St. John's and with both old and new friends, Dorothy's grades suffered. She earned three B's, five C's, and a D in her first-semester courses.[59] Mercita Thailing, a friend of Dorothy's, recalls that after Dorothy received her report card from the dean she retreated to a back stairway and burst into tears.[60] She must have later realized that she had to "hit the books" a bit more because her grades in succeeding semesters were never quite as low as those first-semester marks.

Another event occurred at the end of Dorothy's first semester at St. John's that would affect her much more, however, than receiving unexpected low grades. She would meet someone who would play an important role in her life for the next few years.

Shortly before Christmas 1957 while working in the men's department at Bailey's, Dorothy met Donald Kollenborn, a young soldier from Bakersfield, California, who was stationed on a missile base in Willowick, Ohio. Dressed in his uniform, Don appeared in Bailey's one day to buy a sweater. Dorothy immediately captured his attention because she was very attractive.[61] But he was also "just taken with her personality. She was outgoing, but she was still very reserved."[62] Before he left the store, Don told Dorothy that he would return to see her. She later told Mercita, who was also working at Bailey's that day, that she doubted he would come back.[63] When Don indeed returned to Bailey's the next day and asked Dorothy for a date, she refused him. He then stopped at the store everyday for the next three weeks and asked her out until she finally agreed. Dorothy and Don then began to see each other on a regular basis.

In the meantime Dorothy was still corresponding with Russ Smith, who was overseas with the Marine Corps. He, however, came home for his first leave in the spring of 1958. Although Dorothy had never mentioned Don in her letters, Russ, "got a feeling things were more and more vague"[64] in her correspondence. Dorothy, though, intended to continue seeing Russ when he came home until Don said to her, "I'm not going to see you again until you decide *who* you are going to see. If you decide to see me, then he's not going to be a part of your life."[65] After a difficult period of discernment, Dorothy told Russ that she was not going to see him anymore. He accepted her decision and "decided to walk away from the whole thing."[66] However, unknown to Russ at the time, he would meet Dorothy again, but it would not be until many years later.

When Dorothy told Malvina of her decision to end her relationship with Russ to pursue one with Don, her mother was not pleased. Malvina liked Russ very much and thought he would make a good husband for Dorothy.[67] He was also Lithuanian and Catholic. Because Don did not share Dorothy's ethnic background — he was of German descent — and at the time was not a member of any organized religion, Malvina disapproved of him.[68] Several of Dorothy's friends, who were also friends of Russ, opposed Dorothy's decision to break up with him. Her mother's and her friends' opinions did not, however, deter Dorothy from doing what she had chosen to do. She and Don then resumed dating.

*　*　*　*　*　*　*　*　*

Several of the education courses students completed while in the Cadet Program required that the teacher in training spend a "laboratory" period each week in an elementary classroom. One such course was "Child Development and the Educative Process I-II" which the students took in the spring session of their first year in the program. For this course they did a case study on a particular child and then produced a formal written report. Students also satisfied the lab requirement by doing practice teaching for various methods courses.

Dorothy chose to spend her laboratory hours in classrooms at the parochial school at St. Robert Bellarmine Catholic Church, her parish. The school was staffed by the Ursuline Sisters of Cleveland, and although Dorothy had come into contact with Ursulines at St. John's,[69] she did not personally know any Ursulines until she came to St. Robert Bellarmine School. There she got to know Anna Margaret Gilbride in whose first-grade classroom she did her case study; she later became friends with Helen Marie Davidson in whose classroom she did some practice teaching.

* * * * * * * * *

Throughout her second year at St. John College, Dorothy steadily dated Don Kollenborn. They spent most of their time together with Dorothy's friends, going bowling, picnicking at nearby parks, and seeing movies. Because nobody had very much money, they often played chess and cards at the Kazel home.[70] But Dorothy and Don also went places alone just to sit and talk. St. Robert Bellarmine Church was their favorite meeting place. Here at night, in the back of the church, they would sit for hours and "just talk about a lot of things."[71]

As the year progressed, and Dorothy and Don's relationship grew, their love for each other deepened. Partly as a result of Dorothy's influence,[72] Don began instructions in Roman Catholicism in the fall of 1958. He and Dorothy then began talking about getting engaged, and during the spring of 1959, Don asked Dorothy to marry him one day while they sat together in St. Robert Bellarmine Church. She accepted his proposal as well as the pearl engagement ring he presented to her.[73] That August Dorothy went to California to visit her aunt and uncle, Natalie and George Radauskas. At the time Don was on leave, visiting his parents in Bakersfield. Dorothy joined him there and met his parents.

* * * * * * * * *

After completing the Cadet Program in the summer of 1959, Dorothy got a job teaching the third grade at St. Robert Bellarmine School. She loved teaching and gave each of her forty-three students personal attention by bending down hundreds of times during the day and attentively listening to each child's request or concern. A hard worker, Dorothy could often be found in her classroom long after the school day ended.[74] Don helped her whenever he could by doing artwork, putting up bulletin boards, and correcting papers.

Despite her heavy teaching load, Dorothy spent time making plans for her wedding. She and Don set the date for August 5, 1960, and reserved St. Robert Bellarmine Church for the wedding Mass. Together they chose a hall for the reception, paid a deposit for its rental, and picked the members of the bridal party. They also discussed where they would live after they married and mutually decided to remain in Ohio. Dorothy and Marilyn Friga, a close friend who planned to marry in October of 1960, periodically met to talk about their wedding plans. They agreed to be each other's maids of honor.

* * * * * * * * *

In the midst of making all of her wedding preparations, however, Dorothy was entertaining the thought of entering the convent. Except for Helen Marie Davidson, with whom she taught at St. Robert Bellarmine School, and Marianist Father Eldon Reichert, and Father Eugene Best, her confessors, Dorothy shared her thoughts and feelings of confusion with nobody. Not even Marilyn Friga and Fran Harbert, who had been her friends since childhood, had any idea that Dorothy was concerned with much else except her upcoming marriage.

Don also had no inkling of what Dorothy was considering and along what confusing lines her thoughts were running. During the first semester of that year, 1959-60, Dorothy attended several retreats[75] at the St. Joseph Christian Life Center and at other retreat houses in Cleveland. Don recalls that when she would come back from one of her retreats, she would be different for a couple of days.[76] Inevitably, though, Dorothy would always return to her "old self," and Don would forget about the effects the retreats had had on her.

* * * * * * * * *

When his military service ended in January 1960, Don returned to California to continue his college education. Over the next few months he and Dorothy corresponded quite frequently, but in her letters, Dorothy never mentioned anything about entering the convent. This is fairly obvious from the following excerpt from one of Don's letters in February 1960: "I think that I am a pretty lucky guy to have such a wonderful girl as you. Just remember I do love you, and if you feel you need me, remember I need you twice as much!"[77]   In this letter Don also thanked Dorothy for a Valentine card she had sent him.

Sometime between January and early March of 1960, Dorothy made a retreat for engaged women that convinced her of the reality of her religious vocation. She called Don in March to tell him that she was seriously thinking of entering the convent and that she wanted to break their engagement. Responding first to her announcement in "absolute, total disbelief"[78] and then in anger, Don refused to continue the conversation over the phone and flew to Cleveland that evening. He stayed at the Kazel home for a week, and he and Dorothy spent many hours discussing her desire to become an Ursuline Sister. Although Dorothy did not return Don's engagement ring at this time, she and he concluded that a religious vocation was a very real factor in her life but one that needed further reflection.[79]   Don then left for California with the hope that he and Dorothy would maintain their relationship and that he would see her again that summer.

Apparently, though, choosing religious life was becoming more of a reality to Dorothy, for two months later, when the lay teachers with whom she worked at St. Robert Bellarmine told her they wanted to give her a shower, Dorothy asked them not to because her plans to marry had changed.[80]   In May she asked Father Joseph Wagner, assistant pastor at St. Robert Bellarmine Parish, to write her a letter of recommendation for entrance into the congregation of the Ursuline Sisters of Cleveland. In his letter, addressed to Mother Marie Sands, the General Superior of the Cleveland Ursulines at the time, Father Wagner wrote, "Dorothy has taught in our school this past year and has been an inspiration to the children by her prayers, her devotion, and her daily communion. I have no doubt that she is morally and spiritually well qualified for the religious life."[81]

On June 29, 1960, one day before her twenty-first birthday, Dorothy formally applied to the Cleveland Ursuline Congregation.[82]   With her Aunt Lucy, she flew to Palm Springs, California, in July to visit her Aunt Natalie and Uncle George. While there, she met Don several times, and they debated about her religious vocation a long time.[83]   After they *both* reached the conclusion that entering the convent was the right move for Dorothy to make,[84] she returned Don's engagement ring. He drove her and her aunt to the airport when it was time for their return to Cleveland. Lucy boarded the plane while Don and Dorothy said good-bye and then parted. When Dorothy got on the plane and sat next to her aunt, she was visibly shaking.[85]   Lucy said to her, "Dorothy, you were in love with Don, and now you're giving it all up to God. You must understand that there may come days when giving up the world will be a terrible temptation for you."[86]   Dorothy firmly replied, "Yes, I understand, but I must do what I feel I have to do."[87]

Although Dorothy and Don never saw each other again, they continued to write throughout the rest of the summer. In his letters[88] Don expressed how difficult it is for him to deal with his separation from Dorothy: "I have thought about coming back to see you in the time between school sessions, and I have a terrible desire to call you. [Doing] these sorts of things would only make my adjustment that much harder, though."[89] And he, of course, wondered why circumstances turned out the way they had: "It's really funny the way that life can change. I never thought for a minute that we would end up the way we did." Don concluded this particular letter with "I still love you (darn it)."[90]

Out of sensitivity to Don's feelings, Dorothy remained in touch with him throughout the summer. She insisted, however, that once she joined the Ursuline Sisters, they should have no contact. Don agreed but told her that he would wait for her for one year.[91]

Dorothy spent the remainder of the summer of 1960 enjoying social activities with friends and preparing for her move to the Ursuline Motherhouse. In July, she, Fran Harbert, and Mercita Thailing went on a vacation to Kelly's Island near Sandusky, Ohio. Shortly after, Dorothy "took up smoking Pall Mall (unfiltered) cigarettes."[92] Towards the end of the summer, her friends had a going-away party for her. And on the night before she left for the convent, Dorothy asked several close friends to go with her to the horse races. None of them, including Dorothy, had ever been to the races, and when they asked her why she wanted to go, she replied, "I want to do something I've never done before and might never get a chance to do.[93] So they accompanied Dorothy, who was smoking cigarettes all the way, to a racetrack in Northfield, Ohio.[94]

*   *   *   *   *   *   *   *   *

On September 8,[95] 1960, with nineteen other young women, Dorothy entered the novitiate[96] of the Ursuline Sisters of Cleveland at the congregation's motherhouse in Pepper Pike, an eastern suburb of Cleveland. Here she spent the first five years of her religious formation: one year as a postulant, two years as a novice,[97] and two years as a junior professed[98] Sister. During these early years of religious formation,

Dorothy became acquainted with religious life generally and the Ursuline life specifically.

As a postulant, Dorothy was introduced to the prayer and communal life of the congregation. With the other members of her "set"[99] and the novices, she rose each morning at 5:20 and went to chapel for the recitation of morning prayers from the congregational prayer book, a half-hour period of meditation, and Mass. Breakfast followed Mass, and then the novitiate returned to the chapel for the Morning Hours of the Little Office of the Blessed Virgin Mary.[100] At fixed times throughout the rest of the day, the remaining hours of the Little Office were scheduled: Midday Hours[101] after lunch; Vespers or Evening Hours at 5:00 p.m.; and Compline or Night Hours before retiring. The Little Office was always chanted by the postulants and novices, who sat together in the first benches in the chapel. Aside from participating in communal prayers, each postulant and novice made a "Holy Hour," an hour of private prayer, and read books on various spiritual topics. When not at prayer, the postulant spent time doing "charges," such as washing dishes, working in the main kitchen, the laundry, and the infirmary, and cleaning the novitiate area and other parts of the motherhouse. The postulants and novices also gathered each night after supper for an hour of recreation[102] together.

Dorothy's religious formation included learning about the Cleveland Ursuline Congregation, religious life, and spirituality. Anna Margaret Gilbride, who in 1960 was appointed the assistant to novice directress, M. Kenan Dulzer, lectured the postulants once a week on the life of Saint Angela Merici, foundress of the Ursulines, and on the history of the Cleveland Ursulines. Required reading included the Rule, Counsels, and Testament of Saint Angela and *The Broad Highway: A History of the Ursuline Nuns in the Diocese of Cleveland, 1850-1950* by M. Michael Francis Hearon, a member of the congregation. The postulants expanded their background in theology by taking dogmatic theology, sacramental theology, and scripture courses, also taught by Sister Anna Margaret.

Besides taking theology courses, the postulants also took standard college-level courses towards a bachelor's degree. They attended classes in the motherhouse and were taught by Sisters from Ursuline College, which was then located on Cedar Hill in Cleveland Heights.[103] Dorothy and her set took courses in philosophy, English literature, European civilization, elementary French, and speech.[104] With the theology courses, they averaged fourteen-to-fifteen credits a semester. Because she had had college courses at St. John College, Dorothy took some upper-level courses in addition to the freshman-level courses the other postulants took. She was, therefore, in class with both second-year novices and postulants.

Dorothy was distinguished as a postulant by the outfit she wore: a mid-calf length black skirt, black blouse with white collar and cuffs, black cape, a small black cap edged in black ribbon, heavy black nylons, and "sensible" black oxford shoes. When her period of postulancy ended, however, on August 12, 1961,[105] she was formally accepted into the novitiate and received the Ursuline religious habit with a white veil.[106] On this day, her "Clothing" as it was then called, Dorothy dressed in a long black serge habit with a stiffly starched guimpe and bandeau.[107] The habit had a yoke, double pleats in the front and back, and wide, rolled sleeves, under which nylon "undersleeves" were worn. A leather cincture and large rosary worn around the waist made the habit complete. At her Clothing, Dorothy was also given the title "Sister" and the religious name "Laurentine," preceded by "Mary."[108] The original Sister Mary Laurentine had been an Ursuline Sister of Valenciennes, France, who was martyred during the French Revolution.[109]

On the day after the Clothing ceremony, the families and friends of the Sisters who had received the habit attended a reception for the Sisters in the motherhouse. Mary Jo Lackamp, who had entered the congregation with Dorothy but had left several months before the Clothing, came to visit the members of her set. When Mary Jo saw Dorothy and heard what her religious name was, she asked, "Who was Laurentine?" Dorothy replied, "Oh, she was an Ursuline martyr from the French Revolution. And if they think I'm going to be a martyr, they have another thought coming!"[110]

*　*　*　*　*　*　*　*　*

Don and Dorothy had not communicated with each other during the preceding year, but he had called Malvina at Christmas to ask if Dorothy was still in the congregation.[111] At the Clothing reception, Malvina told Dorothy that Don had called again, this time to find out if Dorothy had received the Ursuline habit. Learning that she had indeed been "clothed," Don nevertheless decided to wait for Dorothy for another year.[112]

*　*　*　*　*　*　*　*　*

Soon after Clothing Dorothy began her Canonical Year.[113] As a Canonical novice or a "Canonical," she attended lectures given by Sister

Kenan on the vows and all aspects of the spiritual life: prayer, meditation, and the cultivation of virtues. The Canonicals read and studied The Rule[114] and The Constitutions[115] of the congregation to prepare themselves for commitment.[116] And to learn about religious decorum, or the behavior expected of an Ursuline Sister, they also read *Ursulines in Training* by Gertrude Ftechschulte, O.S.U., of Toledo, Ohio. What the Canonicals were taught in lectures was reinforced in the spiritual books they read.

During their Canonical Year the novices did not take a full course load from Ursuline College. So that they could devote more time to prayer and service to the motherhouse community, the Canonicals took only music theory, ethics, liturgical music, and general crafts.[117] They also took the following theology courses, taught by Sisters Kenan and Anna Margaret: the theology of grace, the spiritual life, and the Catholic Church, the mystical Body of Christ. When they were not attending private and communal prayer and lectures or completing assignments for their courses, the Canonicals did charges in all areas of the motherhouse. Each night they also recreated with the other novices and the postulants.

When her Canonical Year was over, Dorothy resumed her college studies full time. As second-year novices, Dorothy and her set continued to take theology courses, and on every Saturday night they met Sister Kenan for lectures on that Sunday's Epistles and Gospel.

This second formal year in the novitiate was also one of intense preparation for the profession of religious vows, which Dorothy and her set, or the "Profession Set" as they were then called, were scheduled to make the following August. Their religious training, therefore, also included special meditations and readings on the vows and the observance of certain religious "practices," such as keeping strict silence every Friday in memory of the Passion of Christ. The aim of this final stage of religious training was not only to prepare the second-year novices to consecrate their life to God but also to help them fully to understand the meaning of such a commitment.

*   *   *   *   *   *   *   *   *

For their professional training, the postulants and novices took general and survey college courses toward an undergraduate degree. Although they knew that they would someday teach, nobody knew while she was in the novitiate if she would teach on the elementary or secondary level. Shortly before they professed vows, however, the General Superior determined what level each Sister would teach. If assigned to elementary education, the Sister would attend St. John College; if assigned to secondary education, she would attend Ursuline College. During the summer before profession, each novice received from the General Superior a written "obedience" or appointment that informed her of the college at which she would complete her degree and earn the appropriate teacher certification.

Because she was already certified to teach elementary school, Dorothy fully expected to return to St. John College. In June of 1963, she received the obedience from Mother Marie Sands, the General Superior of the Ursuline Sisters at the time, to study at Ursuline College.[118] The reasons why Mother Marie assigned Dorothy to secondary rather than elementary education can only be surmised, for in the early 1960s in the Cleveland Ursuline Congregation, novices were not asked their preference in terms of apostolic work. And although Dorothy was confused and disappointed by her appointment, she would never have questioned a General Superior about her motives. What is fairly certain, though, is that in the mid 1960s Mother Marie was concentrating on increasing the religious faculties of the congregation's three high schools[119] and consequently assigned to them quite a few young Sisters.[120]

* * * * * * * * *

On August 13, 1963, with fifteen young women who remained in her set, Dorothy professed the traditional religious vows of poverty, chastity, and obedience, as well as a special fourth vow of Instruction of Youth[121] for a period of three years.[122] As one who had taken temporary vows, Dorothy was considered a "junior professed" Sister, or a "junior." At her profession ceremony she received the black veil of a professed Sister in place of the white veil of a novice. To complete the transition, Dorothy moved out of the novitiate section of the motherhouse to the "juniorate," the area in the motherhouse designated for juniors.

Shortly after profession, Dorothy registered for courses at Ursuline College. At some point during the summer, she had been advised to major in business. Perhaps Mother Marie had looked at Dorothy's transcript from Notre Dame Academy and noticed that she had taken several business courses and knew that in the near future either Sacred Heart Academy or Villa Angela Academy would need a business teacher.

So, for the next two years Dorothy took numerous business and secondary education courses and accumulated quite a few credits in the area of social studies.[123] On June 1, 1965, she graduated from Ursuline College with a bachelor of arts degree and an Ohio State Four-Year Provisional High School Teaching Certificate in the fields of stenography-typing and comprehensive social studies.

* * * * * * * * *

What was Dorothy like in the novitiate and juniorate? Kathleen Cooney, who was in Dorothy's set and later became a close friend of hers, recalls that she was "outgoing, friendly, very animated, and energetic. Everyone was her friend, and she was everyone's friend."[124] Mary Catherine Cummins, who was also in Dorothy's set, describes Dorothy "as someone easy to get along with, a happy person. Most of the time she had a smile on her face."[125] Because she made friends easily, Sister Kenan Dulzer viewed Dorothy as "a bonding member of her group, one who kept the group cohesive."[126] Ann Letitia Kostiha, another member of Dorothy's set, agrees:

> Dorothy had a real sense of mothering about her. When we had small crises within our set, whether it was dealing with difficult situations or relational types of things within the group or outside the group or just trying to understand why we were here in the first place, she really had a listening ear. And if you were crying, she'd cry with you; and if you were laughing — well, in the end you'd wind up laughing because she just seemed to spark a sense of something that was deeper than the sorrow that was there, and she'd help you carry that load.[127]

The semi-cloistered life Dorothy lived in the novitiate and juniorate apparently did not stifle her exuberance, enthusiasm, and love of socializing, for whatever parties, plays, and other activities were planned by the novitiate and juniorate, she was in the middle of all of them.[128] Nor did the structured style of religious life of the early 1960s and its demands change her. She retained her sense of good humor and is remembered as a joyful person and a lot of fun and one pleasant to be around.[129] Nor did Dorothy allow her new religious lifestyle to make her into someone other than the Dorothy she and others had come to know. She simply was herself in any situation.[130]

As for community involvement in the novitiate and juniorate, Dorothy participated in everything.[131]   Sister Anna Margaret Gilbride recalls that Dorothy was a hard worker: "I would see her with her apron on, bustling around doing things. She was never one to shirk her duty or sit back.[132]   Mary Jo Lackamp agrees: "She was not afraid of work. If something had to be done, she was right in there doing it."[133]   But Mary Jo also adds that Dorothy "could make fun out of almost any assignment or task."[134]   Sister Kenan remembers how often Dorothy took the initiative when there was work to do: "She was always the first one there helping; the first one there cleaning up; the first one setting up things."[135] And because she was responsible, Dorothy was often asked to perform tasks that others in her set were not asked to do, such as driving the Generalate[136] places.

In the novitiate, Dorothy seemed very secure in her vocation.[137] Sister Kenan's recollection is that Dorothy "had always a stability about her, a maturity: it was 'I came here, I know what I am doing, I made a choice, and this is what I am following.'"[138]   To Mary Jo, Dorothy seemed "very stable, and she was probably one of the people who had the best and clearest motivation for being in the convent. I think it was ministry."[139]   Dorothy's novice directresses and peers agree that she seemed to have a confidence about her as well as a sense of who she was and where she was going.[140]

*   *   *   *   *   *   *   *   *

In June 1965 Dorothy was appointed to teach at Sacred Heart Academy on Euclid Avenue in East Cleveland. Founded in 1904, Sacred Heart Academy, or the Ursuline Academy of the Sacred Heart as it was then known, had educated thousands of young girls in what was once an upper-middle class, all-white suburban area. But a shift in population occurred in Greater Cleveland during the 1960s so that by the time Dorothy arrived at the Academy, the residents of East Cleveland were predominantly black, economically deprived, and few of them were Catholics.[141]   Sacred Heart's enrollment consequently dropped, and by 1965 the Sisters were actively recruiting students for their school.[142]

During her years at Sacred Heart, Dorothy taught mainly in the business department, and on the average, usually had five preparations a day which included the following courses: typing I and II, shorthand I and II, general business, accounting, and office practice. She taught in a small garage or "portable," as it was called by the faculty and students, in the back of the school. The portable had a porch and four steps that led to double doors. The building contained only two small rooms: one room was used for typing; the other for business and secretarial courses.

Fellow faculty members recall Dorothy passing between the two rooms in her characteristic energetic fashion as her classes changed each day. Since the portable was cold and drafty, during the winter months Dorothy's students could be seen sitting at their typewriters in coats, scarves, and sometimes, even gloves, as Dorothy similarly clothed, instructed them as though nothing were at all unusual about the situation. And because of her positive, fun-loving presence, Dorothy's students did not seem to mind the cold. Many would even remain after school was over for the day and talk with her, oblivious of the time. Sister Vincent de Paul Witchner, then principal of Sacred Heart, fondly recalls seeing Dorothy standing on the steps of the portable, saying goodbye to the students who had gathered in her classroom. After they left, Dorothy would hurry back in, lock the rattling windows, cover the typewriters from the view of possible intruders, and sweep the porch and steps of the building. She would then briskly walk across the yard to the chapel in the convent for Evening Prayer.[143]

The Sisters with whom Dorothy taught remember her fearless nature, evident whether she performed such minor tasks as operating their "Model T" mimeograph machine which leaked ink that inevitably appeared all over her hands and face,[144] or more serious tasks such as investigating the school for possible burglars. On one occasion when the burglar alarm went off at 2:00 a.m. in the school, Dorothy ran over with a few of the other Sisters. She encouraged them to laugh and talk loudly as they passed through the halls so that intruders would believe that a very large, bold group of people had come to find them. Arriving at the school's main office, Dorothy cautiously pushed open the door, flashed on the light — and saw no one. The Sisters then very audibly breathed a sigh of relief and *quietly* returned to the convent.[145]

When the burglar alarm went off again, the Sisters called the police, and this time Dorothy received a surprise, but it was not, however, the burglars she again anticipated. One of the officers who was dispatched to the school was Russell Smith, her former boyfriend, who, unknown to Dorothy at the time, was working for the East Cleveland Police Department. Russ also did not know that Dorothy was teaching at Sacred Heart. Consequently, when the two met, he was visibly stunned, as

Dorothy was dressed in the *long* Ursuline habit which left only her face and hands visible. Throughout the next several years Russ saw Dorothy on a few other occasions, but naturally, none of these had quite the effect on him that the initial one had.[146]

* * * * * * * * *

Former students of Dorothy's remember her as an excellent, well-prepared teacher whose good sense of humor and attentive manner managed to make them feel comfortable and confident. Probably for this reason she was assigned a freshman homeroom each year. One former student, Patricia Maresco, a nervous freshman in Dorothy's homeroom, recalls Dorothy's introduction: "My name is Sister Laurentine, and you'll be able to remember it because it rhymes with 'quarantine.'"[147] Immediately the girls laughed, and the tension in the room evaporated.

Other students considered Dorothy a warm and loving friend who was always ready to listen: "After school every night I would do typing work for her, and we would sit and talk, and if there was ever a problem, Sister Dorothy would always listen and help."[148] Another recalls, "She was a good teacher and much, much more. Her understanding and compassion were her two greatest qualities, and her fun personality, her quick grin and laugh made her the most popular nun at school."[149] For some former students Dorothy is the first teacher they think of when they remember their years at Sacred Heart: "When I think of high school, my fondest memories are those of the times spent with Sister Laurentine. What a lovely, sincere woman! I idolized her and loved her as such a compassionate person."[150]

* * * * * * * * *

Despite her heavy teaching load, Dorothy found time to participate in other activities at Sacred Heart. In the 1967-68 academic year, she taught ninth-grade religion in addition to her regular typing and business courses. Two years later, Dorothy, along with Kathleen Cooney, coordinated the "Beatitudes in Practice" program, placing Sacred Heart sophomores in community service agencies during the school day as part of their education. The agencies at which the students volunteered included hospitals and homes for the elderly and the physically challenged.

With others from Sacred Heart, Dorothy attended ecumenical religious services and retreats at various non-Catholic churches in the area. She looked upon such services and retreats as a way of helping to alleviate religious discrimination.[151] For about three years Dorothy was also involved in the Charismatic Movement and attended prayer meetings at St. Joseph High School, Cleveland. Extra-curricular activities of the school likewise took up much of Dorothy's time. On weekends she went on camping trips with the Girls' Athletic Association and accompanied groups of girls on overnight retreats.[152]

Dorothy, however, did not limit her service-oriented activities only to Sacred Heart. From 1966 through 1968, she taught Catholic doctrine to deaf children at St. Philomena Parish in East Cleveland on Saturday mornings. To learn the skills necessary for effectively teaching the deaf, she attended workshops on special education. At a workshop held at the Mercy College of Detroit, Michigan, Dorothy learned sign language and fundamentals of the psychology of teaching the deaf.[153] On Saturday afternoons during the 1968-69 year, she volunteered at the Martin de Porres Center[154] in Cleveland.

*   *   *   *   *   *   *   *   *

While serving at Sacred Heart Academy, Dorothy completed her initial formation in religious life. Her temporary vows expired on August 13, 1966, and she renewed them for an additional two years. On August 13, 1968, Dorothy pronounced her final vows and at the time also returned to the use of her baptismal name.[155]

*   *   *   *   *   *   *   *   *

Responding to frequent papal requests for missionaries to Latin America,[156] the Diocese of Cleveland sent two priests to open a mission in the Diocese of San Miguel, El Salvador, in August 1964. At this time, Cleveland's Archbishop Edward F. Hoban suggested that religious congregations of Sisters might also consider sending volunteers to El Salvador. So, in August 1966 the first group of Sisters, three Dominicans of Akron, Ohio, departed for San Miguel.

The Ursuline Sisters decided during the summer of 1966 to support the foreign missions, and in 1967 they agreed to assign two Sisters to El Salvador every five years. Mother Annunciata Witz, General Superior at the time, then asked for volunteers from the congregation. Sisters who were interested were to write a letter of application in which they discussed their desire to go to El Salvador and the qualities they believed would qualify them for missionary work.[157]

On November 4, 1967, Dorothy wrote to Mother Annunciata and asked to be considered for the Cleveland Latin America Mission (CLAM) Team. Dorothy's request was denied, however, because in 1967 she was in temporary vows, and the congregation had determined that only finally professed Sisters could go to foreign missions. In the summer of 1968, the first two Ursuline Sisters were sent to El Salvador. The other Sisters who had volunteered, including Dorothy, were assured that they would be considered to serve as replacements in the future.

* * * * * * * * *

Dorothy told nobody at Sacred Heart of her desire to be a missionary until after she had written her letter to Mother Annunciata. When she did tell the Sisters that she had volunteered for El Salvador, she explained, much to their surprise, that being a missionary was what she *really* wanted to do.[158]

With this in mind, Dorothy investigated missionary options in the United States. Between 1967 and 1969 she made various inquiries about working with Native Americans in the Southwest.[159] She eventually found a summer program: teaching Catholic doctrine to Native Americans of the Papago Tribe in Topawa, Arizona. From June 15 to August 7, 1969, she worked in this program with priests from Santa Barbara, California, and lived at St. Catherine Convent with Sisters of Christian Charity of Manitowac, Wisconsin.

From Monday through Thursday mornings, Dorothy taught Catholic doctrine to first and second graders in the town of Sells, Arizona. She also visited outlying missions with Father Michael Schneider, O.F.M. In the afternoons Dorothy helped out with the cooking and cleaning at St. Catherine Convent. On Fridays she and the other Sisters made the seventy-mile drive to Tucson to do weekly grocery shopping. They also went swimming at the convent pool at St. Mary's Hospital.[160]

For the entire summer she spent in Topawa, Dorothy kept a diary that consists of brief sketches of what she did each day and where she went: "a.m. — catechism; p.m. — drove to Tucson in truck . . . went swimming at seminary; ate at Furrs Cafeteria; came home about 10:00;[161] "went with Fr. Michael to Our Lady of Guadalupe Mission; ate dinner: bread, chili, Kool Aid; picked up the children; came home, relaxed, and did some chores the rest of the day";[162] and "a.m. — catechism; cleaned up; p.m. — washed car; 8:00 p.m. — Fr. Camillus hurt his leg; needed ride to hospital; went to St. Mary's Hospital; stopped at 'Sands' Coffee Shop."[163]

Mary Jane Mertens, S.C.C., who lived with Dorothy at St. Catherine Convent has happy memories of the time she spent with Dorothy and is able to fill in some of the "gaps" Dorothy left in her diary. For example, where Dorothy wrote, "birthday dinner for Fr. Michael; angel food cake flopped! German chocolate cake became crumbs! Ugh!"[164] Mary Jane explains:

> Dorothy decided to bake a cake for Fr. Mike's birthday. She found a package of angel food mix, and she baked it. Well, the cake looked beautiful on top, but the center caved in. Dorothy threw it out to the dogs. The cake was so tough they couldn't bite it! So, we made a chocolate cake. That was too rich — it fell apart as Dorothy took it from the pan, so we put it together with toothpicks! It tasted great.[165]

A week later on June 30, Dorothy's thirtieth birthday, she again baked an angel food cake, but this time it turned out well, as she recorded in her diary: "p.m. — birthday party for me; successfully baked an angel food cake!"[166]

One weekend in July, Dorothy and Mary Jane decided to go up to Sedona in the mountains to make a short retreat. In her diary Dorothy wrote: "Spiritual Life Institute: beautiful people! Slept outside under the stars."[167] Mary Jane describes the experience in a more detailed fashion:

> We set up our sleeping bags in a quiet (or so we thought) spot. Soon a family came and asked if they could pitch a tent nearby. Well, it got so noisy that we picked up our air mattresses and climbed a small hill to another spot we had seen earlier. Spreading them out, we collapsed in exhaustion only to hear "s-s-s-t" as the air went out of Dorothy's mattress. A cactus was the culprit! We slept anyway and woke up at dawn with tents all around us. It poured rain the second night so we slept in the car.[168]

In her diary Dorothy also inserted brochures from the various sightseeing trips she took. Although the diary certainly yields an accurate record of what Dorothy was *doing* during her missionary experience, it does not reveal how she *felt* about the missionary work she was doing.

*   *   *   *   *   *   *   *   *

Throughout the late 1960s the Sacred Heart faculty sought creative ways to combat the decreasing enrollment of the school. In the 1967-68 academic year, they began a laboratory-work curriculum geared to the particular needs of the students[169] but also aimed at attracting future students. Called the "Thrust Program," this innovative approach integrated school and community educational resources. Community leaders and other residents were consulted regarding program planning and development, and modular scheduling made possible the application of concepts learned in the classroom.[170] Dorothy was very involved in the Thrust Program as many of her students were placed in nearby businesses to gain practical experience.

Even though the Thrust Program had run smoothly and had benefitted the students, Sacred Heart's financial situation reached crisis proportions in 1968-69 as the enrollment continued to drop. Meetings with the faculty and representatives of the East Cleveland Board of Education, Ursuline Superiors, Bishop William M. Cosgrove, pastors of parishes, alumnae, students, and parents[171] were held throughout most of the year. The faculty also set up a committee composed of three Sisters to recommend solutions to the school's financial problems. Dorothy was one of the Sisters picked for the committee. A financial drive to solicit funds was agreed upon, and as a result, on February 12, 1969, the Sisters decided to keep Sacred Heart open for at least another year.[172]

* * * * * * * * *

In the summer of 1970, Dorothy began graduate studies in guidance and counseling at John Carroll University, Cleveland. Her motivations for choosing a field so remote from business education are unclear. It was known that Dorothy did not like teaching business but did enjoy working with young people. Friends, colleagues, and students also considered her a good listener. Perhaps doubting that Sacred Heart would remain open for many more years, Dorothy decided to think about options other than classroom teaching. Or maybe she just "looked for a way to serve that would fill a special need."[173]

* * * * * * * * *

For more than three years, the Sacred Heart faculty poured much time and energy into efforts to sustain the school. They sought financial assistance from alumnae, the federal government, and private foundations. The Sisters conducted a door-to-door visitation in East Cleveland for recruitment of students.[174] After their 1969 decision to keep the school open, the Sisters also received no salary. But despite their efforts, the Sisters were unsuccessful in obtaining sufficient outside financial aid, and Sacred Heart Academy closed in June 1972.

During the summer of 1972, an auction was held to sell furnishings and other articles from the school. The Sisters packed books and items that would be sent to other schools and convents. On her last evening at Sacred Heart, Dorothy sat in tears on the steps of her typing room and asked the other Sisters, "Don't you wonder what God has in mind for us down the road?"[175]

*   *   *   *   *   *   *   *   *

In May 1972 Dorothy was assigned to Beaumont School for Girls in Cleveland Heights. She taught personal typing[176] but spent the majority of her time in the guidance department. As she had been at Sacred Heart Academy, Dorothy was well-liked by both the faculty and student body of Beaumont, and because she was an effective counselor, many students relied on her for direction and advice. Giving her time freely, she was often involved with some of the more troubled girls until all hours of the night.[177]

Besides teaching and counseling, Dorothy continued her graduate studies at John Carroll University. She completed her practicum in guidance at Beaumont and graduated with a Master of Arts degree on May 26, 1974. In July she received a school counselor certificate from the State of Ohio Department of Education.

*   *   *   *   *   *   *   *   *

In the spring of 1974, Dorothy was chosen to serve on the Cleveland Diocesan Mission Team for a five-year term. Martha Owen was also selected for the team, and together they were the second pair of Cleveland Ursulines to go to El Salvador. At that time, too, Father Kenneth Myers of the Cleveland Diocese was appointed to the team.[178]

In July Dorothy and Martha were assigned to the parish of Nuestra Senora de Guadalupe (Our Lady of Guadalupe) in Chirilagua, located in southeastern El Salvador, and one of three parishes served by the Cleveland Team. At the time of Dorothy and Martha's arrival in Chirilagua, the other team members stationed there were priests William Gibbons, Denis St. Marie, and John Dailey (from the Youngstown, Ohio, Diocese) and lay volunteer Rosemary Smith.

The other two parishes staffed by the Cleveland Team were San Carlos Borromeo (Saint Charles Borromeo) in La Union, located near the Gulf of Fonseca in the southeast corner of El Salvador, and Immaculate Concepción Parish (Immaculate Conception) in La Libertad (the "Port") on the Pacific coastline in the southwestern part of the country. In 1974 the Cleveland Team members who ministered in La Union were Father James McCreight and Dominican Sister Bernadine Baltrinic, then known as "Madre Maria." Those stationed in La Libertad were Father Paul Schindler and Saint Joseph Sisters Mary McNulty and Cynthia Drennan. Besides ministering at the main church of each of these parishes, the Cleveland Team also served thirty or more outlying villages and casarios[179] of each parish.

Dorothy and Martha arrived in El Salvador on July 29, 1974. In the first of a series of audiocassette "letters" Dorothy made for her family throughout her entire time in El Salvador, she relates her initial impressions of the country:

> Our plane came in early. It was about 4:00 [p.m.]. We had a beautiful flight . . . the scenery was gorgeous. Flying over the water was beautiful. We were a little bleary-eyed through the whole thing, but it was really a very nice flight down; it wasn't too bumpy in spots . . . . The country is really exquisite. It's mountainous and green — very green right now. . . It really is beautiful.[180]

After they left the airport, Dorothy and Martha got their first close look at El Salvador, as well as their first experience of traveling the narrow, unpaved roads of the country. Dorothy describes their journey:

> When you pull into Chirilagua, you just pull off onto a dirt road which is really rocky and pitted. So, if you don't have a case of the shakes before, you're totally jiggled, inside out, by the time you get into the little village of Chirilagua which is really very quaint. It's a cute little village but extreme poverty is all over. But it's just the lifestyle of the people. You just have to get used to seeing the very, very poor houses.[181]

Later, she comments on the farm animals that not only live in the yards around the houses but also freely roam the entire village:

Really, it is amusing to see these pigs trotting around: big pigs, little pigs, big cows, little cows, big bulls, little bulls — all over the place — chickens and roosters. I used to believe that the rooster crowed at dawn. Well, I don't believe that anymore. They crow every hour on the hour and continue crowing all day and all night. It's different.[182]

*   *   *   *   *   *   *   *   *

Dorothy and Martha were to begin their missionary work after taking an intensive course in Spanish at the Language Institute in Santa Jose, Costa Rica. Before leaving for the Language Institute, though, they spent about a month with the CLAM Team members in Chirilagua. Dorothy kept a diary of this period, and the entries are typical of her writing style. In brief passages she told what she did but gave very little personal commentary: "Arrived San Salvador; entire team met us. Had Coke in terminal and chatted. Drove to Chirilagua (had supper). Got to bed after midnight. Awakened 4:00 a.m. by serenaders (beautiful)!"[183]   9:15 a.m. went with Rosemary [Smith] to meeting with women in Caritas Program[184] at El Cuco. Ate 'corn starch soup' and corn. Then went over to Pacific and swam in underwear";[185] 9:30 a.m. headed to San Miguel. Took sick lady to hospital. Stopped at San Lucas. Went shopping in new market. Went to Burger King for Whoppers. Drove to volcano and San Miguel (coffee) and had a picnic";[186] and "Saw smoking volcano. 8:30 La Libertad — city church in marketplace; very noisy and hot; like inner city."[187]

Some of the letters Dorothy sent to her parents shortly after her arrival in El Salvador mirror narrations from her diary. In her first letter to her mother and father, Dorothy wrote:

> We made it in one piece. The team met us at the airport. After eating, we headed to Chirilagua. After getting to bed after midnight, we were awakened at 4:00 a.m. by our serenading church group. It was really lovely.
>
> We then slept to about 10:00, got up, "showered" in our bird house, and ate at the priests' house. They took us around Chirilagua today (a very poor place). We then went to Mass at Candlera, another poor village, and then had Mass here again at 7:00 — by candlelight, as it rained and knocked out the electricity!
>
> All is going well — there is much to see and learn. Will write again. Love, Dorothy[188]

In the first taped letter she sent to her parents, Dorothy described the "new market" she had mentioned in her diary entry of August 1, 1974:

> We went into San Miguel proper which is the third largest city here in El Salvador, and it's very interesting. It's very much like the capital [San Salvador] in the sense that the streets are very narrow, and the sidewalks are a half-inch wide so you have to walk single file down them.
>
> The marketplace is rare. Now, we just learned that we were in the new marketplace — they [team members] didn't take us to the old marketplace. Rosemary [Smith] didn't think we were ready to face that yet. But the new market — everything is literally out on the road, and they must've had two billion watermelons they were trying to sell. I don't know who's going to buy them all! They have all their food in the open — their bananas and peaches and watermelons; all kinds of clothing were also in the open. . . . It's nothing like our convenient department stores. . . .
>
> The other interesting thing is the boys are boys, and the girls are girls in the sense that the girls all do wear dresses here, and the boys, of course, wear their slacks. But the mod fashions haven't really hit here as they have in the States. The guys' hair is a reasonable length — you don't see guys running around with ponytails. The girls, on the whole, have very long hair, and they wear it straight and pulled back.[189]

*　*　*　*　*　*　*　*　*

On August 24, 1974, Dorothy and Martha left for the Language Institute in Santa Jose, Costa Rica, to study the Spanish language. While in the program, they lived with a native family and commuted each day to school.

During the three months she spent in Costa Rica, Dorothy kept a diary in which she composed abbreviated commentaries of her activities: "Went to town — all day. Opened checking account. Got home at 6:00.[190] Called home! School till 11:15. Left for Puntarenas on train; took four hours; stayed at Tioga Motel; ate at Chinese place; relaxed";[191] "Swam in Pacific; truck ride; showered under the waterfalls";[192] and "Climbed mountain with cross! Fantastico!"[193] In this diary Dorothy did not describe her experience of learning Spanish at the Language Institute.[194]

*　*　*　*　*　*　*　*　*

On December 13, 1974, Dorothy and Martha left Costa Rica to begin their ministry at the parish of Nuestra Senora de Guadalupe in Chirilagua. Their work in Chirilagua and at the other two parishes where they would eventually be assigned was mostly pastoral: planning and organizing celebrations of the Eucharist and other liturgies, playing the music and conducting choirs for the liturgies, preparing both adults and children for the reception of the sacraments, and training native lay persons as catechists. They also managed the Caritas Program and visited the sick. In the early years of their missionary experience, Dorothy and Martha tutored the people in reading and writing.

*   *   *   *   *   *   *   *   *

At the time Dorothy was in El Salvador, there were usually two priests and a comparable number of women, both lay[195] and religious, assigned to every parish the CLAM Team served. Each priest celebrated Mass and administered the sacraments at the main church of his parish, and in addition, visited ten or more outlying villages and casarios once a month to perform the same services. One or two Sisters and laywomen accompanied him.[196] Every week, then, the missionaries visited three or four cantones[197] in the area. If these villages and casarios were in very rural areas, as was often the case, the missionaries traveled by jeep. Otherwise, a van served as transportation.

Whereas a priest could only visit his entire area once a month, the Sisters and lay women visited their area — all ten or more outposts — weekly, alone, and usually on horseback or by motorbike because of the rough terrain. These frequent visitations were to remind the parishioners of upcoming Masses and other liturgical celebrations and to determine with them at whose house in the village or casario the services would be held. The women then relayed this information to the parish priests. Since they served as such a vital link of communication between the parish and its parishioners, the Sisters and lay women, in a sense, guided the work of the parish.[198] They also maintained constant contact with the parishes through the Caritas Program, which they coordinated in the outposts of their area.

Because the main goal of the Cleveland Team was to develop the lay leadership,[199] they spent much time training native lay persons as catechists so that the work of the Church would continue when the missionaries were gone. The priests, Sisters, and lay women first identified the native people they thought would make good catechists;[200]

then they held cursillos[201] at a large training center for catechists[202] or at a particular village and taught Catholic doctrine. At the cursillos the designated catechists learned how to teach doctrine to their people and how to prepare them for the reception of the sacraments of the Eucharist, confirmation, and marriage. They were also instructed in conducting communion services and the Liturgy of the Word. If a village or casario had the Eucharist,[203] the lay catechists would daily call the community together, and they would celebrate a communion service.[204] If they could not be "nourished by the Eucharist . . . they had the opportunity to worship together and to be nourished by their reflection on the Word of God"[205] through the Liturgy of the Word.[206]

In other areas of their ministry, the CLAM Team educated the native people so that they would ultimately help each other. The Sisters and lay women taught the native men and women how to read and write with the hope that they would in turn teach others in their village; in the Caritas Program they first taught the women how to properly care for and nourish their children and then how to pass along this vital information to other women. So, according to Martha Owen, "There was constant working with the people, empowering them, trying to get them to do the teaching and coordinating.[207]

*   *   *   *   *   *   *   *   *

The length of Dorothy and Martha's ministry in Chirilagua was cut short because of an unanticipated staffing problem in nearby La Union. The parish there, San Carlos Borromeo, was supposed to get three Sisters from Costa Rica in January 1975 to join Madre Maria, who had been stationed in La Union alone for the past year and a half. Since Maria had ministered at the parish a total of eight years, she was planning to return to Cleveland after spending a few months training the Costa Rican Sisters. As it turned out, though, the Sisters could not come to San Carlos Borromeo. The Cleveland Team then concluded that some other arrangement would have to be made. On April 2, 1975, they mutually decided that Dorothy and Martha would go to La Union.[208] In a tape she recorded for her parents on April 12, 1975, Dorothy explained why she and Martha were chosen to replace Maria and how the transition would best come about:

> Since we were still brand new in Chirilagua, the team decided that it would be better that we come to La Union, and Maria would stay with us and work with us with the programs and

then she would be able to go back. But we're not sure when she is going to go back — it might be in August; it might be later. We talked about it, but so much just depends on us being able to pick up Spanish well and understand the people well and figure out the programs.[209]

Dorothy then described La Union and where exactly she and Martha were living:

La Union is a very lovely place; it's a place that we call the suburbs. It's like a city; it's got a great big, beautiful church here — it's called the Church of St. Charles of Borromeo, but they really honor Our Lady of the Immaculate Conception here. And here is where we live: in the church. The left side of the church is the priests' quarters, and the south side is the nuns' quarters. We are at the top of the church — it's just a wing stuck on at the top of the church. It's really fantastic, but we do have our own rooms here, and it's a lot roomier. . . . We do have a bathroom that Martha and I share, but La Union also has a terrific water problem. They have to store water . . . well, the water used to come on at least once a day, and now it doesn't even come on, or else it comes on so low that there's not enough pressure to get the water upstairs so we have to carry the water up. . . .[210]

In La Union Dorothy and Martha worked with Cleveland Team member Father James McCreight and two Salvadoran priests, Miguel Montecinos and Leonel Cruz. On February 4, 1976, Vincentian Sister of Charity Christine Rody, another Cleveland Team member, joined them. In addition to the same type of pastoral work they had done in Chirilagua, Dorothy and Martha also visited rural schools in the La Union area and taught basic Catholic doctrine to the children.

The times the missionaries shared with the people and with each other were happy and uncomplicated. On December 11, 1976, however, in a tape to her parents, Dorothy refers for the first time to Salvador's unpredictable political situation — one that would become even more problematic and unstable in only a few short months.[211] She framed her comments in reply to her parents' request to come to Salvador to visit her:

I think you're going to have to wait because. . . . we think the elections, the presidential elections, are around the middle of February — around the 20th — and you never know what's going to happen. There could be a coup; there could be a demonstration; there could be trouble.

So, what we think we're going to do is go and study during the month of February and come back in March just to get out of here. Jaime [Jim McCreight] is going to go home for a two-month vacation [during February and March]. And we're just going to go for a month to Guatemala, probably the first part of February and into March.

We can't really have too many meetings and things going on during the elections because they're just a precarious time around here. So, it's probably better that we just go and study.[212]

*   *   *   *   *   *   *   *   *

In December of 1977, the parish of San Carlos Borromeo was transferred back to the native clergy. Father Jim McCreight then returned to the Cleveland Diocese, and Dorothy, Martha, and Christine were assigned to the parish of the Immaculate Concepción in the port city of La Libertad. Also ministering at the parish were priests Paul Schindler and Ken Myers and Sisters Cindy Drennan and Loretta Schulte.

Although Dorothy, Martha, and Christine would be operating mainly from the parish church in La Libertad, they decided to live in Zaragoza, a village a short distance from the Port. This way, they reasoned, they could offer a religious presence to the people in another area besides the Port proper where Cindy and Loretta lived. Zaragoza was also a canton of the parish, and Ken Myers lived there.

Soon after Dorothy, Martha, and Christine moved into a house Ken rented for them in Zaragoza and were then ready to begin their ministry, they and the other team members divided the large parish of La Libertad into four zones to better facilitate their pastoral responsibilities. The team also determined that Dorothy and Cindy would work with Paul in La Libertad and its surrounding areas, and Martha and Christine would work with Ken in and around Zaragoza.[213] Because she was scheduled to leave in June of 1978, Loretta worked with both groups where she was needed. And when Cindy left in July of that year, Dorothy acquired her areas and programs and continued to work with Paul.

*   *   *   *   *   *   *   *   *

During the fall of 1978, the team received word from the Cleveland Mission Office that a young woman who was interested in becoming a member of the Cleveland Mission Team would be visiting El Salvador in the near future. Her name was Jean Donovan, and she arrived on October 10 for a ten-day visit. The team members in La Libertad, with whom Jean associated the most, introduced her to the types of work they were doing. After spending a few days with Jean, Dorothy offered her first impressions of her:

> She went to Case Western Reserve [University], and she's been living in Cleveland. She's working there right now in a computer processing company. She's quite the smart little girl and comes from a family with money, actually. Her parents live in Sarasota, Florida. They have a suite in Disneyland [laughs]. So we like that! Maybe we can use it sometime!
>
> Jean's really cute — a typical twenty-five-year-old kid. She's very pleasant and friendly and seems really settled in her mind to come down here and work and is willing to. . . . She's interested in working with the Caritas Program, possibly, which would be nice, and also a little bit of the evangelization, too, like doing First Communion classes or working with the youth or something like that. . . . So, we shall see what happens . . . We've been taking her around to the different places and letting her see what it's all about . . . .[214]

*   *   *   *   *   *   *   *   *

In tapes to her family, Dorothy rarely mentioned Salvadoran politics, and because she did not want her family to worry, she hardly ever discussed any incidents she or the other team members may have had with the Salvadoran military. However, in a tape to her family in February 1979, Dorothy revealed how she and the team in La Libertad were regarded by the military. She prefaced her comments with "Maybe I shouldn't tell you this so it doesn't scare you out of your liver":

> There have been things going on, and we have not been directly involved. They [the military] haven't been against us except that I have just been called a Communist, and Pablo [Paul Schindler] has just been called a Communist on Sunday, but so, what's new? They always call us Communists. . . .

The Guardia are like the National Guard, I guess you'd translate it as. They're the group that does all the killing all the time. They're right outside the church — right across the street from us. So, anytime anything's going on in the church, they certainly can hear and listen to what we're saying, and we're not saying anything "bad" or communistic as they claim we are.[215]

*   *   *   *   *   *   *   *   *

The summer of 1979 marked the end of Dorothy's and Martha's assignment in El Salvador. Each had served her five-year term. By this time, however, the Ursuline Congregation had decided that one of the Sisters of a pair assigned to El Salvador would always remain in the country for an additional year to help train and also offer community support to the new Ursuline assigned to the CLAM Team. Mother Bartholomew McCaffrey, General Superior, left it to Dorothy and Martha to determine which of them would stay in El Salvador for the extra year. A situation regarding team personnel enabled them to quickly arrive at a decision.

Since Cindy Drennan and Loretta Schulte had left La Libertad a year ago, Dorothy had been working with Paul. If she left, obviously Paul would have to work alone; whereas if Martha left, Ken would still have Christine with whom to work. Keeping this staffing situation in mind, Dorothy and Martha mutually decided that Martha should go and Dorothy should stay. They then informed the other team members of their decision. Martha recalls that Dorothy was so excited about staying,[216] for she really wanted to continue doing missionary work.

*   *   *   *   *   *   *   *   *

Later in the summer of 1979, and several weeks after Dorothy returned to Salvador from her annual vacation in the States, she made her mother and father a tape in which she again mentioned Salvador's political situation. This time, however, she assured her parents that she was fine and not in danger. Malvina, who apparently had read about the escalating violence in El Salvador and was understandably worried about Dorothy, called her on July 16. Dorothy's tape is her response to their telephone conversation:

Hello. This is me, your dear daughter who is still alive and safe and sound here in El Salvador. It is now Monday evening, and you just called me this afternoon so I thought I would at least make part of a tape and send it with Christine [Rody] so that you will know that I *really* am okay.

Really, as I say, you get more nervous when you're back home because you people read more about what's going on in the papers than we probably even know about. We are really alright, so don't worry about it. . . .

I just wanted to send you something so that you know that we are A-OK. . . . Everything is fine. You know, things are not perfect in this country, but we're alright. You do not have to worry, okay?[217]

2

A Record of a Death

*Overcome fear of . . . laying down my life in very service of
others . . . letting the cross of Christ cut into my very soul:
Love the cross — accept it totally — it is He. . . .*

Journal, November 1, 1970

In order to fully comprehend the nature of Dorothy's missionary
work, particularly in her last years in El Salvador, and ultimately, the
context of her murder there, one must be generally familiar with the
historico-political background and of the major forces at work on the
contemporary Salvadoran scene.[1] What follows is a brief description
of these elements. This narration, however, is in no way a definitive
analysis of the complex political situation, nor does it offer a solution
to its resulting problems.

*   *   *   *   *   *   *   *   *

El Salvador has had a long history of domination by a ruling
oligarchy. In 1525 the area which is today El Salvador was conquered
by Spain, and soon after its central region was partitioned into colonial
plantations that grew trade crops of balsam, cacao and indigo.[2] Large-
scale development of the plantations was delayed, partly as a
consequence of isolation, and the Spanish permitted the native
population to maintain much of their traditional system of communal
lands.[3] In 1821 Central America gained its independence from Spain,
and by 1839 El Salvador and the other countries of Central America
became separate. During these years of the fledgling republic, however,
the landed oligarchy began to initiate efforts to dissolve the system of
communal lands.[4]

With a decline in demand for indigo in mid-century, the oligarchic
families, who by now had become the "famous fourteen families,"[5]
proposed a full-scale privatizing of the communal lands held by the

native inhabitants in order to increase export production.[6] Large tracts of communal land used for internal production were, therefore, turned over to cash or export crops — indigo, cotton, sugar, and coffee.[7] Forced to then lease lands from the new landowners, the native people's only source of money was to work as seasonal laborers on the newly enlarged plantations.[8] This new pattern of land use and land ownership, established over one-hundred years ago by men whose heirs still own and exploit it, remains fundamentally unchanged today.[9]

By the late nineteenth century, coffee became the major export crop and the source of wealth for the oligarchic families. The majority of the native population was increasingly impoverished by the growth of the large coffee estates, and because many began to rebel, a National Guard was created in 1921 to furnish the landowners with a rural police force charged with control, coercion, and oppression of farm workers.[10] During the 1920s, however, the number of workers' organizations increased, and in 1930 Farabundo Marti founded the Salvadoran Communist Party (PCES).

With the Great Depression of 1929 came a drop in coffee revenues and a consequent reduction of wages throughout the countryside. These factors created widespread unrest among the workers, which was met by extreme repression. On January 22, 1932, a revolt led by Marti resulted in the massacre of 30,000 native people by the army. The Salvadoran people call this uprising and its aftermath "la Matanza" — the Massacre — while the landowners refer to it as the Communist Rebellion.[11] Since the Massacre, military governments have held power in El Salvador.

Such extreme resistance to the military government did not appear again until the early 1970s. At this time left-wing opposition groups,[12] composed of militant peasants, students, teachers, and workers, and supported by the Salvadoran Catholic Church,[13] emerged to campaign for basic social and economic reforms.[14] The members of these groups were viewed by the government as anarchists, terrorists, fanatics, and communists. Among the latter group the government included priests, Sisters, and lay catechists.[15]

Organized left-wing terrorism likewise made its first appearance in the early 1970s when two small guerrilla groups sponsored a campaign of kidnaping among the wealthy families and the foreign business community.[16] To combat such terrorism, the landowners established and armed a rural civilian vigilante organization called ORDEN, with groups in every hamlet, village, and community to provide the "ears" and the "fingers" for the National Guard, the police, and the army.[17] Tension in the country mounted when in 1973 and in 1976, the landowners succeeded in blocking even the most moderate proposals for agrarian reform. And in 1972, 1974, and 1977 the military destroyed all possibility of the development of a democratic opposition of the center through systematic electoral fraud.[18]

Also in 1977 government violence grew to epidemic proportions. The first attack against the Catholic Church occurred in March of that year with the murder of Rutilio Grande, a Salvadoran Jesuit. Organized, systematic persecution of union members, professionals, and teachers, as well as of laborers and campesinos,[19] began in the spring with the appearance of the first professional death squads, the "escuadrones de muerte." Composed of former and present members of the military, these roving squads took their orders and received money from some of the best-known names in the country.[20] In order to frighten the people, they published death lists and disfigured and dismembered the bodies of their victims.

Despite authenticated reports of death-squad atrocities and other government-sponsored barbarisms, such as torturous murders and unexplained disappearances, the United States approved a $90 million loan in military aid to the Salvadoran government in November 1977. This action inaugurated America's entrance into the internal affairs of El Salvador. The year also brought, however, the appointment of Archbishop Oscar Romero to the diocese of San Salvador. He would become the voice of his people, speaking out in justice and compassion against the repressive, oppressive oligarchy. And like so many of his murdered brothers and sisters, Romero would ultimately suffer their own fate.

* * * * * * * * *

During the fourteen months or so before Dorothy's death, the violence and political upheaval of El Salvador reached several crescendos. A bloodless coup occurred on October 15, 1979, in which a group of young military officers overthrew the government and formed the first junta,[21] the "Revolutionary Military-Civilian Junta."[22] On January 3, 1980, however, it collapsed, and on January 9 the military announced the formation of a new government, a second junta composed of the military and of Christian Democrats.[23]   The United States supported this second junta, believing that it was the force of moderation, "the beleaguered center, beset by violence from both the Left and the Right."[24]   What this description neatly ignores, however, is the reality of right-wing violence directed and carried out by the junta's security forces,[25] notably the assassination of Archbishop Oscar Romero on March 24, 1980.[26]

As the military nature of the repression in rural areas expanded, members of the Social Democratic Party, dissident Christian Democrats, and the Marxists of the popular organizations, together with the major trade unions, united in April 1980 to form the Revolutionary Democratic Front (FDR). Formed for the purpose of providing an alternative to the second junta, the FDR presented the only hope for an end to the slaughter and the development of a democratic government committed to social justice for the entire population.[27]   The second junta, however, continued its oppressive tactics, and in May security forces inaugurated a campaign to uproot members of the popular organizations and guerrilla groups from their rural bases in the North.[28]   This antisubversive campaign developed in practice into a program of terror, aimed at depopulating the regional villages and destroying crops in order to create starvation conditions.[29]

The conflict between the guerrillas and the army, which gradually grew into a full-blown counter-insurgency war, and the civil war between the guerrillas and ORDEN produced large numbers of refugees fleeing from their villages and cantones often with little more than they could carry. A particular area or town was frequently the scene of confrontations between the fighting factions. One such town was Chalatenango. Because the guerrillas had established bases in the mountainous terrain and the surrounding mountains of this northern town, it was victimized by the counter-insurgency tactics and retaliation of the security forces.

Government violence and terrorism increased as 1980 drew to a close. In October the government launched a "definitive military operation"[30] against the guerrilla stronghold in the northeastern province of Morazan. About 5,000 troops of the army and security forces were deployed, and for the first time the Salvadoran Air Force was used in counterinsurgency. Thousands of refugees fled as their villages were randomly bombed.[31]   On November 27 six of the most prominent leaders of the FDR were assassinated by security forces.

These acts of murder, however, would not be the final ones committed by the government that year.

*   *   *   *   *   *   *   *   *

In the midst of the political turmoil happening all around them, the members of the Cleveland Latin American Mission Team tried to conduct their pastoral duties as normally as possible. However, they and their lay catechists did occasionally experience firsthand the increasing threats against the Church from the Salvadoran military, as Paul Schindler related:

> The people are getting used to threats, and they haven't stopped them in most parts. The threats are getting a lot more violent, though.
>
> We had one catechist beaten up by the Guardia. And last Saturday in La Lima, the Guardia were there when I got there [for Mass], about a block and a half from the house where we were, and they just stood there through the whole Mass. They sent word — they wouldn't talk to me — to the owner of the house that I was only allowed to be there a half an hour. I sent word back with one of the kids. I told him to say, "The padre's [priest] going to be here until noon — or about two hours." There were no repercussions afterwards, but the Guardia is getting a little bit bolder in their threats.[32]

A few weeks later in a tape to Martha Owen, Dorothy referred to the growing seriousness and complexity of Salvador's political problems, and for the first time in any of her tapes, she commented on the military aid the United States has been sending to El Salvador. Dorothy's remarks are in response to some newspaper articles Martha had sent to her.[33] She said:

> The articles you sent down on El Salvador are very interesting, especially this one, "El Salvador Falls Apart," where they say that in September arms are expected to come in regularly. Oh, it just makes you sick! And you really wonder how true it is and what's going to happen. I mean, there's so much going on that you really, really wonder how much longer we can survive.[34]

Despite El Salvador's uncertain political situation, though, Dorothy was committed to remain there, as she claimed later in the tape: "I could not leave Salvador, especially now because I am committed here for another year, and I am committed to the persecuted Church here."[35] Projecting into the future, Dorothy then wondered what she will do when she returns to the States the following year. Her lack of direction led to some unsettling feelings, but ones which were not overwhelming to her at the time. She shared her thoughts with Martha:

> I'm just on high Q and very emotional, but right now I feel better [because] I went to Mass, and then I stayed and prayed awhile . . . really, I just don't know what God is wanting me to do or where to go with stuff [I'm thinking about] . . . but I feel peaceful about it.[36]

*   *   *   *   *   *   *   *   *

Jean Donovan arrived in El Salvador on August 10, 1979, to begin her ministry in the Immaculate Concepción Parish of La Libertad with Dorothy, Christine Rody , Paul Schindler, and Ken Myers. At this time the Cleveland team members at La Libertad were attempting to take care of five additional parishes which brought the total number of their parishioners to 140,000. The team also maintained contact with two North American Maryknoll Sisters who worked within a fifty-mile radius of La Libertad: to the northwest in Santa Ana, Madeline Dorsey single-handedly ran a health clinic and ministered to the needs of some four-thousand slum dwellers; to the northeast in the village of Tamanique, Joan Petrik ran a small rural parish which had been without a priest for sometime.[37] Tamanique was one of the areas Paul visited on a monthly basis to celebrate Mass.

After getting settled in Zaragoza with Dorothy and Christine, Jean began working closely with Dorothy in the parish since it was the understanding among the team members that she would take Dorothy's place when Dorothy left La Libertad in a year. So, throughout the remaining months of 1979, Jean learned, with Dorothy's guidance, the workings of the parish and got to know the parishioners in its outlying areas.

In the meantime, because of political upheavals occurring in the country and with the signs of approaching civil war clearly visible, the Salvadoran Church was already making plans for refugee centers in which women, children, and the elderly, fleeing from the violence in their villages, could be sheltered and protected from the assaults of security forces and groups like ORDEN.[38]

The CLAM Team was also considering running refugee centers when and where they would be needed. In a letter she wrote to Mother Bartholomew McCaffrey in November 1979, Dorothy mentioned that her and the team's discussions of plans to operate the centers were influenced by the Maryknoll Sisters whom they knew quite well and who had served in Nicaragua during its civil war.[39] Toward the end of the war, in May 1979, the Sisters had run a refugee center in Leon, Nicaragua,[40] and in her letter Dorothy explained, "Since then they have given us lists of things to have ready for our potential refugee centers here. For instance, the school in La Libertad would be an ideal place — and possibly the church in Zaragoza. Anyway, this is how we are thinking right now."[41]

Under the direction of Archbishop Oscar Romero, the first refugee center was established at the end of January 1980 on the grounds of the archdiocesan seminary in San Salvador. The CLAM Team, however, played no part in the foundation of this center. They, in particular, Dorothy, Jean, and Christine, would not become actively involved in refugee work for another few months.

*　　*　　*　　*　　*　　*　　*　　*　　*

In January the mission team received word that James A. Hickey, bishop of Cleveland, and Father Alfred Winters, director of the Cleveland Diocesan Mission Office, would arrive in El Salvador on the thirty-first for visitation with the team. Also that month Dorothy, Jean, and Christine accepted an invitation from the Maryknoll Sisters they knew in Leon, Nicaragua, to come for a short visit. They, along with newly arrived Cleveland Team member Vincention Sister of Charity Elizabeth Kochik, left by ferry from La Union on January 20 for what they thought would be a four-day trip. To facilitate their travels once they arrived in Nicaragua, the women took with them on the ferry the team's microbus.

Some time after the trip, in a lengthy letter she sent to her family and friends, Dorothy describes in colorful detail her and her companions' "vacation" and the unexpected surprises it held for them. To preserve the integrity of her narrative, it is printed in its entirety below.

We left La Libertad and drove to La Union to catch the ferry to Nicaragua on Sunday, January 20. We arrived in La Union at 2:30 p.m. and left on the ferry at 1:00 a.m. Monday. The ride over was beautiful — the heavens were full of stars and the milky way was close and heavy. The Southern Cross rose over us. Cris [Rody] and I slept on the outside benches while Jean and Elizabeth [Kochik] stayed inside the micro.

We arrived in Potosi, Nicaragua, about 6:30 a.m. Monday. It took about one and one-half hours to get into the country. The "muchachos" [young, Nicaraguan soldiers] are not as organized as they should be. We then drove to Chinandega and on to Leon. It was an exhilarating feeling being in Patria Libre [free country]. There were signs of reconstruction everywhere. It was good to see red and black Sandinista flags and signs around. In Leon Pat Murray, Julie Miller, Gerri Brake, and Rita Owczarek took very good care of us and gave us the royal war tours, ending with a grand visit to the refugee center. On Tuesday we all drove to Managua to visit with Pattie Edminston, Peg Dillon, Jean Robertson, and Julianne Warnshuis. Again, we got a total tour of the war-torn areas as well as the 1972 earthquake ruins. We also stopped at what used to be a private home of Somoza that they made into a cultural center. Luckily, the Nicaraguan chorale was there so we were able to enjoy some beautiful singing in five voices or more. We also took a shopping trip to Masaya and passed through Moning Bo which was a center of war activity. We also stopped to see a beautiful volcano. Nicaragua's topography is hillier and more volcanic than Salvador. On Thursday we spent the morning at the "polio pit," the home(s) and pool and tennis courts of some friends of the Maryknollers in Leon. The owner of the place had done a lot to help the Sandinistas during the war. Afterward, we did a little more shopping. On Friday at 4:00 a.m., we arose and had a scrumptious breakfast before leaving for Potosi to catch the ferry. We arrive there at 6:30 a.m. and got all of our papers processed to leave. About 8:30 a.m. we learned that the ferry may *not* be going for a few days. What to do! Well, we decided to send Cris and Elizabeth in a dug-out canoe with a

motor and fifteen other people over to La Union. It would be
about a five and one-half hour trip. But they were our
connection with the "outside world," as there was no means of
communication for 80 kilometers. However, after we sent
them, we were worried, as neither of them swim — and being
in one these canoes on the open ocean does leave something to
be desired. However, thanks be to God, they did make it —
and got safely home by the next day.

Meanwhile, Jean and I stayed with the microbus — it
became our "mobile home." We lived through Friday,
Saturday, and Sunday pretty well because the promise was that
we would leave the latest by Sunday night. First of all, in
Potosi there is no drinking water or lavs. Also the one water
spigot they had to use to wash up with did not work after
Friday. There were only two comedors [restaurants] — and
one was a greasier spoon than the other. This, of course, forced
us to a three-times-a day potty schedule. We would get up at
4:30 a.m. while it was still dark; at noon we visited a friend's
outhouse; then again before we went to sleep, we hit the beach.
We would eat in the comedor once a day — and try to share a
meal. However, the truck drivers thought we didn't have
enough money, so they would offer to buy us our meals. In the
mornings we usually waited to hear the news of the day about
the ferry. Then we would go down to the beach for our dip in
the ocean and then go to the fresh water river to wash up. This
is also where the people wash their clothes, their kids, and
themselves — along with the cows and horses. Usually in the
late afternoon we would go back down to the ocean and sit on
the rocks and read or write or whatever. It was good getting to
know the people there — there was hardly a person we talked
with who had not lost a loved one in the war. One evening we
even had a rifle demonstration. Three of the muchachos
working there showed us everything one needed to know
about rifles. The littlest one also carried the heaviest rifle! He
was eighteen and had been in training for two years. It truly
was a war won by "tots." The truck drivers were also an
interesting group. When they know you're a religious, they
all want to talk about God — so that we did. We even talked

about forming catechists out of some of them. Most of them were Salvadorans who drove the huge cargo trailers. They were dependent on the ferry also because they had Salvadoran license plates, and with those you cannot cross through Honduras because we are still at "war" with them (since 1968!). Now Sunday we thought would be our last day there because they kept telling us it would leave that evening. So Jean and I took our last river bath (in which we used her $20 bar of Estee Lauder soap!) and put on our clean clothes. Well, Sunday night came and went — and they were promising Monday. Well, then they started saying it might be another 15 days because the motor was really bad . . . Well, then they said, "*No*, Tuesday morning it will leave." So we hung on till about 11:00 a.m. on Tuesday — then they again started saying Tuesday night. And we kept thinking, "We've *got* to get back — the Bishop [James Hickey] will be in Salvador on Thursday, and we'll still be in Potosi."

So we decided to chance going through Honduras. The worst that could happen is that we would have to return. So we had to *re*-process our papers and get back *in* to Nicaragua so that we could leave another way. We passed through the Nicaraguan frontera [border] without any trouble. As I pulled into the Honduranian frontera and got out of the car to go to Immigration with our passports, the man said he could do nothing for us because of the Salvadoran plates. So I talked to the jefe [chief] there who told me I had to go to Culuteca to get permission from the commandante to pass through. I asked if he could be called — they said they had no means of communication. I asked if they were sure he would be there — they said yes; if not him, one of the others could do it. I asked, "How do I get there?" They said, "Take a taxi." I asked, "How much does it cost?" They said, "Twenty-five dollars." I said, "Who's going to pay for that? I don't have that much money!" So I finally got a man in a pick-up truck to take me in for ten dollars.

We first went to one cuartel [army barracks] and then got sent to another. They told me the man I needed to see went to Tegucigalpa and *nobody* else could help me. Then they said he should be in by 5:30 p.m. (this was 3:30 p.m.). Meanwhile my truck driver friend had to leave — so there I sat waiting. At 5:40 they proceed to tell me that he most probably wasn't coming back because it was late. I was not too happy at this point. They told me to come back the next morning. I left *very* upset looking for a taxi in a city where I had never been. I then ran into three civilians and exasperatedly asked them where I could get a taxi. So, they told me to wait right there and then asked what was the matter. So I told them my plight. And they encouraged me and said I certainly should be able to get help before going back. So they told the taxi driver my plight, and he took me to the personal home of Captain Aguilares. He, of course, was *not* home but his son said he just left so he should be somewhere near. Well, we went looking around for him and couldn't find him. So, we went to another captain's house, but he hadn't come home yet. So we returned to the first place. This time his wife and second son came out to talk to me to hear my plight. So, the son went with us to find him. After looking in every park, restaurant, and bar in town, we finally found him in front of a delicatessen drinking a Pepsi with two buddies. So he came back to the house in the taxi with us. After listening to my story, he proceeds to tell me there is *nothing* he can do for me. He instead, sent me to the head of Transito [department where papers are processed]. This man was bien amable [friendly]. When I walked in, he said, "What can I do for you?" I said, "Help me! I've got to get back home," and I told him my plight. He kept holding his head and assuring me that he would think of something. So he said, "I can't help you, but I know who can."

So he sent me with one of his blue-and-white uniformed men *back* to the place where I had been sitting originally. This is now about 6:50 p.m. Around 7:00 in walks some captain. All the soldiers there stood up and saluted, and the guy at the desk told him my whole story without pausing for a breath. He then went into his office for awhile. When he came back out, he sent one soldier to buy vitamin pills for his little girl. Then he proceeds to call his wife and chit-chat with her.

Meanwhile I'm beginning to get a bit upset, thinking this is the man I'm supposed to talk with. Well, luckily, it was not! About 7:15 the soldier at the desk tells me to go inside to talk to the commandante (Head of the Army in Culuteca).

Well, it was like a movie. I walk into this huge warehouse-sized office with air-conditioning. There was a huge desk in the middle with this enormous gentleman behind it with cigarette holder and cigarette. Behind him is this very red drape. To his left was a huge map of Central America; to his right was a drawing board; to the right center was his television. I could hardly believe it. He, too, was bien amable and asked, "What can I do for you?" I said, "I've *got* to get home! My problem is that I have a car with Salvadoran license plates." Well, he then reiterated all the laws that tell I can't pass through Honduras. I said, "But I've *got* to!" Then I told him our whole Potosi story and how the ferry wasn't working, and we didn't have water, etc. So he had one of his "peons" working there give me a big glass of ice cold water, and he started making the necessary phone calls, etc. Well, he finally got me cleared through and gave me a note to take to some colonel. Before I left he said, "Do come back again — but when you don't have such problems." He was really dear. I was so grateful to finally get the okay to pass through. My taxi driver and I finally got back to the frontera about 9:15 p.m.

Meanwhile, Jean had been babysitting the micro. Neither of us had been signed into the country — but here we were. Before I even got back, the jefe who made me go to Culuteca assured her that I would get permission. This was because he had received the information from the commandante. Because it was too late to pass through, we spent another night in our micro. The next morning we had to take the front plate off, and because we couldn't get the back one off, they just covered it with paper and tape. Then we had to have a soldier go with us to the other border. Two others came along to get dropped off at other places. At the other Honduran border they were waiting for us and processed us through as quickly as possible. Then we had to put on the front plate and uncover the back plate and pass into the Salvadoran frontera. This was quite a treat for them because cars with Salvadoran plates *never* pass through Honduras. So they asked, "How did you do it?" I said, "With *great* difficulty!" But we made it — thank God! Our four-day trip to Nicaragua took six days to get home![42]

* * * * * * * * *

True to plan — and just one day after Dorothy and Jean arrived home from their Nicaraguan excursion — Bishop James A. Hickey and Father Al Winters arrived in La Libertad on January 31 to visit the CLAM Team. The topic of conversations among the team members, Bishop Hickey, and Father Winters repeatedly turned to El Salvador's chaotic political situation and its possible outcomes. Just one week before the bishop's arrival, members of the popular organizations and their political allies had been shot down by the National Guard and the police as they had peacefully marched through the streets of San Salvador in commemoration of the 1932 uprising. This act of violence was only one of many that would be attributed to the newly formed second junta during the next few months.[43]

The CLAM Team members who had been working in El Salvador for a number of years also discussed the extent of their responsibility to new team members[44] in light of the country's unstable condition. Dorothy expressed her own concern about new team members to Mother Bartholomew in a letter dated February 15, 1980:

> Regarding the situation and all, I did talk seriously about it with the bishop. I'm not sure of exactly how to explain it in a letter but I will try. My thinking is this: because (or IF) there is a possibility of an insurrection in the near future, what is our responsibility to the new team members here? I personally would feel terrible picking up and leaving them to make it on their own. Maybe this is over-protective — I don't know. Different people, team members included, keep asking me if I couldn't stay on — at least for awhile. Whether this is even a possibility — or even necessary — is what I am not sure of. That is my dilemma.[45]

Despite her thoughts about remaining in El Salvador, however, Dorothy was planning to return home in June 1980 when she would have completed her sixth and final year of missionary work. In the same letter to Mother Bartholomew quoted above, Dorothy explained what she intends to do immediately after she leaves El Salvador:

> I don't know if I mentioned this to you before or not, but I am thinking of spending 10-14 days at the Maryknoll Cloister in Gallup, New Mexico, for some "quiet time" before coming home. It is something that I *definitely* need. The other *definite* thing I did was sign up for 2-3 weeks of study at Maryknoll, New York. I talked with Al Winters about this, and he thinks we all should take something upon returning. So I signed up for "Socialism and Christianity" from July 27-August 1 and "On Being a Christian in a Capitalist Society" from August 3-8.[46]

Dorothy did not discuss in this letter the type of work she wanted to do when she returned to Cleveland, for at this point she did not know what it was. She concluded the letter with the following statement: "Any comments or help you can give to sort out and straighten out any of the above would be appreciated."[47]

In approximately six weeks Dorothy would receive the help she requested "to sort out and straighten out" her feelings concerning her responsibility to new CLAM Team members. The answer to her dilemma, however, would not come directly from Mother Bartholomew.

*   *   *   *   *   *   *   *   *

On February 17, in response to a newspaper article about United States military aid to El Salvador, Archbishop Oscar Romero wrote the following letter to President Jimmy Carter:

> In the last few days news had appeared in the national press that worries me greatly. According to the reports your government is studying the possibility of economic and military support and assistance to the present junta government. . . .
> I am very worried by the news that the government of the United States is studying a form of abetting the arming of El Salvador by sending military teams and advisors to "train three Salvadoran battalions in logistics, communications, and intelligence." If this information from the newspapers is correct, the contribution of your government instead of promoting

greater justice and peace in El Salvador will without doubt sharpen the injustice and repression against the organizations of the people which repeatedly have been struggling to gain respect for their most fundamental human rights. . . .

If it is true that last November "A group of six Americans were in El Salvador providing $200,000 in gas masks and flak jackets and instructing about their use against demonstrators," you yourself should be informed that it is evident that since then the security forces with better personal protection and efficiency have repressed the people even more violently using lethal weapons.

For this reason as well as my obligation as a Salvadoran and as Archbishop of the Archdiocese of San Salvador to see that faith and justice reign in my country, I ask you, if you really want to defend human rights, to prohibit the giving of this military aid to the Salvadoran government and to guarantee that your government will not intervene directly or indirectly with military, economic, diplomatic, or other pressures to determine the destiny of the Salvadoran people. . . .

It would be unjust and deplorable if the intrusions of foreign powers were to frustrate the Salvadoran people, were to repress it and block its autonomous decisions about the economic and political path that our country ought to follow. It would violate the right publicly recognized by the Latin American bishops meeting in Puebla: "the legitimate self-determination of our people that permits them to organize according to their own genius and the march of their history and to cooperate in a new international order."[48]

In support of Archbishop Romero, on February 20, members of the Cleveland Latin American Mission Team, along with the Maryknoll priests and Sisters and Franciscan Sisters of Perpetual Adoration who were also ministering in El Salvador, wrote the following letter to President Carter:

We are United States Catholic missionaries, priests, Sisters, and lay people working in various parts of El Salvador. Some of us have been here for more than fifteen years and have seen unfold firsthand the history of this nation over the years. We appreciate our role as U.S. citizens working for the cause of peace and justice along with spreading of the Gospel of Jesus in whom we believe. Therefore, we feel it is urgent to support the stance of Archbishop Romero in his letter to you of February 17, 1980. Our experience of working with the poor has enabled us to independently arrive at the same conclusion: that giving more military aid will bring about greater violence and oppression. In our work we have shared in the sorrow of families whose members have disappeared, been tortured and killed. We have noted, too, that under the present junta, suffering, violence, and repression have not been stopped but greatly increased, despite its honest efforts.

We agree with the archbishop that it would be "unjust and deplorable" if foreign intervention frustrated the efforts of the people of Salvador to decide their own destiny. It is because of our own love of liberty and justice for all and the belief in the right of self-determination of nations springing from our religious and national roots that we make known to you our full support of Archbishop Romero's request.[49]

*   *   *   *   *   *   *   *   *

As the early months of 1980 progressed, the number of political killings also rose. Those who were murdered by security forces were mostly rural people in villages supporting labor organizations. On March 13 the Salvadoran Human Rights Commission published a list of 689 murders that had been committed since the beginning of the year; on March 21 Amnesty International reported 1390 cases of killings during the second week of March.[50]

Also on March 21 Dorothy had an encounter in which she experienced firsthand the murderous acts being performed by the security forces in many areas of the country. A week later, in a tape to Martha, Dorothy described her experience in graphic detail:

On Friday I had to go to Chaquiton because I wanted to talk to Carmen [lay catechist] about First Communion classes. So, I go out on my motorbike, and as I'm driving in, I see these people clustered outside Julianne's house and two other people walking up from the playa [beach]. Well, it's a husband and wife: the guy is 22 years old, and the girl is 18. He had a bullet lodged in his face! What the Guardia does is they shoot them in the face, and the bullet goes through one cheek bone and into the other. So, the bullet is not in a part — the brain — where it would kill you, but it's through the face.

So, here he comes, walking like a zombie, and here comes his wife with her legs blown off: the calf of her leg, huge hole, flesh hanging down, full of dirt because they were from the playa. They said that the soldiers from the San Carlos cuartel were there last night around 9:00 or 10:00, and evidently — they are somewhat organized there, and I guess it's a campesino group that's a branch of FAPU [United Popular Action Front] — they had asked for a raise in salaries, and they had gotten it. So, they don't know if this is just a repression or just what the problem was. But anyway, the soldiers — not the Guardia — came.

When I ran into these two, I thought, "My God, what can I do?" I first had to find Carmen because she has been involved in some of this stuff, and I didn't know if she was dead or alive. I found her, and she said that she was okay, and she told me about what had happened the night before. I then ran back to the Port on my motorbike, found Pablo [Paul Schindler], got the pick-up truck and some sheets, and we both went back to Chaquiton. We put the man in the front of the truck with Pablo, and I stayed in the back with the woman. And you never know if you're going to go by police and are they going to stop you. We've had police on the road every day since January when the airport opened.[51] Usually they do not stop us because they know who we are now. But, you just never know what's going to happen. . . .

Anyway, the girl knows absolutely zero about zero. She doesn't know anything about organization: she didn't know if her husband was involved or anything. She, I guess, got scared and started running, and that's when they shot her.

I can't believe how these people can endure all of this. They [husband and wife] were truly in a state of shock, but, My God, I didn't find them until 10:00 in the morning — twelve hours later. By the time we got them to the University,[52] it was about 12:30 or 1:00. But as we were getting into the capital, she had started relaxing, and she was really going into pain.

By the time we got her to the University, she was really miserable. But anyway, they took her in, and they were going to take care of her. Pablo went back the following Monday, and he didn't see them, but those at the University said they're okay — whatever "okay" means. The girl will probably lose both legs . . . the bone is there, but there isn't any flesh.[53]

Barely recovered from her experience of March 21, three days later Dorothy learned the shocking news of Archbishop Oscar Romero's murder. Shortly after 6:00 p.m. on March 24, as he was celebrating Mass in the chapel of the Hospital of Divine Providence, Romero was shot by a young man in street clothes who had been hiding behind a pillar at the entrance to the chapel. After being rushed to the nearby Policlinica hospital, Romero died minutes later of heavy internal bleeding, the result of a single bullet the assassin had fired into the archbishop's chest.[54]

On the same tape to Martha quoted above, Dorothy related how she and the other team members in Zaragoza had heard about Romero's "dramatic murder," as she termed it. She then expressed her own disbelief at Romero's murder as well as her feelings of deep grief:

On Monday [Father] Jim Kenny and the Chirilagua team members were coming in because Jim was going to leave [for the States after visiting the CLAM Team] . . . . Well, they came around 6:30 or so, and right before they came, Ken came over and said he had heard that the archbishop had been shot . . . and the next thing we knew, he had died. . . . Here we were, going to go out, too, to have a big dinner with Jim. Well, we couldn't. We couldn't believe it. I thought, "Oh, it can't be," and I still can't believe that it's really happened. . . .

Ken rang the bells, and we had a very lovely Mass. The whole pueblo [village] came. Everybody had heard. This guy, Pedro, an old man here, got up at the homily — Ken invited people to get up and say something if they wished — and he just gave a beautiful testimony to the Archbishop, and he broke up. It was very touching.

Everyone is just in a state of shock because he had just given this beautiful, beautiful homily on Sunday — very strong. The radio had been destroyed by bombs, but it came back on Sunday morning. . . . His message was very strong. He said, "And to the soldiers I have a special message. I beg of you, I plead with you in the Name of God, stop the repression. Don't kill." And you know, then here he is [begins to cry and stops recording] . . . .[55]

Sometime later that day Dorothy continued her tape to Martha and narrated in great detail the memorial Masses and other commemorations held in Romero's honor in the days following his murder and her and the team's role in these events.

On the evening of the archbishop's funeral on Sunday, March 30, Dorothy and Christine resumed the recording to Martha, and they each gave their eyewitness account of a riot that had occurred during the funeral. Explosions and gunfire had erupted in the square outside the cathedral in San Salvador, causing the large crowd gathered there to rush into the building for safety. At this time Dorothy, Christine, Elizabeth, and Jean were in the cathedral, on the right side, near the spot where Romero would be entombed. Dorothy explained, "We were told to put our head down because there was gunfire going on. So we did, but in the meantime, I was taking pictures, trying to see something. . . . When it was all over, there were eight or nine people dead in the cathedral — crushed to death."[56] During the stampede into the cathedral, a total of thirty people had actually been killed, and countless others were injured.

At the conclusion of her tape, Dorothy made a request of Martha: "Would you do me a huge favor and just hold onto this tape? I might want it for details later on if I need to remember something." She continued: "This is why I'm trying to give you as much detail as I can about *what* happened *when* — just in case I need it for anything."[57]

*   *   *   *   *   *   *   *   *

Archbishop Romero's funeral brought Bishop James A. Hickey once again to El Salvador. After he witnessed the riot at the archbishop's funeral, Bishop Hickey realized that new CLAM Team members would have difficulty handling the violent situation existing in the country. He also noticed how the Salvadoran people had come to trust the present team members, who offered them some stability in the midst of so much political turmoil and death.[58] With the team members, therefore, Bishop Hickey discussed the possibility of their remaining in El Salvador for an extended period of time beyond their actual term.

When he returned to Cleveland, the bishop called Mother Bartholomew to ask her to consider reappointing Dorothy to El Salvador for another year. Mother Bartholomew told Bishop Hickey that the decision to stay was up to Dorothy. On the evening of the day the bishop had called Mother Bartholomew, Dorothy also called her and said, "I'm wondering if Bishop Hickey has talked with you since he got back from El Salvador?" Mother Bartholomew replied, "We're ahead of you! He already called and requested that you stay in El Salvador, and I said, 'Yes, if *you* want to stay.'"[59] Dorothy then excitedly called out to the other team members who were in the room with her, "Oh, I can stay!"[60]

*   *   *   *   *   *   *   *   *

In the months before his death, Archbishop Romero had asked the American Church to send seasoned missionaries to serve the Church in his archdiocese. Maryknoll Sister Carla Piette, who had had extensive missionary experience with the poor in Chile, decided to answer Romero's request. She arrived in El Salvador on the day on which he was assassinated. The end of March 1980 also saw the arrival of Maryknoll Sister Teresa Alexander from Panama who came to work with Joan Petrik in the Port. Several weeks later yet another Maryknoll Sister, Ita Ford, who had worked with Carla in Chile, came to El Salvador.

After spending a month becoming acquainted with El Salvador, Carla and Ita decided to volunteer their services by helping refugees in one of the most war-torn areas of the country: Chalatenango. They planned to move into the rectory in the town of Chalatenango, but until the rooms in the crumbling old building could be readied for habitation, Carla and Ita stayed with the Assumption Sisters who lived across the street from the rectory. From this base they visited different parishes in the area to coordinate the relief work and commuted to San Salvador to check on supplies and funding requests and to meet with archdiocesan personnel.[61]

On May 22 Dorothy and Christine met Carla and Ita for the first time. In a tape Dorothy made for her parents on June 4, she described the meeting:

> We went to Santa Ana to see them . . . there's another one who just came up from Panama, Teresa, who is with Joanie in the Port. . . . So, we went out to visit Madeline [Dorsey] and Carla and Ita — one of them is named Ita Ford. . . . She's real cute. She's tiny and very Irish, and her name "Ita" is an Irish name. We went out to be with them, and we went up to Cerro Verde, to Izalco, the pretty volcano. And we just walked around up there, and they had made a picnic lunch, so we ate lunch up there.[62]

In the months that followed, Dorothy, Jean, and other members of the CLAM Team occasionally helped Carla and Ita, who had no jeep, to move food, supplies, and sometimes refugees to refugee centers in the Chalatenango area. By this time Dorothy and Jean had already been going up to the northern parts of the country, where the army was doing sweeps, and bringing refugees to centers around San Salvador. Paul Schindler remembers that Monsignor Ricardo Urioste, vicar-general of the archdiocese, had asked him if Dorothy and Jean could accompany the refugees. With their obvious "American" looks, Dorothy and Jean could protect the people from harm just by their presence, he reasoned. Paul agreed because even he felt a little safer around Dorothy and Jean: "Urioste and I used to tease about how safe it was to be around blonde, blue-eyed American women because they [the military] were killing priests like crazy, and so we'd constantly have these debates: 'Should we go out here, or should we go out there? Are you going to be safe, Paul?' We had a rule that either Dorothy or Jean had to go with me all the time."[63]

During the week of June 1, the same week that Dorothy made the tape for her parents quoted above, she also made a tape for Martha. On the tape she briefly mentioned meeting the Maryknoll Sisters but then explained in great detail events of the past week--incidents she did not speak of to her parents. She began the tape in this manner:

> Lots of things have been happening that I want to tell you about, and again, I wish you would hold onto this tape for me.

Please don't tape over it. Just save it for me — I will make another one for my parents — because I want to go into detail on some stuff with you so I remember dates and all, and I don't want [my parents] to hear all the detail because it's kind of gory in spots.[64]

Dorothy then related one of the "gory" situations she referred to above. The episode, one of several she described on the tape, involved two young men, Julio and Pastor, from the nearby village of Santa Cruz who had been abducted, brutally tortured, and killed by eight members of the death squad. The incident happened on the evening of Thursday, May 22. Dorothy, whose tone of voice shifted back and forth from anger to compassion, and finally anger again, told the horrifying details of the story:

There is a tienda [store] on a corner of the road by the river that sells a lot of liquor, and on the other side of that little road is this other tienda. Well, they [death squad] went to this other store first and set off a bomb to blow the door open, and they went in and took the man who was about forty or forty-five years old — didn't say why — then they went to Julio's and Pastor's houses . . . [which] are on the main road, but of course, there's no traffic at that hour of the night — but it just drives you wild. Julio's mother and his other brother were sleeping in one part of the house, and he was in the back part. So, they [death squad] went in and took him out. . . .

Then they went to Pastor's house. Pastor lives with his mother Mercedes, and his father is blind. . . And he had just made this little house for them where they were living, and I guess they [death squad] came banging on the door, and of course, the mother and father were put at gunpoint. Poor Mercedes just sees the whole thing as — their faith just knocks you over, it is so powerful — she said, "He was just like Jesus being led to the slaughter — the innocent lamb. They dragged him out and told him to lie down, and he lay down; 'stand up,' and he stood up; 'put your hands behind your back,' and he put his hands behind his back. . . ."

So they took him out, and they took Julio and this guy Antonio [whom they had taken from the store]. . . . They returned to the first tienda and blew up the door and went in and robbed the place — stole a lot of liquor then left. . . .

Well, on Friday, the twenty-third, they found their bodies. And Martha, they were hacked. Julio's eyes were pushed out, he was scalped . . . There were bits of skin — they had tried skinning him; one of them was decapitated. It was just gruesome, just gruesome. You know, it's just *why*? *Why?* There was no connection between this man [Antonio] and these two kids. And the only thing we're worried about is that these kids have been with us for the celebrations [of the Word] and all and interested in being catechists.

So, to this day we don't know, and who knows if we'll ever know. But the poor, poor families. . . . That was really a grueling thing for us, but it's over with, and we're still living with the sin of it. . . . We went out [to Santa Cruz] on Wednesday [May 28] to see how the people were doing, and that's when I talked to the mothers, and really, as I say, their faith is so great. . . . Julio was a good kid — a really good kid. . . . Really, I could vomit every time I think about it. . . .[65]

After she described a few more incidents that occurred in the days following the killings in Santa Cruz, Dorothy said on June 2:

Something's been happening every week. Everyday in the paper — I got the paper today: ten bodies found in Santa Ana, five with EM ["escuadrone de muerte," or death squad] written on them, another twelve in San Miguel, and these are just the ones that they put in the paper. There are so many more. I think I told you that Christine and I came across those two bodies [last week]. It just gets to be too much sometimes. It's so sad and so out-of-control.[66]

Later that day on the same tape, Dorothy told of two events that brought the threat of military-sponsored violence another step closer to the team members in La Libertad. On May 28, at about 3:00 p.m., after she had spent the afternoon in Santa Cruz comforting the families of Pastor and Julio, Dorothy returned to the Port to wait for Christine who would accompany her to the airport to pick up Rosemary Smith who was returning to El Salvador from her vacation in Cleveland. As Dorothy drove into the outskirts of the city, she encountered roadblocks on all the main roads. Finally discovering a clear, smaller road to take, Dorothy drove through the deserted streets and empty marketplace of the city and immediately began worrying about Paul and his whereabouts, especially since the army had been in the Port the day before asking questions about him. Her anxiety diminished when she saw Paul walking down one of the streets.

When they met, Paul told Dorothy that the Guardia had placed La Libertad under an alert and that they were stationed around the area by the church. They had also dismissed the children from the parochial school which was located on the property. By this time Christine had arrived, and after Paul assured them that he would be fine, they left for the airport. In the next couple of hours, however, an officer from the Guardia approached Paul and told him that the commandante wanted to talk with him.

When Dorothy, Christine, and Rosemary returned to La Libertad from the airport at 5:30 p.m., they learned that Paul was with the Guardia. Dorothy related the rest of the story to Martha as follows:

> After waiting a few minutes, I went over to talk to a couple of the guards who were around [Paul's] house, and I said, "I want to ask about the padre." One of the guards said, "He's fine. He's just talking." I said, "Well, I'm just concerned." And he said, "Don't worry. He'll be back."
>
> So we went and sat in the truck outside, looking down the road, waiting for him. Well, he finally came out about forty-five minutes later, and we went in [his house] and talked. The commandante had said to Paul, "You are very suspicious. You are always in and out, and we don't know where you're going and what you're doing."[67] Paul does go in and out for Masses, and he goes in and out and drops people off. We've been going out late at night to pick up people, and that one night I got stuck in the mud and didn't get back until 10:30 or 11:00. . . .
>
> Anyway, Paul had to show the commandante his calendar and tell him exactly where he's going and what he's doing all this week, and he told him we were going to have a Mass in

Santa Cruz this Wednesday. . . And the only places that the commandante mentioned — this is very strange — were Santa Cruz — you know, like he wanted to know what we were doing there — and Tamanique because also in Tamanique, just within the last couple of days, three guys were shot in the head. And when they found their bodies, the men had all sorts of propaganda — organization propaganda — in their hands. Now whether they had had it really, or it was put into their hands afterwards, who knows. Well, those were the only two places he mentioned. . . .

Anyway, Pablo talked to the commandante and tried to pacify him and tell him everything he could to let him know that we are innocent. So, you know, that's the thing that kills me. If they [Guardia] really did kill our guys in Santa Cruz just because of incorrect information, it really makes me want to vomit because they were innocent, *too* . . . that's what makes me sick.[68]

Although Dorothy certainly could have felt helpless and hopeless in the face of so much evil happening around her, she did not, as the next section of her tape, which she recorded on June 4, reveals. Here, she made several requests of Martha, ones which would enable her to serve the suffering people of Salvador in additional ways during the next few months:

What I need is money for medicines. We're trying to buy medicines to have on hand. We are going to have this first-aid course this Saturday and next Saturday . . . which I want to go to. That's the other thing: this may sound gross, but if you can find me any information — any strategic first-aid information — on gun wounds, knife wounds, things like that — what to do about them, what kinds of medicines to use. Hopefully, we'll never need to use them, but it's just good to have them on hand — at least know something about. I think basically we'll get that, but if you come across anything or know of anybody who has anything or any kind of information you can find for me and have ready for me when I come home, I would be grateful.

I don't know if maybe Ursula Ann [Hanna, O.S.U.] or Ann Joachim [Barbara Lusnak, O.S.U.] or any of the other nurses at the motherhouse — how much they know about these kinds of things — but if you can talk with them; if they could give me a half of a day and teach me how to do some things when I come home . . . without alarming anybody — don't tell anybody else — just talk to them. It's just that if I know a little bit of something in case of emergency, it would be helpful. But *please* don't panic the whole world, and don't say anything to anybody else.[69]

Dorothy ended this long, event-filled tape with one final request of Martha: "Please hold onto this tape for me, and keep the information to yourself. I don't know how much I'll tell my parents. I just mention things to them, but I never go into detail with them as I do with you on tape because I don't want them to worry unnecessarily."[70]

* * * * * * * * *

Six weeks after the murders of Pastor and Julio, the team members in La Libertad again experienced the murder of two other young men from their parish. This time, however, they were men the missionaries knew very well: Armando Arevalo and Carlos Gonzalez Jerez. Armando was the sacristan of the church in La Libertad and the leader of its choral group; Carlos was Paul's adopted son whom he had rescued from the streets seven years earlier and helped to educate.

Around ten o'clock p.m. on July 6, Armando and Carlos walked Jean home after seeing a movie with her, said good-bye to her in front of her apartment above the parochial school,[71] and began to leave for home. As they stepped out into the street, they were approached by three assailants, who shot them both in the head.

Shortly after the murders, Dorothy left Zaragoza, where she had been living with Christine and Elizabeth, and moved in with Jean in La Libertad. At this time Joan Petrik left El Salvador for the United States. Since Teresa Alexander who had lived with Joan was now alone, Dorothy invited her to stay with her and Jean in La Libertad. Terry accepted Dorothy's invitation and remained with her and Jean for two months.

* * * * * * * * *

According to Paul, the night of the murder of Armando and Carlos "was the hardest time we ever had together."[72] The murders also spoke, however, a very direct message to the members of the Cleveland Team "to back off from their commitment to help and support the people of La Libertad."[73]

*   *   *   *   *   *   *   *   *

On July 14 Dorothy returned to Cleveland for her annual month-long vacation. Parties and picnics with her family, friends, and Ursuline Sisters occupied her time as well as several celebrations in honor of her forty-first birthday which had been June 30. While in town Dorothy also made a week-long retreat at the Ursuline Motherhouse, and from July 27 until August 9, she took two courses at the Maryknoll Institute, New York.

Meanwhile, back in El Salvador, Maryknoll Sister Maura Clarke arrived in Santa Ana to live and work with Maddie Dorsey. Another experienced missionary, Maura had spent many years with the poor of Nicaragua. In Chalatenango, to the northeast of Santa Ana, Carla and Ita finally moved into the parish rectory. The building became their home and the official headquarters for their refugee operation which they called "The Emergency Committee of the Vicariate of Chalatenango."[74] Carla and Ita also acquired a jeep by this time that enabled them to move more quickly and freely without having to depend on the availability of the parish jeep or the town bus.[75] So, feeling settled in their new home and new country, they continued to lovingly minister to the suffering, displaced refugees of Chalatenango until tragedy struck in late August.

On the evening of August 23, Carla and Ita were asked to pick up a released prisoner from the army base in Chalatenango and return him to his village in the hills.[76] Rain was imminent when they left the base, but as they reached the El Chapote River about ten minutes outside of Chalatenango, it started raining heavily. While Carla and Ita began to cross the river, a wall of water struck the jeep in which they were riding and turned it over on the driver's side. Carla, the driver, pushed the slight body of Ita out through the half-opened window. Ita was then carried by the current for several miles down the river until she managed to grab hold of some tree roots and pull herself up the slippery bank. She was found the next morning, as was Carla's broken, twisted body, which had washed ashore nine miles from the spot where the jeep had overturned.

Shortly before Carla's death, Dorothy left Cleveland to return to El Salvador, despite pleas from her family and friends to stay home for good that summer. She usually flew from Cleveland to Florida and took another plane from there to El Salvador. In late August, however, Dorothy drove to Tampa, Florida, with her brother Jim, her sister-in-law Dorothy, and their six children to drop off her niece Colleen at the University of Tampa, where she had enrolled. The trip to Tampa in the Kazel family van was filled with plenty of food, fun, and jokes. After they arrived in Tampa, the Kazels checked into a nearby hotel and spent several relaxing days at Clearwater Beach.

Concerned about being picked up at the Comalapa International Airport when she arrived in the country, Dorothy called her fellow missionaries in La Libertad on August 25, the day before she was due to depart from Florida. At this time she learned about Carla's death by drowning. Although visibly upset by the news, Dorothy remained firm in her resolve to return to El Salvador.

*   *   *   *   *   *   *   *   *

September found Dorothy and the other CLAM Team members involved in refugee work besides their usual pastoral duties. In a letter he had addressed to the Diocese of Cleveland, Paul Schindler stated why the team's ministry had expanded to include work with refugees:

> As we continue to work, we see a steady strengthening of faith in the lives of so many of our people. Here in La Libertad many of our activities have been modified and new expressions of apostolate have risen to meet the needs of the times. With so many people having to flee from the war zones of the country, we find Sister Christine Rody, Jean Donovan, and Sister Dorothy Kazel working with transportation to and organization of refugee centers. Father Ken Myers has been housing in the casa comunal children who have been separated from their families.[77]

On September 5 in an uncensored letter[78] to Martha Owen, Dorothy further described her and the team's work at the refugee centers. She also explained the readjustment in assignments of the Maryknoll Sisters as a result of Carla's death:

First of all Chris is working (managing) a refugee center in San Roque in San Salvador. Carla got her involved. It's been a good thing for her but is exhausting. She's there Monday through Friday and then comes to Zaragoza on the weekends to help with confirmation charlas [talks], etc., and to eat and sleep decently. Her bed there is an examining table in the clinic — a very narrow one! So she *needs* to come back once a week. The place is a church in the process of becoming — *not* quite done — but it serves the purpose. The people are from Chalatenango. She had 134 but twenty- nine left to go back to their pueblo. Hopefully they will be okay. Caritas does a lot of providing for the centers — there are seven — we've also been helping out, too. Al [Winters] knows about this now so it's safe to talk about — except in letters — unless they're being delivered personally. Jean is mailing this from Florida as she'll be on vacation as of Tuesday. It seems as though Jean and I will be helping Ita and Maura out in Chalatenango when needed. Maura is a lovely person who came to accompany Maddie in Santa Ana. Since Carla's death, she has volunteered to be with Ita in Chalatenango, and Terry (who was here with Joan Petrik) will go to Santa Ana.[79]

In this same letter, Dorothy also gave the details of a scene of violence that had recently taken place in the parish:

On Friday I went out on my motorbike to advise our catechists about confirmation charlas. Just past Cangrejera and Chaquiton there were three cadavers. I didn't stop because people were there — I thought I'd go to Valle Nuevo first and stop on my way back. Well, as I pulled in to Valle Nuevo — where the health clinic is — there were lots of people, and I saw the candles and the caja [coffin]. Here they also shot and killed the father of Margot (the girl catechist who helps us). He was the caretaker of the center. It seems a group of masked men came in about midnight and shot him. A seventeen-year-old son and an eight-year-old boy were there, but they hid in a bathroom that doesn't work and luckily weren't found as these guys hung around until four-thirty a.m. There was one other killed from Valle Nuevo, one from Cangrejera, and one from Los Planos — but no one we knew.[80]

Enraged by such senseless killings and also by an incident that occurred on September 22, 1980, Dorothy felt a responsibility to express her anger to the President of the United States. So on September 23, 1980, she wrote the following letter to President Jimmy Carter:

My name is Sister Dorothy Kazel, and I am a North American missionary working in the Central American country of El Salvador. I have been here for six years, and I have seen the oppression of the people grow worse each year.

My reason for writing this letter comes from an experience I had yesterday afternoon. I realize my experience is a very *common* happening here, but it's one that truly makes a person sick. And it makes a North American even sicker because of the help our country has given to the government here — as it was stated — for "vehicles and communication."

Early Monday morning [September 22, 1980], the army soldiers of El Salvador made house searches in San Jose Villa Nueva. This in itself is a terrorizing tactic when at one o'clock in the morning, when everyone is sleeping, soldiers with rifles and equipment come pounding at your door. Of course, if you do not open the door, they will knock it down. You then have to present your papers proving who you are, etc.

It seems that this group (of soldiers) kept going further up the isolated road to the cantones above in their *high-powered trucks* with their *communication* equipment.

About 6:00 or 6:30 in the morning, they killed ten or more people in one canton and then went farther up (the road) and killed another ten or more people. One old man was coming down the road with three cows — he got killed. One young man was going to wash down by the well — he got killed. One young girl about twelve years old had in her hands the words of a song which had been written in honor of one of the priests who had been martyred. They (the soldiers) claimed she was a subversive and killed her.

There were three masked men with the soldiers pointing out the houses to them and naming the people in them. When taking a man from his house, the soldiers never asked him if he was the "name" they were looking for. When a wife asked, "Where are you taking him?" or "Why are you taking them?" there was no answer. No words of explanation were ever given.

Now I realize these soldiers are looking for "subversives," and they may have a right to do that — but do they have a right to do it in this manner? Do they realize how many really *innocent* people they kill because they have received wrong information? Do they investigate the information they receive before they come and kill people?

And the most appalling thing to me is that I am a North American, and *my* government gave them money for the "durable equipment" they have so that it's relatively easy to get into the worst cantones without much trouble and kill innocent people because of the wrong information they have received.

I really would like to know what you think of this situation, Mr. President, and whether you really realize how many innocent people we are helping to kill. How do you reconcile all of this?[81]

* * * * * * * * *

In spite of the unrelenting violence all around them, Dorothy and Jean continued their parish work as well as assisting Maura and Ita in Chalatenango. With their white Toyota van, Dorothy and Jean, who had been dubbed "The Rescue Squad" by Maura and Ita, traveled through the hills, transporting refugees and supplies. They were well aware of the danger and were fearful,[82] especially when driving alone in isolated areas. But because they looked so American with their blonde hair and blue eyes, Dorothy and Jean believed they were safe. Jean used to say, "They [the military] don't shoot blonde, blue-eyed North Americans."[83] Echoing Jean's opinion, Dorothy would claim, "Being a gringa [North American] is an asset. They wouldn't do anything to you."[84]

* * * * * * * * *

The tumultuous political climate of El Salvador and genocidal killings of the Salvadoran security forces continued to weigh heavily on Dorothy's mind during the month of October 1980. In a letter she wrote to her parents on the ninth, Dorothy made brief mention of the chaotic situation: "Things are still as absurd as ever. To know[85] how this will ever end."[86] On October 21 on a tape to Martha, Dorothy claimed that the news from El Salvador "is not very good . . . . It's miserable, as a matter of fact."[87] She then added, "To know what the truth of all the matter is. . . . We never know anything of the truth."[88] Dorothy also told Martha that she had written to Jimmy Carter and explained why: "We are still responsible for these people being killed. Now, how do we reconcile ourselves to all this?"[89] After then graphically depicting some gruesome murders recently committed by the death squads, Dorothy angrily exclaimed, "[It is] really disgusting, really sick . . . I mean, sick, sick stuff. Oh, it just makes you ill. You wonder — it's just so damn diabolical, you just — oh, it makes you want to weep."[90] Towards the end of her tape, Dorothy described the guerrilla "forces" that the government claimed are such a threat to them and the well-being of the country:

> They're like Daniel Boone, you know. This is worse than rinky dink cowboys and Indians. It's like Indians against the United States Marines today. Really, I don't know how these guys are ever going to win this war. These guys are nothing but campesino guys . . . [they] all either had rifles or pistols, but the rifles were like overgrown BB guns. I just wonder how this is all going to turn out. . . . And, you know, my heart just aches for these people when I see what they've got to work with. And they're really hoping to win. I just don't know how these guys think they're going to do it when we're giving money, even if we're just giving it for communication equipment and huge trucks and such, so they [the military] can get up there easier to kill these guys. . . . It just makes me ill when I see us doing this kind of garbage.[91]

To lift their spirits, the Cleveland missionaries and the Maryknoll Sisters had a Halloween party on October 28. Two days later, in a letter to her parents, Dorothy gave the details of the party:

> On Tuesday we celebrated Halloween here. We went to the beach all day. The Franciscan Nuns from Sonsonate came

along with all our Maryknoll people. Then in the evening we had a "dress-up" party — t'was fun. I took some pictures — hope they come out![92]

* * * * * * * * *

As November rolled around, Dorothy seriously began to consider her permanent return to the United States. She planned to leave El Salvador in mid-March 1981 but would not arrive home until May because she wanted to vacation in Brazil, Bolivia, and Chile and then make a retreat at the Maryknoll Cloister in Gallup, New Mexico. In a letter of November 2 to her parents, Dorothy asked for help regarding her trip to South America:

> Would you please call Air-Paraguay (there's an 800 number)? Find out how much it would cost to fly from Miami to Sao Paolo, Brazil, to La Paz, Bolivia, to Santiago, Chile, and could it be done as one trip, or do you have to change planes in Asuncion, Paraguay, to go to the different places.[93]

She concluded the letter with the following comments: "As you can guess, we're [she and Christine] planning our vacation-trip home. Nothing for sure yet — just lots of *fun* ideas."[94] To Martha on November 5, Dorothy wrote:

> We've been planning trips home. I'm not sure when I'll leave yet — maybe by mid-March. I'd still like to get to Bolivia if possible and then spend a few quiet weeks at the Maryknoll Cloister in New Mexico. We shall see. Chris is all set, except now she's talking about going to Bolivia with me if we went in January--*to know* what we will really do![95]

In the midst of making her travel plans, Dorothy received a reply to the letter she had written to Jimmy Carter on September 23. The reply, dated November 7, had not been sent by Carter but rather by John D. Blacken, Director of the Office of Central American Affairs. In his letter Blacken sympathized with Dorothy and offered justifications for the American policy towards El Salvador but completely sidestepped the issue of American military aid to the Salvadoran government:

We deplore the violence in El Salvador which is continuing at a high level. We have made clear to the Salvadoran Government our hope and expectation that it bring the violence under control from whatever source, right or left, official or unofficial. As you undoubtedly know, it is being carried out by both extremes.

However, the leftist opposition has refused both the government's offer of amnesty announced October 15 and the Conference of Bishops' offer to mediate announced October 18. The FMLN [Farabundo Marti Peoples Liberation Front] has announced what it terms as the "final offensive." In such situations involving widespread violence from a variety of sources, it is tragic that innocent people become the victims. Nevertheless, the government's plans for elections and reforms are moving forward and may succeed in alleviating some of the conditions which have spawned the violence.[96]

In early November Maura and Ita also received a "letter" which emanated from the "conditions" that continued to spawn even more violence. Posted on the door of the rectory in Chalatenango was a sign that pictured a knife embedded in a human head. A stream of blood spurted toward the text that read, "This is what will happen to anyone who comes to this house because priests and nuns are Communists."[97] Although some of the parish workers left Chalatenango after this warning was issued, Maura and Ita remained and continued their work which had now expanded to include housing refugees in the rectory until Dorothy and Jean could make more permanent arrangements for their transportation and protection.

Meanwhile, Maura and Ita were finalizing plans to attend the annual regional assembly of Maryknoll Sisters from Panama, Nicaragua, and El Salvador which had been scheduled for the last weekend of November at the Diriamba Retreat House in Managua, Nicaragua. Maddie Dorsey and Terry Alexander, who also planned to attend the meeting, sent Maura and Ita a telegram towards the end of the month, telling them of the reservations they had made for their flight back to El Salvador and suggesting that they all return together on Tuesday, December 2.

*   *   *   *   *   *   *   *   *

On November 14 Dorothy made the last tape her parents would ever receive from her.[98] On this tape her voice was hoarse, and she explained why: "I am tired. . . . My voice keeps going, but it's just because we've been running around a lot."[99] Dorothy then related to her mother and father that in the weeks since she had sent them her last tape (October 24 and 26), she had been getting medicines for the sick and then transporting them to various hospitals and makeshift clinics in addition to her usual pastoral work. She also mentioned that she and Jean have been transporting quite a few refugees:

> We're pretty much into this refugee problem. These people are mostly women, children, and older men who are families of the organized, but they cannot stay up in the hills. . . . On Tuesday we'll be taking medicine and stuff up to Chalatenango. That's another area that's bad news, but anyway, it's just one of those things you've got to do so you do it.[100]

When she had any spare time at all, Dorothy told her parents that she returned to the centers to visit with the mothers and play with the children she had transported.

Later in her tape Dorothy tried to update her parents as well as she could about her plans for her final trip home to the States in the spring of the following year. Because she was considering numerous options, though, Dorothy did not have definite information to give to them:

> I don't know if you found out anymore about airplanes for me. I've been thinking about all kinds of things and trying to figure out just really what I'm going to do and about coming home and all, and absolutely nothing is definite . . . I'm aiming to be home by May. I might even leave by mid-March. I don't know. . . . I'll just hang in and do what I can here and then leave when I can . . . I'm still considering going to Bolivia. . . . I'm also still thinking that I'd like to go out to New Mexico for retreat. . . . It's all up in the air. . . .
>
> Nothing is ever definite, and that's where I'm still at. As things gel, I will let you know. But right now I'm still not too sure of just what I'm doing or where I'm going or when I'm even leaving. But there are just all kinds of ideas in the air. . . . And nothing will probably happen.[101]

Dorothy concluded her tape with a request and a reassurance: "Do keep praying for us. We are all fine."[102]

*   *   *   *   *   *   *   *   *

Maura and Ita left Chalatenango on Monday, November 24, for a few days of relaxation before their meeting. Early in the day of Wednesday, November 26, Maddie and Terry drove their jeep to La Libertad and left it in the parish parking lot so Dorothy and Jean could keep their eye on it during Maddie and Terry's absence. Dorothy and Jean then drove the two Maryknoll Sisters to the Comalapa International Airport and promised to pick them up from there on December 2 at 4:00 p.m. Since they had not heard otherwise, Maddie and Terry told Dorothy and Jean that Maura and Ita would also be returning with them on the same flight from Nicaragua.

*   *   *   *   *   *   *   *   *

After a Thanksgiving ecumenical service held on Wednesday, November 26, Dorothy, Jean, and the other team members met the American ambassador Robert White and his wife Mary Anne for the first time. Towards the end of the evening, when the topic of conversation had turned to the Salvadoran political situation, the Whites invited the entire CLAM Team to dinner the following Monday, December 1, to continue the discussion.[103] They advised the missionaries to pack an overnight bag and to plan to spend the night because they did not want the team to travel at night on the dangerous road back to La Libertad.

On Friday November 28, Dorothy wrote a letter to Martha Owen in which she disclosed her plans for her return to the States: "I hope to be home by May 18 the latest — my sister-in-law [Dorothy Chapon Kazel] is graduating from Ursuline [College] then. Right now I'm thinking about leaving here mid-March but nothing is positive. I hope to travel around and make a *quiet* retreat before coming back — so we shall see. I *may* stay until Easter — depending on *need* — saber [to know]!"[104]

*   *   *   *   *   *   *   *   *

As they had planned, Dorothy, Jean, Christine, and Paul dined with Robert and Mary Anne White on Monday, December 1, at their residence in the American Embassy. As a result of many stimulating hours of discussion that revolved around the Salvadoran situation and U.S. foreign policy,[105] the dinner ended late, and the missionaries were forced to stay overnight at the embassy residence. Unknown to the team at the time, a second anonymous threat was slid under the door of the rectory in Chalatenango that night.

After breakfast the next day, Tuesday, December 2, Dorothy and Jean left the embassy and drove to San Salvador to do some shopping for the children's center in Zaragoza before going to the airport to pick up the Maryknoll Sisters. On the way they dropped off Christine at her refugee center in San Roque. In Chalatenango that day, a death list with Ita's and Maura's names and the names of every person on the Chalatenango parish staff, except for the cook, was shown to a lay worker by an unidentified man who said, "Here is a list of the people we are going to kill — and today, this very night, we will begin."[106]

*   *   *   *   *   *   *   *   *

At 3:00 p.m. Dorothy and Jean reached the airport. When the 4:00 LANICA flight arrived from Nicaragua, only Maddie and Terry got off the plane. After welcoming their Maryknoll friends, Dorothy and Jean asked why Maura and Ita were not with them. Maddie and Terry explained that the other two Sisters did not get reservations on the same flight but on a COPA one that was scheduled to arrive at 6:00 that evening. They then repeated what Ita had told them shortly before they left Managua: "Tell Dorothy and Jean not to worry about returning to the airport to pick us up. We will take a taxi."[107] As Dorothy and Jean would not hear of such a thing and because they had also planned that Maura and Ita would stay with them that night in La Libertad, they simultaneously responded, "We will go back for them."[108]

As the women left the airport, a National Guardsman on duty telephoned his post commander Deputy Sergeant Luis Antonio Colindres Alemán.[109] The four women then proceeded to La Libertad so that Maddie and Terry could get their jeep, which had been parked in the parish parking lot for the past week, and then return to Santa Ana. The drive along the costal highway was uneventful. Terry later recalled that she had expected to see soldiers and perhaps be stopped along the way, but not one appeared.[110]

After making sure that Maddie and Terry's jeep started and that they were safely on their way to Santa Ana, Dorothy and Jean left again for the airport and reached it at about 5:30 p.m. to meet Maura and Ita's 6:00 flight. The National Guardsman who had telephoned Deputy Sergeant Luis Antonio Colindres Alemán earlier that afternoon called him again. Colindres then ordered five guardsmen to change out of their uniforms into civilian clothes and to accompany him with their service rifles and ammunition. Meanwhile, in the terminal Dorothy and Jean learned that the flight from Managua would be an hour late. So, they sat and waited for it.

The plane safely landed at 7:00 p.m. Dorothy and Jean greeted their two friends and then proceeded to the baggage claim station. While waiting for Maura's and Ita's baggage, the four women chatted with a group of Canadians who had just flown into El Salvador to attend the funeral scheduled on the following day for the six leaders of the Revolutionary Democratic Front (FDR) who had been murdered by security forces on November 27. Other church and human rights representatives and news reporters from the United States and Central America had also just arrived and were milling around the station. As the Canadians secured their luggage and bid Dorothy, Jean, Maura, and Ita goodbye, they would never have imagined that they would be the last people to see the women alive.[111]

*   *   *   *   *   *   *   *   *

At about 10:00 that evening, along the road to Santiago Nonualco, about twenty minutes northeast of the airport and in the opposite direction from La Libertad, four campesinos in a pineapple field witnessed a white van passing. Because it was dark, they could not tell who was in the vehicle. From the road the van turned off onto a dirt lane, continued another half mile and stopped by an isolated area.[112] The campesinos then heard several gunshots. Fifteen minutes later the van passed them again, but this time the lights inside of the van were on, the radio was blasting, and the campesinos counted five bare-headed men.[113]

*   *   *   *   *   *   *   *   *

What actually happened to Dorothy, Jean, Maura, and Ita in the interim after the arrival of the flight from Nicaragua until the time of their deaths — about two-and-a-half hours — is questionable even at this writing.[114] One theory is that they were abducted in the airport terminal, questioned there first, and then taken to another military base where they were further interrogated and physically and sexually abused. From that location the five guardsmen took the women to the rural area by Santiago Nonualco and murdered them there.

Paul Schindler believes this first but less accepted theory to be the most plausible. He bases his opinion on his own investigation of the women's murders and familiarity with the Salvadoran military's treatment of persons from La Libertad who had been kidnaped and tortured but had survived the ordeal.

Shortly after the women were murdered, Paul questioned the people he knew from La Libertad who worked at the airport and were there on the evening of December 2. One of the workers Paul knew used to sleep at the airport because he got off work too late to make it safely home before the curfew.[115] This man told Paul that he had seen the Maryknoll Sisters being taken to Immigration as Dorothy and Jean waited nearby.[116] A little while later, according to Paul's witness, several guardsmen came for Dorothy and Jean. By this time the airport was empty because the flight from Managua had been the last one to come in that evening, and travelers and workers alike had already left the airport to reach their destination before the curfew began.

Paul believes that all four women were questioned together at the airport and then taken to army barracks in the nearby city of Zacatecoluca[117] which was the center of death squad operations in that area. Here they were further questioned, physically mistreated, and finally, raped. And because the security forces never killed anyone where possible witnesses could be found, the guardsmen forced the women back into their van and drove them to the deserted outskirts of the town of Santiago Nonualco. Paul had also interviewed people who lived along the road leading to the town, and they claim to have seen the van pass at around 10:00 p.m. and then return about fifteen minutes later.[118]

The most commonly accepted belief regarding the women's abduction, however, is that they left the airport terminal and were stopped by Colindres and the other guardsmen at the first toll station outside the airport. Here the women were ordered to vacate their van and were then interrogated. According to *The Churchwomen Murders: A Report to the Secretary of State* by Judge Harold Tyler, Jr., the following events then occurred.

After the guardsmen questioned the women, Colindres ordered them back into the van with three of the guardsmen, one of whom commenced to drive the van in the opposite direction from La Libertad. Colindres and the other two guardsmen followed the van in the National Guard jeep.

In a short while the jeep developed engine trouble, and after a brief stop for temporary repair, the two vehicles made it to the National Guard Command Post at the town of El Rosario de la Paz. Here Colindres telephoned the airport and instructed his second-in-command officer to send another vehicle to El Rosario to retrieve them. The jeep was then left at the guard post in El Rosario with one of the guardsmen to watch it.

The other five guardsmen crowded into the van with the four women and proceeded in the direction of the town of Santiago Nonualco to the deserted area where they would murder the women. When they arrived at the spot, a dirt lane by an empty field, the van came to a halt, and Colindres ordered the women out of the van. The guardsmen proceeded to rape the women. Then at Colindres' orders, they killed the women execution-style[119] and left the bodies along the roadside.

In the meantime another two guardsmen had left the airport in a blue Customs Police pick-up truck for Rosario de la Paz. Arriving in the town they found the stalled jeep and the guardsman who had been left there to guard it. The three men then waited for Colindres and the four other guardsmen. At approximately 11:00 p.m. they arrived, and climbing into the cab of the pick-up, Colindres instructed the guardsman at the wheel to drive the truck back onto the coastal highway in the direction of La Libertad.[120] Followed by the white van, the pick-up proceeded along the road until Colindres ordered it to stop. After removing several items[121] from the van and putting them in the truck and taking off the vehicle's license plates, three of the guardsmen took a small can of gasoline from the van and poured the gasoline on the inside and outside of the van. One of the guards then set it on fire, and the vehicle was consumed by flames.[122]

*   *   *   *   *   *   *   *   *

At 7:30 in the morning of December 3, a campesino from Santiago Nonualco found the bodies of the four women sprawled along the roadside. He then contacted the local militia commander to report the discovery. At 8:30 a.m. two National Guardsmen and three policemen arrived at the scene and ordered the preparation of a common grave. The militia commander also summoned the local justice of the peace who authorized the immediate burial of the women as "unknowns."

As the guardsmen silently stood by with their rifles in hand, four of the local residents began to dig a shallow, common grave. Several other campesinos, out of respect for the women, dressed them in their slacks, which they had found crumpled on the ground. After gently pushing the bodies into the grave, the villagers covered it and placed a simple cross made out of two tree branches, one nailed on top of the other.[123]

* * * * * * * * *

Because Paul Schindler had expected Dorothy and Jean to return to La Libertad the evening of December 2 with the Maryknoll Sisters, he was a bit puzzled when he went to their apartment at 5:30 p.m. and did not find them there. To reassure himself of their whereabouts, later that evening he called Ken Myers in Zaragoza, as Dorothy and Jean often stayed there with Christine and Elizabeth. Ken told Paul he would check to see if the two women were there, but before he could get back to Paul, the phone lines went dead. Paul then called the Assumption Sisters in San Salvador where Maura and Ita stayed when they visited the capital. The Sisters told Paul that they expected Maura and Ita at 11:00 the following morning for a meeting. Assuming Dorothy and Jean and the others were in Zaragoza, Paul made no more phone calls that evening.

The next morning, Wednesday, December 3, Paul again telephoned Ken who told him with certainty that Dorothy and Jean were not in Zaragoza. He then called the Assumption Sisters who informed him that Maura and Ita had not arrived for their meeting. Thinking the four women might have gone to Santa Ana with Maddie and Terry, he called them. When he was unable to reach the two Maryknoll Sisters, Paul left a message for them to return his call. Around noon Christine called Paul from her refugee center in San Roque to ask him if Jean were in the Port because she was supposed to have brought some refugees to the San Roque Center that morning and had never appeared. When Christine learned that nobody had seen either Dorothy or Jean since the day before, she decided to come to La Libertad and join in the search for the women.

By early afternoon Maddie and Terry had contacted Paul. When they told him that Maura and Ita had not traveled with them from Nicaragua, Paul placed a call to the Maryknoll Mission there to find out if Maura and Ita had ever left Managua the day before. Learning from Paul that Dorothy and Jean had never returned from the airport,

Maddie and Terry decided to join the Cleveland missionaries in La Libertad. In the meantime Paul telephoned the archdiocesan office and Robert White at the American Embassy to report that the women were missing, although at the time, he did not know if they were looking for only Dorothy and Jean or for all four women. A little while later Ambassador White informed Paul that he had called Minister of Defense General Jose Guillermo García to request that he send out an all-points alert for a white Toyota van.[124]

Throughout the rest of the afternoon, the CLAM Team anxiously awaited the phone call from Nicaragua, for at this point they still did not know if they were looking for two or four people. At about 5:00 p.m. Christine and Elizabeth decided to drive to the airport to find out for themselves if anyone could offer some information regarding the missing women. Along the side of the road, about four miles outside of La Libertad, they spotted a burned, wrecked vehicle that several armed policemen were inspecting. Something about the shape of the vehicle caught the women's attention, and they stopped to examine it, although there was very little to see, as the tires, windows, and all flammable parts were gone. The dents in the fenders of the burned-out hulk looked vaguely familiar to the two women, however, so Christine said to the policemen, "I think this is our van."[125] But since she and Elizabeth could find no other identifying marks on the wreck, Christine added, "But we are not absolutely sure that it is ours."[126] They then resumed their drive to the airport.

Once inside the busy airport terminal, Christine and Elizabeth wasted no time inquiring about their friends. When they showed photographs of Dorothy, Jean, Maura, and Ita, three people admitted to having seen all of the women at the airport the night before. Now knowing for certain that they were looking for four people instead of two, Christine and Elizabeth hastily left the airport. When they returned to La Libertad, they relayed their news to the other team members and also told them of their discovery of the burned-out van. Paul immediately looked up the van's serial numbers, and accompanied by several local policemen, went to the site where the wreckage stood. The numbers listed on the van's registration papers matched the numbers stamped on the motor block of the abandoned burned-out vehicle.

*   *   *   *   *   *   *   *   *

Early in the morning of Thursday, December 4, a villager[127] in the parish of San Vicente told his parish priest of the burial of four foreign women wearing sandals[128] and of the location of the gravesite. The priest called the Archdiocese of San Salvador with the news, and Bishop Arturo Rivera y Damas called the American Embassy. He then tried to call the parish house in La Libertad but was unable to get through because of trouble with the phone lines.

The news, however, quickly reached the convent of the Assumption Sisters in San Salvador where Heather Foote, a staff member of the Washington Office on Latin America (WOLA), was staying after attending the funeral of the slain FDR leaders. Heather subsequently called WOLA in Washington D.C. and told Maryknoll Sister Peggy Healy that the bodies of four North American women wearing sandals had been located. Peggy then notified the Maryknoll Sisters Center in Ossining, New York, and around noon was able to get through to La Libertad.

When Ken Myers answered the phone in the parish house and called out to the other team members in the room, "It's a call from Washington," everyone grew still. Ken listened quietly to the caller, and after several long minutes he asked the group if Dorothy and Jean were wearing sandals when they were last seen. Christine remembered with certainty that Dorothy had been wearing them. Hoping that what they had just heard was a hoax, or at the least, untrue, the CLAM Team tried to telephone the archdiocesan office in San Salvador. After three attempts, they reached the office. Personnel there told the missionaries that the news they had heard was not a rumor and that the archdiocese had been trying all morning to get through to them. They then told the CLAM Team where the bodies had reportedly been located: on the Hacienda San Francisco near the town of Santiago Nonualco. Several cars of newspaper reporters accompanied Paul, Ken, Elizabeth, Maddie, and Terry to the area. Christine remained in La Libertad to answer the phone. Gathering some sheets, she left for the burial site about an hour later, accompanied by Maryknoll priests John Spain and Ronald Michels who had come to La Libertad seeking information about the location of the bodies.

Arriving at the hacienda, the missionaries immediately decided that they must open the grave to discover if the women were truly buried there. When Paul began to dig, however, the campesinos who had gathered around grew frightened and claimed that exhuming bodies without permission from the local justice of the peace was unlawful. Ignoring the people's protests, Paul continued his task. After he had dug about three feet and reached the first body, which he identified as Jean's, Ambassador White arrived. He asked Paul to stop until he could send for the justice of the peace to authorize the disinterment. Two embassy security men then went to Santiago Nonualco and brought the justice of the peace to the burial site. He showed Ambassador White and the missionaries the entry in his record book where the burial had been reported, and he then gave his consent for the bodies of the women to be exhumed and then transported from the site.[129]

Under the hot midday sun, the bodies were unearthed and pulled out of the grave, one by one, with ropes — first Jean, then Maura, then Dorothy, and finally Ita. Dorothy's slacks were on backwards, and she was wearing only one sandal. Jean was unrecognizable because the bullet had collapsed the bone structure of her face. Her body was badly bruised, as was Ita's, whose left arm also appeared to be broken.

As bloody bandanas and the women's panties were also pulled from the grave, the spectators silently acknowledged what the women's final moments must have been like. They then reverently covered the bodies with palm branches.

*   *   *   *   *   *   *   *   *

Throughout the afternoon the missionaries remained at the hacienda waiting the arrival of a hearse from the funeral home La Auxiliadora in San Salvador which Archbishop Rivera y Damas had requested be sent to the burial site. By 4:30 the hearse had not arrived, and because the curfew would soon be in effect, the missionaries who still remained at the spot, Paul, Elizabeth, and John Spain, decided to take the bodies themselves to the funeral home.

So, with the help of some of the local campesinos, the missionaries wrapped the women's bodies in the sheets Christine had brought, and they carefully loaded them into the back of the team's pick-up truck. Along the road to San Salvador, two different groups of the Guardia stopped the truck. When Paul produced the transport papers the justice of the peace had issued earlier that day, the Guardia allowed the truck to pass without further question.[130]

When Paul, John, and Elizabeth arrived at the funeral home, Monsignor Urioste joined them. As the funeral director prepared to embalm the bodies, the missionaries decided that an autopsy should also be performed.[131] They mentioned their request to the director, but none of the doctors he knew would come. The missionaries next found a local doctor who did come, but after he looked at the bodies, he also refused to conduct the autopsies.[132] Finally, through the intervention of the archdiocese, a local judge came to the funeral home and authorized the autopsies.[133] Doctor Carlos Cuellar Ortiz, the official medical examiner of San Salvador, soon arrived and performed each of the autopsies. In his report about Dorothy's autopsy, after Cuellar described the general appearance of her body and the clothes she was wearing, he wrote: "She had a wound on the region of the temple of the skull, right side . . . with destruction of the brain mass. It is believed that this wound was the cause of death."[134]

*   *   *   *   *   *   *   *   *

On Friday, December 5, at 4:30 p.m. at the parish of San José de la Montaña in San Salvador, Archbishop Rivera y Damas concelebrated the Mass of the Resurrection for the four slain women. The bodies of Dorothy and Jean were then taken to La Libertad for an all-night wake. Escorted by more than a dozen jeeps, vans, and cars, the bodies of Maura and Ita were driven to Chalatenango. According to Maryknoll tradition, they were buried among the poor with whom they had worked and died.

Paul Schindler celebrated a second funeral Mass for Dorothy and Jean in La Libertad on Saturday, December 6, at 5:00 a.m. When the Mass ended, CLAM Team members lifted Dorothy's and Jean's caskets to carry them to a waiting limousine that would transport them to the airport for their final trip back to the States. Inside the church the congregation lined the aisles, and as the caskets passed through the crowd, from hand to hand and shoulder to shoulder, the people stood on the benches and began to applaud. Outside the church the thousands of Salvadorans who were lining the streets of the city leading to the airport road also began to applaud. When the caskets appeared, men struggled for the privilege of carrying them; women reached out their hands to touch them. They were then loaded into the limousine, and as it slowly moved between the lines of people, the applause continued — thunderous in volume, triumphant in tone.

*   *   *   *   *   *   *   *   *

In late November 1980 Dorothy had written the monthly CLAM Team letter to the Diocese of Cleveland. She began the letter in this manner: "December is almost upon us. Time surely is moving by quickly — and at times one wonders just *where* it is going!"[135] What then follows is Dorothy's description of the pastoral work in which she and the other team members would engage during December. She afterwards claimed:

> All of this goes on as normally and ordinarily as possible. And yet if we look at this little country of El Salvador as a whole, we find that it is all going on in a country that is writhing in pain — a country that daily faces the loss of so many of its people — and yet a country that is waiting, hoping, and yearning for peace. The steadfast faith and courage our leaders have to continue preaching the Word of the Lord even though it may mean "laying down your life" for your fellowman in the very *real* sense is always a point of admiration and a most vivid realization that Jesus is *here* with us. Yes, we have a sense of waiting, hoping, and yearning for a complete realization of the Kingdom, and yet we know it will come because we can celebrate Him right now![136]

Dorothy's family, friends, and fellow Ursuline Sisters received this letter shortly after her death.

"Madre Dorotea," La Union, 1975.

Dorothea Lu, age one.

"Dottie," age four, and brother "Jim," age seven.

First Communion, May 23, 1948.

Dorothy, age ten.

Dorothy as a high school freshman at Notre Dame Academy, Cleveland, Ohio, 1953-54.

In March 1956 Dorothy won second place in a beauty contest at the Rollerdome Skating Rink in Euclid, Ohio.

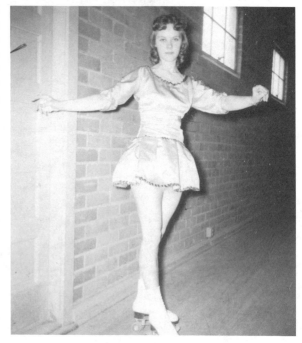

Dorothy and Russell Smith at the St. Joseph High School Senior Prom, May 1956.

Dorothy's high school graduation portrait, 1957.

Dorothy and her fiancé, Donald Kollenborn, attend a dance at St. John College, May 1959.

Dorothy and friends and family enjoy a holiday get-together at her home in Euclid, Ohio, January 1960 (bottom row, left to right): Joe Harbert, Donald Kollenborn, Jerry Friga; (top row): Fran Brezar (Harbert), Dorothy (Chapon) Kazel, Dorothy's sister-in-law, Dorothy, and Marilyn Chapas (Friga).

Dorothy on vacation at Kelly's Island, Ohio, July 1960.

Dorothy as an Ursuline postulant with her mother and father, Malvina and Joseph, outside Merici Hall, the Cleveland Ursuline Motherhouse in Pepper Pike, Ohio, 1961.

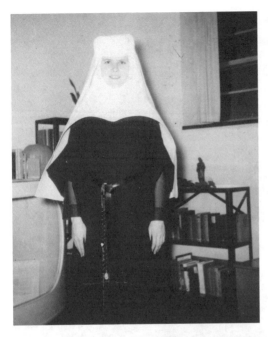

Sister Mary Laurentine, O.S.U., on the feastday of the Ursuline Martyrs of Valenciennes, France, October 23, 1962.

Dorothy, typing and business teacher at Sacred Heart Academy, Cleveland, 1966.

Final Profession of vows as an Ursuline Sister of Cleveland, August 13, 1968.

Taking time out for some sightseeing while ministering to the Native Americans of the Papago Tribe in Topawa, Arizona, Summer 1969.

Dorothy relaxing at a backyard picnic, early 1970s.

Dorothy getting into the spirit of a "50s Day" at Beaumont School, 1972.

Newly assigned member of the Cleveland Latin American Mission Team, July 1974.

Dorothy visiting the people in the beach areas of La Union, 1976. Father John Garrity, director of the Cleveland Mission Office at the time, is on the left.

Dorothy en route to minister in the cantones of La Union, 1976.

*Dorothy resting
in a bell tower in
an old church
in the town of
Panchimalco,
January 1977.*

Ready to tackle the rough terrain of the El Salvador countryside, Zaragoza, 1978.

Dorothy working at her desk at home in Zaragoza, 1978.

Smiling for the camera: Dorothy and "Jaime" in front of Our Lady of the Pillar Church in Zaragoza, 1978.

Dorothy and Martha Owen, O.S.U., traveling to the States for vacation, June 1979.

A happy group on their way to a Eucharistic celebration, August 1979.

The Cleveland Mission Team in La Libertad, winter 1979 (left to right): Christine Rody, V.S.C., Dorothy, Father Ken Myers, Jean Donovan, and Father Paul Schindler.

Dorothy and Paul celebrate an outdoor Mass in the cantones of La Libertad, 1979.

(Credit: MaryKnoll Mission Archives)

Jean Donovan stops to chat with a village woman, 1980.

Carla Piette, M.M.

(Credit: MaryKnoll Mission Archives)

(Credit: MaryKnoll Mission Archives)

Maura Clarke, M.M.

Ita Ford, M.M.

Dorothy dressed as a flower garden, Halloween 1980.

Dorothy with Teresa Alexander, M.M., and Monsignor Ricardo Urioste, vicar-general of the archdiocese, in Tamanique on November 21, 1980. This photo is one of the last that was ever taken of Dorothy.

(Credit: Chris Lafaille, Sipa, Black Star)

Maryknoll Sisters Teresa Alexander (left) and Madeline Dorsey kneel in prayer after the bodies of Dorothy, Jean, Maura, and Ita are exhumed from a shallow, common grave on December 4, 1980.

Dorothy's grave in All Souls Cemetery, Chardon, Ohio. The second date on the headstone (1963) is the date of Dorothy's First Profession of vows as a Cleveland Ursuline Sister.

In 1992 a chapel was constructed on the site where Dorothy, Jean, Maura, and Ita were murdered. The monument in front of the chapel had been erected in the early 1980s by members of the Cleveland Mission Team. Its inscription reads:

North American Catholic Missionaries Dorothy Kazel,
Maura Clarke, Jean Donovan, and Ita Ford
poured out their lives here on December 2, 1980.
Receive them, Lord, into your kingdom.

To the far right, marked by white rocks, is the burial site of the women.

Interior of the chapel: the design and construction of the altar was a collaborative effort of Cleveland Ursuline artist Diane Therese Pinchot and Salvadoran master builder Edilberto Ramos and carpenter Carlos Aguilar. Geraldine Hable, a Cleveland Ursuline artist who was serving in El Salvador at the time, also contributed her expertise.

Ursuline missionaries present and past plant a tree at the gravesite of the four women, summer 1994: Roberta Goebel (far left) and Lisa Marie Belz (far right) are currently serving in El Salvador. Martha Owen (next to Roberta) served from 1974-79, and Sheila Marie Tobbe (next to Lisa Marie) served from 1990-95.

In 1994 a dental clinic in La Libertad was named in Dorothy's honor. The sign reads: "People's Dental Clinic, Mother Dorothy Kazel, Cleaning, Fillings, Pullings, Partial Plates, and All Basic Medical Treatments."

Dorothy, Jean, Maura, and Ita are also remembered in various ways in the United States as in this stained-glass window in St. Maria Goretti Church in San Jose, California. Here the women are depicted with Archbishop Oscar Romero.

3

A Woman of Dimensions: Dorothy's Personality

I accept the fact that I am human and with this human nature strive to become as perfect and loving a woman, Christian, and religious that I can be . . . to accept the person I am with all my weaknesses and not to pretend that I don't have them.

Journal, August 11, 1968

When family, friends, and even acquaintances speak of Dorothy, their initial comments center around her personality. Words that frequently surface include "vivacious,"[1] "sparkly,"[2] "friendly,"[3] "open,"[4] "joyful,"[5] "loving,"[6] and "gregarious."[7] These words evoke a certain dynamism which, Dorothy's relatives and friends readily admit, she clearly manifested. Such dynamism, combined with a strength, and yet a tenderness of spirit, endeared Dorothy to many people while leaving them with a lasting impression of a woman with a multi-dimensional character.

*   *   *   *   *   *   *   *   *

From all outward appearances Dorothy was an extrovert who enjoyed having a good time with people. Her acquaintances agree that because of her outgoing nature, she made friends wherever she went, and many of these friends kept in touch with her throughout her life. Good friends admire the other qualities that were so much a part of Dorothy's personality: courage, independence, creativity, generosity, optimism, and a love of adventure. And all who knew her recall with a smile Dorothy's good sense of humor.

There was also a reserved side of Dorothy that few, except very close friends, suspected in light of her fun-loving, sociable manner; and there was also a struggling, questioning side that scarcely anyone really knew. These qualities, however, rounded out Dorothy's character and made her "just as human as everybody else with frailties and insecurities."[8]

*   *   *   *   *   *   *   *   *

Because of Dorothy's vibrant personality, or as Marilyn Friga termed it, the "good energy"[9] that she possessed, many persons who knew Dorothy can distinctly recall the very first time they met her, whether as a young child, an adolescent, or as an adult. A lifelong friend of Dorothy's, Fran Harbert, describes her initial acquaintance with Dorothy when they began kindergarten together at St. George School:

> Do you know how some children are attractive — that there is just something about them? Dorothy was just sunny, and she matched the way that she looked with the blonde hair and the good smile and the pretty eyes. And everybody wanted to be her friend.[10]

Franciscan Sister M. Helene Balciunas, Dorothy's first grade teacher, claims, "I remember her vividly as though she were in front of me now."[11] With a slight smile she adds, "Dorothy had a chubby little face and was nicely dressed all the time. She was a very good-looking little girl and was quiet but sociable at the same time."[12]

As an adolescent, Dorothy continued to make memorable first impressions on others because of her beauty and bubbly, outgoing personality. Notre Dame Sister Kay O'Malley, a high school classmate and friend of Dorothy's, reminisces about the Dorothy she met in the ninth grade at Notre Dame Academy:

> Dorothy liked to have a good time and really reached out to a lot of people. She was always pretty happy — at least she looked happy, externally very happy — I don't know what was happening on the inside sometimes. To her life was fun. She always had a smile on her face and was full of jokes.[13]

Kay kept in touch with Dorothy until her death. Yet even some of those who did not maintain contact with Dorothy over a lengthy period of time can still recollect their earliest encounter with her. Eileen Best, who taught at Notre Dame Academy during Dorothy's freshman year there and had her only for homeroom, recalls that Dorothy stood out first of all "because she was physically such a beautiful child: very blonde hair, beautiful features and complexion and a very good body in the sense that she was not overweight. I remember a certain shyness about her. I do not think I ever really got to know her, but I do remember *her*."[14] Another one of Dorothy's teachers who had her for only a year at Notre Dame Academy was Notre Dame Sister Muriel Petrasek. Her memory of Dorothy is of "a fresh, vibrant person who was very willing to assist in chemistry class wherever she could. She was a very active individual who stood out."[15]

Throughout her adult life Dorothy sustained her apparently unconscious effort to make striking first impressions on others. In the spring of 1958, when she was a student at St. John College, she arrived at the first-grade classroom of Anna Margaret Gilbride to complete a case study on a child. Anna Margaret clearly recalls this initial meeting with Dorothy:

> I remember when she first came into my classroom — I can still see her — she had on a white pleated skirt with a blue blazer. I was struck by how beautiful she was. And she seemed so unassuming. She didn't seem to know that she was so pretty. She was very vivacious and full of life and very interested in everything.[16]

September 8, 1960, Entrance Day for the Ursuline Congregation that year, was the first time Kathleen Cooney made contact with Dorothy. She recollects that she quickly spotted Dorothy among the crowd of nineteen identically dressed young women who were also joining the congregation. Her image of Dorothy on that day remains lucid in her memory:

> We were all gathering about the front door of the motherhouse. I looked around at the group, and Dorothy was this beautiful, stunning blonde. With her big blue eyes and beautiful smile, she was very striking. And there was an air of maturity about her but also a youthfulness. I looked at Dorothy and thought, "Oh, who's that? Boy, she's pretty."[17]

Ursuline Sister Barbara Jean Sever who taught at Sacred Heart Academy from 1966-72, claims that what she first noticed about Dorothy was her ability to make people feel comfortable, her great sensitivity, and her high energy level.[18] Echoing Barbara Jean's opinion are Christine Rody and Cleveland diocesan priest John F. Loya, fellow missionaries of Dorothy's. Christine first met Dorothy in the spring of

1975 when she visited El Salvador prior to her assignment there the following year. She recalls:

> Dorothy was very friendly and accepting — just made me feel very welcome — I didn't feel like a fish out of water because I didn't know any Spanish. She also made sure that I understood what was going on when we visited villages and casarios for Mass.[19]

John F. Loya also made his first acquaintance with Dorothy in El Salvador. When he flew into San Salvador's old international airport in January of 1980, she and the other CLAM Team members were there to meet and welcome him. John recounts his arrival and memorable first encounter with Dorothy:

> As I got off the plane and walked across the tarmac to the terminal, I saw Dorothy smiling and waving enthusiastically from the observation deck. I was nervous about coming to El Salvador, but upon seeing that my arrival meant something to her and the rest of the team, I temporarily regained some self-confidence. While I was waiting in line for the customs inspection, however, I grew apprehensive again. Everything that had seemed new and exciting about being a missionary was suddenly strange and frightening. I glumly pondered what I had gotten myself into by volunteering to work in El Salvador. In an effort to take my mind off my worries, I looked around and saw Dorothy watching me from the waiting area. She was following my progress through the entrance procedures with keen interest. She waved at me then and every time I looked in her direction. It was as if she knew what I was feeling and was trying to reassure me from where she stood. She also gave me the impression that if I ran into any trouble, help was not far away. For that bit of communication, I was very grateful.
> I do not know exactly how Dorothy did it, but when finally we were close enough to shake hands, she made our first meeting feel like a reunion of old friends. I can remember thinking that if a person whom I had never met could have such a good effect upon me, I should try to do the same for

others. That a quiet and retiring person like me should even think about acting in such a manner, much less attempt a change in behavior, was no small tribute to Dorothy and her exuberant example.[20]

*   *   *   *   *   *   *   *   *

For most people who knew Dorothy, however, the image they retain of her transcends first impressions to that of a woman who was gifted with the unique ability to love and accept practically everyone with whom she came in contact. As Donald Kollenborn claims, "People instantly identified this energy that she had. Everybody seemed to attach to that. And I think they just sensed her strength."[21] Although Donald knew Dorothy only in her young adulthood, those who were acquainted with her for a longer period of time claim that her power to attract others — this certain magnetism she possessed — was an outstanding characteristic of her personality throughout her life.

Marilyn Friga, who attended both St. George School and Notre Dame Academy with Dorothy, recalls that Dorothy "always had people around her. She was just very popular — probably the most popular girl in the class for the whole time."[22] Marilyn also adds that Dorothy was "the kind of kid that you would pick out in any class that was really special."[23]

Dorothy did not express a desire to be special, however, nor did she consciously attempt to make herself stand out. As Fran Harbert claims: "She wasn't trying to attract anybody, but she could just reel them in. Everybody liked her."[24] Fran then relates an incident that clearly illustrates Dorothy's magnetism:

In July of 1960, shortly before Dorothy entered the convent, she and I and Mercita Thailing went on a week-end vacation to Kelly's Island, Ohio. One afternoon we went swimming, and Dorothy met this really cute guy on the beach. He was from Detroit, I believe. Anyway, that evening we went to a dance someplace on the island, and Dorothy met the same guy there. They danced together, and towards the end of the evening, she gave him her address and didn't tell him that she was going into the convent. I guess she never thought he would actually contact her. Well, later that summer, on the day on which we gave Dorothy a going-away party, that guy came to her home. With so many people present, she had to tell him that she was entering the convent.[25]

Years later when Dorothy first arrived in El Salvador and could not speak Spanish, her personality spoke for her. Martha Owen remembers: "Dorothy would walk right up to the people, and she couldn't speak a word to them. But she would talk to them with her smiles and her gestures, and they responded to her very well. I believe she *could* communicate with them without a spoken language."[26]

*   *   *   *   *   *   *   *   *

Dorothy's magnetic personality drew persons of diverse backgrounds and ages to her and around her in an ever-widening circle of relationships, as Fran Harbert affirms:

> She was just a light, some sort of beacon. People just wanted to be around her like moths around a flame because she was just so personable. And she gave you all of her attention when you were together, and you just felt that she cared about you. It sounds like a bunch of platitudes, but that's how it was.[27]

*   *   *   *   *   *   *   *   *

In her introduction to *Women and Creativity*, Dolores R. Leckey notes that a person's available writings serve as one window of insight into what is truly valuable in the person's life.[28] Another window is the personal items a person chooses to save: momentos from childhood, notebooks, books, pictures, scrapbooks, and diaries. Such objects also surely shed light on the person's character.

Like many people, Dorothy's keepsakes serve as concrete reminders of honors earned and goals achieved. Among her surviving personal belongings are the award she was given for being chosen the Valentine Queen of her sixth-grade class at St. George School[29] and a pin she received when she was inducted into the National Thespian Society as a senior at Notre Dame Academy. The programs from Dorothy's senior class play *Cheaper by the Dozen*, in which she acted the part of Anne Gilbreth, and from Father-Daughter Night, another senior-class activity in which she performed and also helped write, are included, as well as programs from roller-skating events and competitions. Also among her memorabilia are her diplomas from high school, college, and graduate school, and yearbooks from St. John College, Sacred Heart Academy, and Beaumont School for Girls.

Although Dorothy did little personal writing, she took careful notes for her college and graduate-school courses and on her spiritual reading.

Several spiral-bound notebooks containing her notes from novitiate theology courses survive as do notes from other college courses such as social thought, social psychology, mental health, and chemistry. Dorothy saved her notes from all of her graduate courses in guidance and counseling at John Carroll University, Cleveland. The most recent course notes are those for the two workshops she took at the Maryknoll Institute from July 27-August 9, 1980.

A small, binder-type notebook bound in black leather holds Dorothy's spiritual-reading notes from her time in the novitiate. Throughout the remaining years of her religious life, Dorothy recorded notes from the spiritual books she read in a few stenographic notebooks or on separate sheets of paper, which she inserted into the backs of the notebooks. None of the spiral notebooks are completely filled. Dorothy also took notes on the conferences given at the retreats she attended. The earliest of these notes dates back to the retreat she made before her Clothing in August 1961 and the latest to another she made in Guatemala in November 1979 with the CLAM Team members. Dorothy took notes for all of her novitiate retreats but later became sporadic in her note-taking as notes for only a few of the annual retreats she made until 1979 exist.

Because of the small number of books Dorothy had in her possession at the time of her death, it is apparent that she was not a book collector. She owned, of course, prayer books and those that related to her life as an Ursuline Sister[30] but few others in comparison to the number most people accumulate in their lifetime. What books Dorothy did save, though, are an interesting assortment: *Four Days: The Historical Record of the Death of President Kennedy*, published by United Press International and American Heritage Magazine; *Christ Among Us: A Modern Presentation of the Catholic Faith* by Anthony J. Wilhelm, C.S.P.; *Prayers for Meditation* by Hugo and Karl Rahner; *Lonesome Cities* by Rod McKuen; *Jonathan Livingston Seagull* by Richard Bach; *The Voice of Those Without Voice: The Living Word of Oscar Romero*, edited by J. Sobrino, I. Martin-Baro, and R. Cardenal; *Puebla: Evangelization in the Present and in the Future of Latin America*, the report of the Third General Conference of Latin American Bishops (October 1978);[31] and *Cry of the People: United States Involvement in the Rise of Fascism, Torture, and Murder and the Persecution of the Catholic Church in Latin America* by Penny Lernoux.

The pamphlets found among Dorothy's personal belongings include: *The Second Vatican Council Decree on the Missionary Activity of the*

Church, December 1965, published by the National Catholic Welfare Conference; *Mission to Latin America*, a progress report prepared by the staff of the Cleveland Latin American Mission; *On the Renewal of the Religious Life According to the Teaching of the Second Vatican Council, June 1971*, Apostolic Exhortation of His Holiness Pope Paul VI; *The Three Apostolates of Modern Woman*, Address of His Holiness Pope Pius XII to the World Congress of the World Union of Catholic Women's Organizations, Rome, Italy (September 1957); *What is Love?* by Jules J. Toner; and *For Adults Only: Some Plain Talk on Enjoying Life* by Walter S. Nosal.

The bulk of the items Dorothy kept are, however, her photograph albums. Some chronicle the special events in her life and activities shared with friends. In a scrapbook she received for Christmas 1954, for example, Dorothy includes pictures of her graduation from St. George School, her first day at Notre Dame Academy, several "Notre Dame Days," and roller-skating shows and competitions. Also illustrated are school dances and a host of birthday, pajama, Christmas, and beach parties Dorothy either attended or gave during 1954 and 1955. A second scrapbook contains pictures of similar events from the year 1956.

Other albums of Dorothy's record her trips to various parts of the United States, and later, her travels in Central America. The earliest one is dated the summer of 1949 when Dorothy journeyed by car to California to visit her Aunt Natalie and Uncle George Radauskas with George's sister Mary Hoover and her husband and daughter. In a small scrapbook with a leather cover stamped "Los Angeles, California," Dorothy neatly arranged the black and white photos of Californian sites and in her large, flowing handwriting penciled in the names of the scenes and the people in them underneath each picture. Twenty years later she memorialized through photographs yet another trip West: the summer she spent teaching Catholic doctrine to Native Americans of the Papago Tribe in Topawa, Arizona.

The most complete collection of Dorothy's photographs, though, are those from her time in El Salvador. A total of thirteen albums provides a fairly complete pictorial history of her life as a missionary from 1974 through 1980; loose photos portray events up until the day before she died.[32] In these albums as in all of her others, Dorothy carefully mounted each photograph and identified it with the date of the event and the names of the people involved. The albums of Dorothy's Salvadoran experience also include scenes of good times enjoyed with friends as the rest do.

Another keepsake of Dorothy's that reveals her personality is her diary of 1956. Many of its entries evidence her love of fun and frequent socializing with friends as well as her general enjoyment of life:

Went to [Marie] Modic's pajama party. Had a great time. Her boys are quite different. One liked me, but I didn't appreciate him. We took a couple walks at night but had to watch for the cops. What a time. We played pool all night. Russ [Smith] got his driver's license! Three cheers![33]

I went to church again (I need it). The history test wasn't *too* bad. Fran came home with me after we went to Franklin's [Ice Cream Store]. At 3:30 p.m. I *walked* her up to Lakeland [Boulevard] and E. 250th. What a great way to exercise. Went skating and had a *ball*!!! Modic's George and friends were there.[34]

Went to Pittsburgh, Pennsylvania, with the St. George Sodality to see the Passion Play.[35] It was pretty good. We had a swell bus driver. The nuns were buggy; all they wanted were draftees for the convent. I bought Russ a can of oil as a souvenir for his car and some cigarettes, gum, a toothpick, and a packet of sugar. We had a great time![36]

Although Dorothy's 1956 diary was the only one she kept while she was in high school, it gives a good sampling of what her life as a high school student was like. The entries also suggest that Dorothy's comments, concerns, and activities were typically adolescent:

Slept until 11:00 a.m. (again); got up, cleaned house. Mare [Friga] and I decided Fran's [surprise sixteenth-birthday] party should be Wednesday and talked about all the stuff. Went to [skating] practice and stayed for session. Mare and I talked through most of it. We had show practice after. I broke the skates I'm using (rather knocked the wheel pin out, as usual). Chuck drove me home and asked me out for Wednesday. But we're having the party (thank goodness) so he asked about Thursday (ugh). So, it looks like I have to tell the dear boy something.[37]

Russ and Jer [Friga] left for the Philippines at 9:30 a.m. We cried like babies because we won't see them for two years.

When we got to school, we were suspended from our office[38] for a month. We still think it was worth it to go see them off.[39]

From August 26 to September 1, 1965, Dorothy attended the annual Summer School of Catholic Action (SSCA) in Chicago, Illinois, with twenty-seven juniors and seniors from Notre Dame Academy and Notre Dame Sister Mary Reean, the group's moderator. Several months later *The Tower*, Notre Dame's newspaper, reported on the scheduled daily events of the meeting:

> Beginning each day's activities, community Mass, said aloud in English by the students, was offered in the Grand Ballroom of the Morrison Hotel. Breakfast and lunch was followed by a number of conferences on such subjects as Catholic leadership, Our Lady and the teen-age sodalists, and courtship and marriage. Activities varying from boat rides to a talent night offered entertainment in the evenings.[40]

In her diary Dorothy gives an account of her last day in Chicago and its evening's entertainment:

> Slept until 9:00 a.m. Sister Reean woke us up. Went to class and then to 11:40 Mass. Shopped some more; had a dance at night. I danced with two boys. One was short and ugly; the other wasn't toooo *bad*. He's going to John Carroll in the fall. Afterwards, we had a *surprise* party for [Dorothy] Klamer. She almost died. Some men (Timber Wolves)[41] were in suite 6 down the hall. Our girls were making out with them. They were *cute*. [Marilyn] Zele got a martini from her buddy. Sister then came down and made us stay in the room. Our *big* chaperone[42] then came *down* and yelled because our blind was open. Then later another came and yelled because we were singing. She said we should be in bed sleeping. We were good then. So [Mary Ann] Gutman happened to hum something, and the chaperone flies in and asks us where we were from and what school! Boy, were we *mad*!!! Got to bed about 3:30 a.m.[43]

For the year 1956 Dorothy wrote New Year's resolutions on a sheet of paper, which she had folded and inserted in the back of her diary. The resolutions offer some insight into the serious or reflective side of Dorothy's character:

1) to remain at 120 lbs.
2) to have patience with others; to understand them
3) to have courage to do what is right
4) to treat Russ as a boyfriend
5) to practice real hard and get someplace
6) to control my feelings!
7) to increase my love for those above (daily rosary)
8) to act sensibly
9) to help make our home a happy one
10) to be a better person all the way through[44]

*   *   *   *   *   *   *   *   *

According to Dorothy's family and friends, a distinguishing quality of her personality was creativity. And a particularly obvious aspect of her creativity was her ability to "make do" with whatever materials were available at any given time and place. Dorothy's mother Malvina recalls an incident that well illustrates this trait of Dorothy's, apparent even when she was a child:

> Around Halloween time, when Dorothy was in the third grade, she did not have a costume for her school party. On the day of the party, when she came home for lunch, Dorothy found some newspaper and cut out a dress and pinned it together. She wore it to school and won first prize for having the most original Halloween costume.[45]

An episode from Dorothy's adolescence also reveals her spontaneous creativity. Marilyn Friga remembers: "We were goofing around at Dorothy's house one day, and she came out of the bathroom wrapped in towels — she had made a dress out of them, and she had one on her head — and she was swinging a towel as a stripper would."[46] And years later in El Salvador, Dorothy once again displayed her flair for creatively using materials at hand. At the last Halloween party of her life, October 28, 1980, she devised her own costume: a flower garden. A photograph from this event shows a smiling Dorothy dressed in a flowing white gown on which she had painted bright yellow and pink flowers. Around her neck and forearms are twined tiny orange plastic bulbous flowers; on her head is perched an arrangement of pink, white, and brown straw flowers and green ribbons cut to resemble leaves. On each cheek and on her chin, Dorothy had painted a huge pink flower.

                    *   *   *   *   *   *   *   *   *

Another obvious characteristic of Dorothy's personality was her appealing sense of humor. Traces of it first appear in her photograph album of the years 1954 and 1955. For many of the pictures in this album, Dorothy wrote captions that are at once clever and innocent in their descriptions of scenes. She labels photos of groups of girlfriends at parties, for example, with expressions such as "The horror show is on," "The Pinups," and "The Colgate Smiles."[47] Underneath one photograph of several girls smoking cigarettes at a pajama party, she wrote the phrase, "The 'Hard' Ones."[48] Dorothy identified pictures of single friends with inscriptions such as "What is it?" "Feed it! Maybe it'll go away," "Hide it! Don't let it spread," and "The Sleeping Beaut [at a pajama party]."[49] In this same photo album, Dorothy also wrote humorous commentaries for a series of photographs she took while on vacation with Marilyn Friga in Port Dover, Canada, in July 1954. Underneath a picture of herself standing in a picnic area is the phrase, "*Ugh*! What a mess"; beneath a picture of herself sitting in front of a lake, she wrote, "Well, it's nice scenery, anyway."[50] Dorothy tagged a photograph of an obese, shirtless man sitting on a bench with the expression, "The Cheesecake of '54" and described a picture of four small children on the lake in an inner tube, which they are paddling with their hands, "The Official Motor and Boat."[51]

When she was an adult, Dorothy's good sense of humor contributed to the unaffectedness of her character. Christine Rody explains: "She was good and sweet, but her personality was not that overpowering 'sweetie' type because of her humor, which at times was borderline brazen."[52] One memorable example of Dorothy's brazen brand of humor was her choice of a name for a cat that she, Christine, and Martha Owen had acquired at one point during their stay in El Salvador. Because the cat had a black mark by his nose, Dorothy decided to call him "Boogers" — "Boogs" for short. Christine admits that she and Martha were at first a little embarrassed by Dorothy's selection of such a name for their cat. They both thought to themselves, "What are people going to say?"[53] After realizing, however, that Dorothy was not embarrassed in the least by the name she had bestowed on the cat, Christine and Martha accepted the name and in time called the cat by it with the same ease as Dorothy. This cat-naming episode, Christine believes, revealed Dorothy's ability "to touch into any phase of life: nothing was beneath her or embarrassing."[54]

Christine also claims that Dorothy could handle situations that would fluster practically anybody else.[55] An incident of this nature occurred during one of Bishop James A. Hickey's visits to the Cleveland missionaries in La Libertad. One night the team decided to take Bishop Hickey out to dinner, and at an appointed time they all met at Ken Myers' house in Zaragoza, where the bishop was staying. A bull that the team had bought to raffle off at an upcoming parish festival was tied to a post in the back yard. While the missionaries casually stood around the animal discussing the raffle, Dorothy suddenly squealed and unzipped her slacks. She then began to frantically feel around one of her pant legs, and the group gathered that something was crawling up her leg. Because she could not find and remove whatever it was, though, Dorothy turned and ran into the house to remove her slacks. Several minutes later she returned to the back yard and in an offhanded way said, "Guess what? It was a cockroach!"[56] The pre-dinner conversation then continued as before.

Another event that exemplified Dorothy's ability to deal gracefully with embarrassing circumstances took place while she, Christine, and one of the CLAM Team priests were doing pastoral work in one of their outlying villages. At the time Dorothy and Christine were teaching the parishioners new songs for the Mass while the priest was hearing confessions. Because the village had no electricity, the missionaries had hung a lantern in the front of the church. Around the lantern fluttered several June bugs. Dorothy happened to be standing near the lantern when one of them jumped down her bra. Immediately, all eyes were focused on her in anticipation of her next move. She nonchalantly turned to the wall where, incidentally, the priest was hearing confessions, smiled at him, flipped the bug out and then turned back around and kept singing.

Dorothy's sense of humor also worked to her advantage in other circumstances. For example, during her early years as a missionary, when her lack of fluency in Spanish put her in some potentially frustrating situations, Dorothy focused on the humorous aspects of the situations and was thus able to laugh at herself. Several days after her arrival in El Salvador, Dorothy recorded two such experiences on tape. She related the first one to her parents:

> Before we began filling out baptismal records, Martha and I decided to run over to the post office and mail all our little cards and letters that we wrote yesterday. So, we trotted over to the post office — just the two of us — which was the first

mistake. We went in, and of course, we did not have enough stamps, but yesterday, when we were in San Miguel, we at least got some Salvadoran money — some colones and whatever the other things are — centavos.

So, we went in with this thing that looks like a five-dollar bill. Anyway, the clerk put the rest of the stamps and things on our postcards. We got that much figured out, and he got that much figured out. The funny part is he ran out of the one twenty-five centavo stamp, so he put on three big, gigantic stamps that covered up the whole postcard! So, if you get postcards, and you can't read them. . . . You may *not* get them because the 'por avion' was covered up. They may be coming on the boat instead. So, hold on for about three months!

Anyway, after he got them stamped, he took out the correct money and gave us back the change, and then we wanted to buy more stamps because we knew we'd be writing some more stuff tonight. Well, trying to get that out in Spanish! He was hysterical, and we were hysterical, but we finally got some stamps out of the guy. And really, we could've bought out the whole store because it's nothing but a little desk and a little man in a little room that's grubby and old and falling apart. And when he was putting on the stamps, he was using what looked like shoemaker glue . . . it just looked grubby. He put it on some of the stamps, and the rest of them he licked.

But anyway, we finally got the stamps out of him, and when we started, it was just the two of us and this little guy, and then a couple of other little guys started coming into the store — this little hut, this little room — and by the time we were through, we were all hysterical trying to figure out what we wanted, and they were laughing with us and at us because all these kids were here, too, trying to figure out what these crazy women wanted.[57]

Three days later Dorothy made a tape for the Sisters at Beaumont Convent and told another "Spanish story":

Well, we're still here in El Salvador, persevering as well as we can — kind of getting used to things. We're beginning our second week. We're celebrating our anniversary today. We've been here for one whole week, and we feel like one-week old babies, and that's no joke. We're still learning lots, and we still have many, many miles to go. It's interesting still trying to communicate with these people. Thank God we can laugh and smile a lot, and they laugh and smile right back with us.

The other night we were at this little village called Intipuca. It's one of the parish villages. We went with Father Bill [Gibbons] for Mass. And all of their churches are very ornate. They have their statues clothed in all kinds of fanciful garments, etc., and they have all kinds of plastic and paper and real flowers mixed in between, and drapery hanging here and there, etc.

Well, we were standing outside the church before Mass, and this little lady comes up to me, and she starts talking. And, you know, me with all the knowledge of Spanish I have, the only thing I can say is "Como se llamo [sic],"[58] you know, "What is your name?" And after that I don't even understand what they say their name is! It really was hysterical.

So, we tried to get what her name was and tried to talk with her, and then all we did was wind up laughing, and Father Bill came over, and he said, "What's going on?" And then she said to him in Spanish, "They're talking to me, and I don't know what they're saying, and I'm sure that they don't understand a thing I'm saying!" So, it was mutual. But we laughed a lot and enjoyed each other.[59]

Some years later Dorothy returned to La Libertad from her yearly vacation in the States with a new hairstyle: a permanent. In a tape to her parents, she described the Salvadoran people's varied reactions to her new look, and once again, revealed her ability to find the fun in an awkward situation and to laugh at herself:

I haven't really told you about my hair. It's been a real riot. When I first came back, people didn't know who I was! They would look at me, and they'd just look past me or something because they didn't realize that it was me because I've never had curly hair before.

So, it's really been lots of fun, and some people just do not like it at all, and they'll come out and tell you, especially some of our kids at the Port, the teenagers — some of them don't like it. But the thing is, you know it's funny. The longer I have it, the more I like it — the more I get used to seeing myself. It's just been fun. It's been kind of a fun thing. My [Caritas] ladies are all teasing me. They told me I'm looking for a boyfriend now with curly hair, and I said, "No, I'm really here to scare them all off!"[60]

Throughout her adult years Dorothy never lost her love of sharing fun and good times with friends. Joan Mury, a Maryknoll Sister who met Dorothy in El Salvador, attests to this quality of Dorothy's personality as well as her engaging sense of humor: "We called Dottie 'Crazy Dottie' as she was always joking, laughing, or coming up with an outrageous idea. She was bursting with life."[61]

*   *   *   *   *   *   *   *   *

Because Dorothy was outgoing and loved to laugh and have a good time, many people with whom she came in contact may have wondered if she even *had* a serious side. Mercita Thailing, who had met Dorothy at St. John College and remained friends with her until she died, affirms this notion:

I think there were many people who would not have thought of Dorothy as being a profound person. They viewed her as "Miss Bubbly" — nothing was wrong with her, and she didn't have a serious thought in her head.[62]

"Dorothy and I, however," Mercita continues, "had some less-than-shallow conversations in the years of our friendship."[63] Agreeing with Mercita, Malvina Kazel claims, "My daughter was very sensitive, and she had a lot of deep inner feelings that not too many people really realized she had."[64] Father Eldon Reichert, who first knew Dorothy when she joined St. Robert Bellarmine Parish and kept in touch with her throughout her life, claims that "Dorothy could be an extrovert and laugh and fool around, but she could also go on a quiet retreat: she worked out of one side just as well as the other. I see her as a good example of the ideal person."[65] He adds, "That kind of a rich person doesn't come down the pike that often."[66]

*   *   *   *   *   *   *   *   *

Those who were close to Dorothy admit that as a friend she was loving and generous and "would do anything for you."[67] Known as a good listener and counselor, she also helped many who struggled with personal problems. But although Dorothy served as friend and confidante to a large number of people, she did not often impart to them what was truly on her mind; nor did she readily discuss difficulties she was experiencing or decisions she had to make.

While in high school with Dorothy, Marilyn Friga noticed Dorothy's lack of self-disclosure. She recalls:

> Dorothy never really blabbed about anything personal. We used to argue about that all the time. She really wasn't either into her feelings or open with them. Dorothy was always bubbly and cheerful, but it was rare that she really talked about things that were bothering her.[68]

Mercita, who met Dorothy several years later, was also aware of her reticence but claims that Dorothy "was not the type of person who would have unloaded her problems to you."[69] She further explains that Dorothy's reluctance to discuss her troubles might have resulted from the way she was brought up: "Dorothy may have learned early on that 'one does not talk about some of those things.'"[70] Barbara Jean Sever's fondest memories of Dorothy center around her accepting attitude and her approachability. "But the other side of Dorothy," Barbara states, "is that she didn't talk about a lot of what was going on inside of her."[71]

In Dorothy's very young adulthood, her unwillingness to discuss personal issues did not seem to be of great concern to her. Marilyn claims that she "told Dorothy about it [her silence] quite a bit."[72] But she recalls that when she did, Dorothy would just shrug her shoulders and say, "That's just the way I am."[73] "And I don't remember her feeling inferior because of it,"[74] Marilyn adds. Some years later on January 15, 1967, Dorothy wrote resolutions for the New Year. One of them may shed some light on her hesitancy to communicate her innermost thoughts and feelings: "*Be* transparent, but be prudent and discreet in revealing self as not all are ready to accept you."[75]

As Dorothy grew older, though, she became aware of her self-censorship regarding personal matters. And she, in turn, struggled with this facet of her character as is apparent from a resolution she composed at the end of her retreat before she took final vows on August 13, 1968: "Help me, Lord, to accept the fact that I *need* others. Give me the grace to let others know I need them."[76] Attesting to Dorothy's difficulties with self-disclosure, Donna Zaller, a good friend prior to 1972, states, "I think her hardest thing was that she couldn't express how she felt. Dorothy felt so deeply about so many things but just couldn't talk about them."[77] Deciding to try to express herself more fully, however, Dorothy wrote the following retreat resolution for 1972: "to make an effort to 'share' myself with others."[78]

*   *   *   *   *   *   *   *   *

Like most people Dorothy had a vulnerable side, one "that didn't have all that strength."[79] And like most people, she tucked this side away, out of the view of the many persons with whom she had contact. "The face Dorothy showed to the world — the happy, sparkly, have-it-all-together one — was a different face than the one inside,"[80] claims Donna Zaller. "And it took me years to find that other face, and I still don't think I really knew her. But because of the friendship we shared, Dorothy did open up some parts of herself to me,"[81] Donna adds.

What were these "parts of herself" that Dorothy rarely revealed to others? They were not so different, once again, from those of most people: a need for self-acceptance and acceptance by others, a lack of self-confidence, and feelings of inadequacy. Moreover, these vulnerable parts of Dorothy, added to those she willingly shared with others, actually contributed to the wholeness of her person rather than detracted from it.

*   *   *   *   *   *   *   *   *

There is evidence, however slight, that points to the fact that Dorothy grappled with self-doubts throughout much of her young adulthood. Donald Kollenborn recalls:

> Whenever Dorothy faced new challenges, like when she began to teach [elementary school], she had that fear that she wouldn't live up to expectations, that she wouldn't be accepted by the children, and that she wasn't going to fall into place. She would work very hard to make sure that she fit perfectly.[82]

Further commenting on Dorothy's lack of self-confidence, Donald claims, "There was a side of her that doubted her own value, that believed she really wasn't worth too much."[83] Donna Zaller also discovered this fact about Dorothy as their friendship grew. Her recollection of Dorothy's feelings of inadequacy echoes that of Donald's:

After I got to know Dorothy, I began to see that she did not have a very high opinion of herself. She really felt inadequate in many ways, which was always so startling to me because people would not think of her that way. She had a lot of doubts about herself, and she was down on herself for a lot of things.[84]

Donna is convinced, though, that Dorothy's vulnerability helped fashion her into "the ultimate human person . . . just as human as you could get."[85]

* * * * * * * * *

According to Donald, Dorothy's vulnerable side "was a deep one where she had this little reservoir of things about her that she kept to herself."[86] On very few occasions, however, Dorothy did commit her self-doubts and insecurities to paper. The earliest example is a resolution she wrote at the end of her retreat before final profession in the summer of 1968. The resolution, which is in fact an acknowledgment of her vulnerability, reads: "to accept the person I am with all my weaknesses and not to pretend that I don't have them."[87] Apparently self-acceptance was still on Dorothy's mind the following year as her New Year's Resolution for 1969 affirms: "I commit myself to becoming a person with all this involves by way of self-awareness and acceptance of myself. . . . I will share mutual human weakness."[88]

Such personal writing does not appear again in Dorothy's journals for several years. In an entry dated January 4, 1974, she claimed, "I still wonder why people don't like me."[89] She then asked herself, "Do I come on too strong?"[90] For the following day, after she mentioned a party she attended, Dorothy declared, "T'was nice, but I felt totally unnecessary."[91] Wondering why she felt this way, Dorothy then asked, "Did I contribute anything? Who really wanted to see me?"[92] A short prayer concluded the entry: "Help me, Lord — there must be something wrong with me."[93] Around the same time period or shortly after, Dorothy wrote the following in another journal:

Sometimes I feel totally incapable of doing anything. Many things that I want are not what God wants for me. I have not fully accepted myself and my limitations. Sometimes I feel I do not belong to this community — I feel people "like" me — they do not love me because I do not have much to offer.[94]

* * * * * * * * *

While on retreat during the summer of 1973, Dorothy reflected on "where she was" at the age of 33. In her journal she recorded that her growth up until that time had "been somewhat 'top-surface.'"[95] She then resolved, "I now need to go deeper."[96]

A year later Dorothy left for El Salvador. Although she does not mention her growth again in the few journals that survive from her years there, remarks about Dorothy's character by several people who knew her well during that time attest to the personal growth she experienced as a missionary.

In Martha Owen's estimation Dorothy was "open, more than anything, and that made her fearless. She also had much self-confidence. These characteristics were all blended together."[97] Another quality Dorothy possessed, Martha claims, is authenticity:

> She had no pretense and never put up barriers. Dorothy was not ever defensive but just very vulnerable. She would reveal her weaknesses and come back strong. That was Dorothy's strength: she would make herself vulnerable and would come back and survive time after time after time.[98]

Christine Rody agrees with Martha's belief that Dorothy was authentic: "She was one of those kinds of people who could go from the sublime to the ridiculous in the same sentence and be just as authentic at either end of the spectrum."[99]

According to Christine, Dorothy was well aware of the growth that had taken place in her during her time in El Salvador. In the few months before her death, she talked with Christine about it and also expressed concern that her friends in Cleveland "would not understand the transformation that had happened in her."[100] Christine recalls Dorothy saying, "One of the things they [old friends] expect me to do is plug-in and be the person I was when I left. I'm not that person anymore. . . . I'm a different person, and they don't see that."[101]

Maryknoll Sister Pat Murray, who knew Dorothy in El Salvador, also remembers her concerns about returning to Cleveland. In the summer of 1980, when Dorothy took courses at the Maryknoll Institute in New York, she, Pat, and Maryknoll Sister Julie Miller often got together. Pat recalls their conversations from that time:

Dorothy talked about how hard it was going to be to return to the States and how much she had changed as a person. She told us how lucky we were because we could come back to Maryknoll where the majority of people had gone through the same experience of having lived in another culture, and we could share that with these people. And she said, "When I go home, there's really nobody to share my experiences with. They don't know what I'm talking about."

So, that was hard for her because she had changed. I don't think she could've done what the Cleveland missionaries were doing in Salvador — finding bodies, transporting refugees, taking care of the wounded — and not change. It was a terrifying time to be alive down there, and it had to change her. She was also concerned that her old friends in Cleveland would not accept and understand this change that had occurred.[102]

One old friend who did realize, however, that Dorothy had changed was Donna Zaller. In August of 1980, she and Dorothy spent a few days together, getting caught up on each other's lives.[103] After Dorothy described to Donna El Salvador's tumultuous political situation and its resulting violence, Donna exclaimed, "Don't go back there! Don't be foolish!"[104] Dorothy calmly replied, "But I really want to go back. I've finally figured it out: I want to work with the poor."[105] "And I think she was much more at peace with herself about what she was doing than I had ever seen her before,"[106] Donna remembers. She then explains: "It was as though Dorothy found Dorothy somewhere in that El Salvador experience. She had come face to face with herself and found that it wasn't as bad as she thought it would be."[107]

* * * * * * * * *

On the underside of the smiling, easy-going Dorothy was a woman who struggled. As related above, she frequently wrestled with her own self-doubts and feelings of inadequacy. But as many people do, Dorothy also struggled with situations about which she felt helpless and with decisions she had to make as well as with ones that had been made for her. And beneath the accepting, self-confident Dorothy was a woman who questioned her own self-identity and motivations as everyone does at some point or other in his or her life: "She just did not have all the pieces together"[108] all the time.

* * * * * * * * *

A condition that troubled Dorothy and one over which she felt she had little control was her father's dependency on alcohol. Although Joe never got belligerent or abusive when he drank — "he would get cheerful and then fall asleep in his chair"[109] — his use of alcohol was particularly disturbing to Dorothy because he and she shared a close relationship. From the time Dorothy was a young child, Joe would affectionately refer to her as "my little blondie."[110] And as she grew older, the bond between them strengthened as he supported her time and time again in her ideas and decisions.

Just as she refrained from discussing extremely personal matters with her friends, Dorothy never did say much[111] about her father's drinking to them. Donald Kollenborn recalls, however, that when Joe drank, Dorothy would get angry and would also feel confused because "she couldn't understand why he was doing what he was doing."[112] Furthermore, Dorothy "disliked the drinking side of her father, and this reaction made her feel guilty because she felt as thought she shouldn't be that way."[113] Barbara Jean Sever remembers Dorothy feeling a sense of loss each time Joe used alcohol: "When he drank and underwent a personality change, however slight it might have been, Dorothy felt she lost him. And this hurt her because she loved her dad so much."[114]

As an adult reflecting on her father's use of alcohol, Dorothy expressed the following to a friend who had also experienced some difficulty because of her father's drinking problem:

> I know how you feel because that's how I felt about my dad. I was angrier, though, when I was a postulant and novice. I had vowed then that until he stopped drinking, I would not drink myself. So, I know how you feel. It does make you sick to your stomach, and there's nothing you can do. . . .[115]

*   *   *   *   *   *   *   *   *

Another struggle of Dorothy's lay in the area of decision-making. Especially during the early years of her religious formation as an Ursuline Sister, Dorothy experienced some frustration about decisions that had been made for her. In June of 1963, for example, when she received her appointment to study at Ursuline College, Dorothy's reaction was shock, initially, followed by disappointment and confusion. She did not want to teach high school and could not understand why she was not being permitted to do what to her was so obvious: complete her training as an elementary school teacher. And when she was told to major in business education, Dorothy also felt disappointed, as business was not her choice of a subject to teach.

Although she ultimately accepted others' decisions for her, Dorothy nevertheless questioned reasons for the decision, or when she was in the novitiate, rules she had to follow. Anna Margaret Gilbride recalls that Dorothy was not afraid to speak up: "She would ask about things or she would question, and she would say, 'I do not understand this,' or 'Why do we have to do that?'"[116] Members of Dorothy's set also remember Dorothy's questioning of the rules as well as the attitude she adopted towards them — one which remained consistent throughout her life. Anita Whitely explains: "I wouldn't say Dorothy broke rules, but she felt comfortable bending them."[117] My sense is that Dorothy was not above the rules," Angelita Zawada adds, "but she never let them hold her down. She always knew where they fit into her life, and she kept them in the right proportion in her life."[118]

*   *   *   *   *   *   *   *   *

Like many people she frequently experienced difficulty making major decisions. And what is fairly obvious from examining Dorothy's life is that she consulted beforehand with very few people — even close friends — about her decisions. She also appeared to "make up her mind at the last minute."[119]

Yet at certain points in her life, Dorothy sought help when she had an important decision to make, and she spent time examining her options. One such period was the 1973-74 academic year when she was ministering as a counselor at Beaumont School. During this year Dorothy had to decide if she would join the CLAM Team in El Salvador the following July.

Those close to her knew that for some years Dorothy had wanted to be a missionary. But after adjusting to Beaumont and enjoying her counseling, Dorothy felt undecided and doubtful rather than excited at the prospect of fulfilling her dream.[120] Should she go to El Salvador when she so obviously felt that she was contributing to a much-needed service to Beaumont School?

To find the appropriate answer to her question, Dorothy sought the aid of priest psychologist Ernest Hepner. During most of the 1973-74 year, she met with him monthly to discuss the various angles of her two options and her motivations for choosing one or the other. Reflecting back on the situation, Father Hepner claims that Dorothy's main concern was "whether going to El Salvador was the right thing for her to do."[121] He explains:

> She wanted to know if becoming a missionary was really a response to a call from God or whether it was just her *personal* desire to go to El Salvador. Her concern was that she was not going there to escape the routine of her life here, but rather, because that's where she really felt that God was calling her. . . . She repeatedly asked herself, "Should I find my fulfillment in living out my religious life here as most Ursulines do, or should I find it in El Salvador?"[122]

By late spring of 1974, Dorothy was ready to make her decision. Through prayer and with Father Hepner's guidance, she had determined that going to El Salvador was indeed God's will for her. "And with all the struggle she experienced and even with some physical manifestations resulting from her concerns,[123]" Father Hepner states, "I feel that when she went to El Salvador, she was fully at peace."[124]

*   *   *   *   *   *   *   *   *

At critical periods in her life, Dorothy questioned her motivations and values. One such time was her final profession summer. In a journal entry dated June 13, 1968, she wrote, "*Why* did I enter?" She then answered her own question with the following:

- running away?
- guilt feeling?
- professional "escape" artist?
- *had* to!! Knew this was the only way *I* could be a good Christian.[125]

Later in this entry Dorothy questions herself again, centering most of her questions around her identity as a Christian. A few refer to her ability to relate to others. The list reads:

- Am I a Christian?
- Am I living a Christian life, or am I resting securely on my laurels?
- People look at me and respect me — why? because I am a Christian? or because I have a loud witnessing outfit on?
- Isn't this easier to do than just being an everyday Christian?
- People give me "credit" for doing a lot more than I really do.

- I profess what the Church teaches. How many listen to the
  Church? How many actually listen to me — "You don't
  understand, Sister — you don't live like we do."
- Am I witnessing to Christ?
- Am I telling others His Good News?
- Do they really hear or see Him in me?
- Am I meeting them as person to person — Christian to Christian?
- Can I really relate to them? Do they accept me as human?
- Am I a person to them — a person who is a Christian — or am I
  preaching to them?
- Am I real?[126]

Because Dorothy was not an avid journal-keeper, such lengthy
entries are somewhat surprising. Donna Zaller remembers, however,
that Dorothy's final profession summer "was a hard one, a very tough
summer"[127] for her. "I think she realized that taking final vows was,
well, the *final* step," Donna claims, "And you just don't go back on such
an absolute commitment all that easy."[128] Although Dorothy questioned
whether she could live under religious vows for the rest of her life, "she
did go ahead and take them."[129] "I don't think she came that close to not
taking them," Donna explains, "but it was a real struggle for her."[130]
Confirming Donna's comments regarding Dorothy's difficult summer,
Ellen Roonan, a friend of Dorothy's who had been a member of the
congregation, sent her a telegram with the following message: "Uniting
my joy with yours that turmoil is changed into everlasting conviction."[131]

Another intense period of questioning for Dorothy was the last year
of her term of missionary service in El Salvador. During this time she
thought deeply about what type of work she wanted to do when she
returned to Cleveland, and she considered other ministry options
available to her. Also on Dorothy's mind were questions regarding her
own adaptability to the structured religious lifestyle of which she would
once again become a part upon her return home.

To Christine Rody and several other close friends, Dorothy confided
her desire to remain in missionary work and confessed that she was
thinking about joining the Maryknoll Associate Program.[132] In a tape to
Martha Owen on Aug. 29, 1979, Dorothy explained that becoming a
Maryknoll Associate was an option she really was considering: "I'm
really thinking about it, and I don't know how seriously.... It might just
be a passing thought except that it has very much been with me, and I see
it as a possibility."[133]

Another of Dorothy's options was to return to Beaumont School for Girls and guidance counseling. While on a retreat in Guatemala from November 11-16, 1979, Dorothy reflected on these options as well as her first summer back in the states.[134]   Under the heading "Listening" in her journal she wrote:

> *End of June*: retreat; interest in St. Francis [of Assisi]; How do the Ursulines follow Francis?[135]   Interest in uniting Ursuline groups (Canada and U.S.A)[136]
> *July:* back to Salvador; Maryknollers — Nicaragua situation; camaraderie, compatibility,[137] encouragement to join Maryknoll — or Associate; Joanie [Petrik] — return first, then decide; Denny [St. Marie][138] — why not stay in Salvador; Beaumont — "We're waiting for you."[139]

At the end of the retreat, Dorothy jotted the following in her journal: "*Ursuline:* 1) habit — optional; 2) Maryknoll Associate; 3) St. Francis of Assisi."[140]   Her mention of the religious habit in this journal entry points to another one of Dorothy's concerns at the time: putting on the habit of the Ursulines of Cleveland and "fitting back into" the congregation.

In 1979 the Cleveland Ursulines were wearing a modified religious habit that consisted of a knee-length black or gray dress and a headdress with a short veil. Because she effectively ministered to the poor in El Salvador for over five years without a habit, Dorothy questioned its witness value. She also believed that the habit in no way determined her self-identity. In a letter of October 2, 1979, to Ursuline Sister Sheila Marie Tobbe Dorothy explains her feelings regarding habit and identity:

> [The issue of] sense of identity should be considered in relation to wearing a habit or not. I really don't know what I'm going to do about that next year — I just can't buy into it. If optional wearing of habit can be agreed to, for sure "sense of identity" will be a number one issue because most people think they will lose their identity without their habit. Is there any *hope* in this area???[141]

Sheila visited Dorothy in El Salvador in December 1979 and recalls Dorothy saying to her then, "How can I ever go back and put on a veil again? I just can't do it!"[142]   Yet the religious habit, Sheila asserts, "was only a symbol of a much deeper struggle for Dorothy — that of conformity . . . having to conform to what other people expected and wanted of her."[143]

In response to a tape Martha had sent her, Dorothy expressed her views regarding the wearing of a habit:

> You were talking about Chapter,[144] and I just got so angry! You were talking about the habit, and you talked with a group of them about doing something about the habit at Chapter. . . . And that's the thing that galls me: they always say it's such an unimportant item and that we have much bigger, major issues to talk about which is the biggest bull I have ever heard, and you know as well as I know, it is such a hot issue they can't even present it. . . . If it was such a trivial, unimportant thing, then we could just make a motion in Chapter and pass it, but it is not. It's super-duper hot. . . .
>
> I was so angry about that stupid habit again because I wish they would just face the reality of it. It's not a "non-important" thing. It's just too important.[145]

Around this time Dorothy also expressed concern regarding her re-entry into community living. On January 6, 1980, in a tape to Martha, Dorothy explains her feelings about living again with a large group of people, particularly the one at Beaumont Convent:

> I got a note from her [Mother Bartholomew] at Christmas, and she said, "You really shouldn't feel an obligation to have to go to Beaumont." After talking to Sheila [Tobbe], there is so much to do there, and . . . it's not that it wouldn't be interesting, but the whole house structure does worry me, and it's been a problem.[146] That's my biggest thing: I don't know if I'm going to be able to put up with this living in community business either.[147]

After she states her uncertainties about Beaumont and community life, Dorothy describes her indecision concerning the type of work she will do when she returns home:

> I probably would like the Hispanic work. . . . I don't know. You know, I just don't know what my problem is — I just don't know — I have no inclination to any special area. . . . I feel obliged and probably feel more inclined toward Beaumont

simply because that's where I have come from, and I have at least some security there. But I don't know that I really want to buy into it. And I don't know — I just don't know. Isn't that terrible? I've been like this for so long, and I keep praying about it, but I just don't know what the Lord has in plan.[148]

*   *   *   *   *   *   *   *   *

On February 9, 1971, Dorothy wrote the following poem, accompanied by no title or explanation. Perhaps it best expresses, though, her own admission of the presence of struggles and questions in her life, as well as her positive attitude towards them:

> Life is a vibrant stream,
>   flowing over sand and rocks —
> Persevering and steadfast
>   in its moving current
>   until it at last becomes one
>   with the body of water
>   that unites many streams.
> Through all its twists and
>   turns and straight ways,
>   it is always onward plunging —
>   never turning back — happily splashing
>   and sparkling over the many
>   rocky boulders it encounters —
>   never fearful that such
>   a one might stop it on its way —
>   but facing it head on —
>   as it continues on in its
>   journey for unity.
> Sandlots bring peace to
>   troubled waters that
>   have had a series
>   of encounters with boulders —
>   allowing for it a time to settle
>   and regain its sense of wholeness
>   before it continues on in its
>   journey for unity.[149]

4

A Woman of Depth:
Dorothy's Spirituality

*I keep watching these two wooden pieces, Jesus. My theory
did not seem to hold true — they did not burst into a
flaming holocaust for you. No, they slowly, quietly became
filled with the heat and burned through the center. Maybe
that's more real, Lord. Maybe we just slowly become filled
with you. . . . .*

Journal, January 19, 1974

Like other personal matters Dorothy's spiritual life was one that
she discussed with few people. Her reticence was not, however, an
indication of a lack of spiritual depth or a lackadaisical attitude toward
developing her spirituality. On the contrary, Dorothy's spirituality was
profound simply because it was such an integral part of her life, as
Christine Rody explains:

Dorothy was one of those kinds of people who lived what we
say we live. And she understood spirituality to the point where
she didn't have to talk about it. She just lived it because it was
a part of who she was. Her spirituality was always integrated
into her personality. It was not apart from it.[1]

Such a strong linkage between Dorothy's self-identity and
spirituality, family and friends claim, was apparent throughout most of
her life. Because she was raised in a family in which the Catholic
religion was valued, Dorothy's spirituality became a natural part of her
life and was very real to her.[2] During her adolescence and young
adulthood, she consequently attended to its growth. Her relationship
with God then became the central focus in her life once she chose to
enter religious life. As an Ursuline Sister, Dorothy further nurtured her
spiritual life through prayer, spiritual reading, and retreats. And her

surviving personal journals prove that she spent time reflecting on her spirituality and strove to make it a priority among her concerns and activities.

*   *   *   *   *   *   *   *   *

Growing up in a home in which participation in the liturgies and the sacramental life of the Catholic Church was stressed, Dorothy early realized the importance of spirituality and developing a relationship with God. With her parents she attended Mass every Sunday and on weekdays went with her class at St. George School. She also frequently received the sacraments. As a child Dorothy acquired a habit of prayer as her parents and teachers emphasized that prayer should stem from everyday occurrences: thanking God for a request answered; asking God for help in finding a lost article; and praising God for the beauty of nature. Dorothy's participation in these devotions, and more importantly her openness to them, laid the foundation for a spirituality that only deepened with time.

While she was a high school student at Notre Dame Academy, Dorothy was a member of both the Notre Dame and the St. George sodalities. As a sodalist she was expected to attend Mass daily and pray the rosary and novenas. Dorothy and her friends faithfully followed this mandate although it was not their sole motivation for participating in Catholic religious devotions, as Fran Harbert explains:

> It just seemed that during high school, Mass was something that we did and enjoyed going to. We had to go everyday in grade school, and it seems a horrible thing to me now because the priest wore black vestments and said a Mass for the dead everyday. But for some reason at that time it didn't turn Dorothy, Marilyn [Friga], or me off, and we continued to go as often as we could during high school.[3]

Apparently, such active practice of one's faith was not unusual, however, for persons growing up in the 1950s. Attendance at Mass and the recitation of daily prayers were familiar activities that few people, including children and adolescents, questioned or resisted. Kay O'Malley further clarifies this fact: "At that point in time, there were a lot of people who went to Mass everyday. And we didn't think it was anything that was different."[4] In agreement with Kay, Fran states:

"Attending daily Mass was just something that we did. All of us used to do it."[5] Regarding daily prayer, she adds:

> And we also said a rosary novena. We would say the prayers
> — different prayers — for each day. We all did that. I mean,
> we would sit around on either Dorothy's bed or Marilyn's bed
> at her house. And if we didn't have the rosary said for that
> day, we would be sure to say it.[6]

On the whole, too, people who grew up with Dorothy did not discuss their spirituality at great length as Kay affirms: "You didn't talk about it — you just did it."[7] She then recalls an incident which illustrates this point:

> I remember that when we would go to pajama parties at
> Dorothy's house, we would get up and go to Mass at 7:00 a.m.
> even though we had been up until 3:00, 4:00, or 5:00 in the
> morning. There were a few of us there who did that. We just
> didn't go to Mass on Sunday, either. If the party was on a
> Friday night, we would go to Mass the next morning.[8]

Like her high school friends, Dorothy did not often speak of her spirituality. That it was valuable to her, though, is hinted at in her 1956 diary. One of her New Year's Resolutions for that year is: "To increase my love for those above (daily rosary)."[9] Sprinkled throughout the diary are other references to Dorothy's relationship with God. In one entry, for example, she states: "We had our championship basketball game, and we won the seniors, 22-19. The dear Lord helped me play. I made about four or five points, and they were all miraculous. Thanks, dear Lord!"[10]

After she graduated from Notre Dame Academy, Dorothy continued to develop her spiritual life. Although she was busy working and attending college, and later, teaching full-time, she went to daily Mass, received the sacraments regularly, and sustained a consistent prayer life.[11] Anna Margaret Gilbride, who first met Dorothy when she was a student at St. John College in 1958, recalls, "Dorothy was a very prayerful person. She had a spirituality that was unusual for a young woman her age."[12]

*   *   *   *   *   *   *   *   *

Although some who knew Dorothy as a young woman characterize her spirituality as "unusual" because of its depth, they readily agree that it was also a healthy spirituality. Marilyn Friga recalls that while she and Dorothy were both in high school, they went to Mass as often as [they] could and said the rosary together.[13] Yet after reflecting on those years, Marilyn claims, "But I thought I was more invested in religious devotions than Dorothy was."[14] She explains, "It was okay to do it, and if Dorothy didn't it was okay, too. I mean, she seemed more well-balanced than I was."[15] Mercita Thailing likewise believes that Dorothy's spirituality was not scrupulous and explains why: "Dorothy didn't ask herself, 'What are people going to think?' and 'Since the Commandments say this, will I be breaking them if I step over this part of the line or that part of the line?'"[16] Mary Jo Lackamp, who joined the Cleveland Ursuline Congregation with Dorothy, describes Dorothy's spirituality while she was in the novitiate:

> I think Dorothy was a lot healthier in her approach to required prayer than some of the rest of us. There were prayers that we were supposed to manage to fit in everyday. And some of us got almost paranoid about the fact that maybe we didn't get them all in. So there would be people up at all kinds of ungodly hours, trying to fit in the prayers. My recollection is that Dorothy was a lot more comfortable in her relationship with God as a personal kind of relationship apart from the rigors of "this many beads" or "that many stations."[17]

As she grew older, Dorothy obviously maintained the depth of her spirituality as well as her wholesome attitude toward it. Contemplating Dorothy's spirituality during her novitiate and juniorate years and in those leading to her death, Kathleen Cooney affirms, "It was deep, but it was natural and integrated into every part of her life."[18]

*   *   *   *   *   *   *   *   *

Because Dorothy's spirituality was intimately bound to her religious vocation, some explanation of the circumstances surrounding her decision to enter religious life is in order. Even at this point in time, though, questions exist for which there are no clear-cut answers: when did Dorothy first consider becoming a Sister? how long did she think about it? why did she refrain from telling her closest friends that entering the convent was on her mind? and why did she not share these thoughts with Donald Kollenborn, her fiance, until she informed him that she wanted to break their engagement?

On the other hand, what is fairly obvious in terms of Dorothy's religious vocation is that she struggled with her decision to become a religious. And although "to walk away and to commit to something like religious life was a very startling thing for Dorothy as well as for everybody else,"[19] she felt a strong calling to do so. Her love for God and her desire to deepen her relationship with God were her primary motivations.

*   *   *   *   *   *   *   *   *

According to her high school friends, Dorothy did not express a desire to enter the convent and did not even appear to be attracted to religious life while she was in high school. Marilyn Friga confirms this truth and adds, "In fact she thought I was crazy when I told her that I was thinking of becoming a nun."[20] Because Dorothy was in "the group in her high school class that didn't talk about the convent,"[21] Kay O'Malley claims, she never mentioned that she thought she had a religious vocation. Kay further explains:

> We went to school with a lot of aspirants.[22] So that was a whole group of people over here, and we were the other group. It was not that we didn't mix — and we tried to mix with them — but they were the ones who were going into the convent, and we were the ones who were well on our way to college and getting married. We were the group that always went to the dances — we always had a date for the dances.[23]

Further proof that Dorothy probably was not considering religious life during high school is her friends' recollection of her indecision regarding a career choice upon graduation from Notre Dame Academy.

Helen Marie Davidson who got to know Dorothy when she did some practice teaching in her classroom at St. Robert Bellarmine School, believes that Dorothy really didn't think about entering the convent until she attended St. John College.[24] Exactly *when* the idea to enter first occurred to Dorothy during this time (1957-59) is not known. But she apparently had not made any *serious* decisions concerning religious life, for she and Donald Kollenborn were engaged in the spring of 1959. However, when Dorothy accepted Don's proposal, she asked that her engagement ring be a pearl instead of a diamond because, according to Helen Marie, "Dorothy told Don that the wedding wasn't an absolute certainty."[25] Although she may have expressed some doubt about actually marrying him, Donald did not feel at the time that their relationship could possibly fall apart.[26] And Dorothy, of course, did not mention her thoughts about religious life to him then.

Shortly after her engagement, however, Dorothy gave the first clear indication that she believed she was being called to religious life. One evening while she was praying alone in her bedroom, she had a strong sense that she should enter the convent. Because the realization was so vivid, Dorothy told her mother about it. Malvina recalls: "Dorothy was saying the rosary at the time, and it just came to her."[27] She adds, "That's the first time Dorothy mentioned to me that she was thinking of the convent, and I think it was after she was engaged unless it was lurking in the back of her mind, and she just didn't say anything about it."[28] For several months afterwards, Malvina remembers, Dorothy prayed "with all her heart and soul"[29] for enlightenment in making the right decision about her choice of a vocation. A retreat for engaged women she attended between January and early March of 1960, though, helped Dorothy clinch her final decision: she would enter the Ursuline Congregation that fall. Dorothy then telephoned Don to tell him of her decision and to break their engagement.

As Dorothy began seriously to consider religious life during the 1959-60 academic year, she also apparently decided that the Ursuline Congregation was the one she would join. On June 29, 1960, she formally applied to the Ursuline Sisters of Cleveland. In response to the question on the application form, "How long have you been seriously considering entering this community?" Dorothy wrote, "one year."[30] She had previously thought about joining the congregation of the Humility of Mary Sisters,[31] according to Helen Marie. "But when Dorothy did her practice teaching at St. Robert Bellarmine School," Helen Marie claims, "she changed her mind."[32] Dorothy was impressed with the Ursuline Congregation as she later explained to several friends. Kay O'Malley remembers Dorothy admitting she had joined the Ursulines "primarily because of the Sisters she had met at St. Robert Bellarmine."[33]

*   *   *   *   *   *   *   *   *

Although Dorothy ultimately *chose* religious life, the choice itself was not an easy one as Mercita Thailing confirms:

People who didn't know Dorothy well believed that the day she decided to enter the convent that was it — that it went along smoothly, and she didn't struggle. But they don't know as Don does, and I saw a bit of that struggle because sometimes the tears came when she couldn't talk with him about it anymore.[34]

The root of Dorothy's struggle lay in opting for one state of life over another. And because they both appealed to her, she obviously "was torn between getting married and entering the convent."[35] Anna Margaret Gilbride further clarifies Dorothy's dilemma:

It seems to me that Don was very ready to be married, and Dorothy was struggling about whether she was supposed to get married or supposed to enter religious life. I think it was more that way. I know that Dorothy liked Don very much, and it was just the choice of a life that was her concern.[36]

Elements of fear and inner conflict also formed part of Dorothy's struggle. To feel a certain amount of fear while choosing a vocation, particularly a religious one, is typical as John F. Loya, Cleveland diocesan priest, writes:

Because accepting a vocation from God launches us into the unknown, it is only natural that we will experience some fear. When we answer a call from God, we do not know everything that will be asked of us. We do not know what awaits us in the future or where God will lead us. We do not know what joys will be ours or what pains we will suffer for the sake of the Kingdom. We do not know what God plans to accomplish through us or how God will do it. When we accept a vocation, we do not even know if we will be able to fulfill the task God has set for us.[37]

At times Dorothy did wonder if she would be able to fulfill the tasks and demands of religious life. In July 1960 when she met Don in California to return his engagement ring, Dorothy further discussed with him her desire to enter religious life and also voiced her concerns regarding her decision. Donald recalls: "We spent probably a good couple hundred hours then, discussing this all night long — talking about the choice and her questioning herself."[38] He then describes what Dorothy was questioning about herself: "She worried about whether she would be able to stand up underneath the rules that she had to live with and was she really supposed to be a nun or not."[39] And even after she entered the convent, Dorothy still questioned. As Donna Zaller remembers: "A little part of Dorothy inside was just not sure that this was the right thing for her."[40]

Dorothy also struggled with her decision to become a religious because she realized that her choice would inevitably affect more lives than just her own. She was mainly concerned about Don and hurting him because she knew she loved him.[41] And according to Mercita Thailing, "Dorothy was also worried about how her decision would influence Don's journey to become a Catholic, and would it sour him on the Catholic religion."[42] Dorothy's fear of hurting Don, Mercita believes, is "why she took so long to even hint to any of her friends that entering religious life was a possibility for her."[43] "She may have thought," Mercita continues, "'Well, what if religious life isn't for me, and I hurt him and didn't need to.'"[44] Another person with whom Dorothy was concerned was her mother. Malvina did not want Dorothy to enter the convent. But because "she was very, very strong in her own mind,"[45] Dorothy set aside her feelings for Don as well as the wishes of her mother and did what she thought she was being called to do.

*   *   *   *   *   *   *   *   *

The struggles Dorothy underwent in terms of her religious vocation in no way diminished her belief that she had been called by God to the religious state of life. To Donald she defined this calling as an "intense feeling."[46] He elaborates: "She felt this pressure in the beginning, and then she felt this desire to do this. Everytime Dorothy would get around the Sisters, or she would go on a retreat, the call was almost overwhelming to her."[47]

Because Dorothy felt this calling so strongly, Donald states that "she did what she needed to do. There's no question in my mind."[48] And although he was heartbroken when Dorothy broke her engagement to him, Donald is now convinced that Dorothy's decision to enter the convent was the right one for her to make. After years of reflecting on Dorothy's choice, he claims:

The plan for all of this was significantly larger than our own. When Dorothy first called me to tell me that she had decided to enter the convent, and I took off and flew to Cleveland to see her, I already knew before I ever got on the plane that what was done was done — that there was no choice. And we talked about it for a long, long time, and Dorothy really felt that while she had doubts in her mind, that entering the convent was what she was supposed to do. And she had to pursue it, and if it was incorrect, she would know.[49]

Donna Zaller agrees that Dorothy felt a very strong call to religious life. She claims:

I think part of Dorothy always loved Don; part of her always wondered what it would have been like to be married, to have kids, and that's something she really would have loved. But because of the calling she experienced, Dorothy felt that she really didn't have a lot of choice in the matter. She felt that there was something that God wanted her to do.[50]

Although Dorothy did not write about her initial call to religious life in the personal journals she kept during her years in the Ursuline Congregation, a notation included in one of her retreat conference notebooks perhaps best explains her strong pull toward religious life. The entry reads: "Nothing can hold you back from the call of the Lord — comfortable human relations, etc."[51]

*   *   *   *   *   *   *   *   *

From the time Dorothy was a child and throughout her young adulthood, prayer was an important part of her spirituality. When she became an Ursuline Sister, however, it formed the backbone of her spiritual life. Through her practice of prayer, to which she committed herself daily, Dorothy strove to deepen her relationship with God, imitate the person of Jesus Christ, and to listen and respond to God's will for her.

It is primarily through her personal written reflections that Dorothy reveals her fidelity to prayer as well as her belief in its importance in her life. The earliest account of Dorothy's opinion regarding devotion to prayer appears in retreat resolutions she made prior to her first profession of vows on August 13, 1963. Prefatory to the resolutions is the question, "How must I act as an Ursuline?"[52]   Dorothy answers: "As one who knows and loves God, for this is my *specialty* and can be achieved through prayer. *All* I do must show this, for this is *my life!*"[53] Under the heading *resolve* she states: "I desire to acquire a 'spirit of prayer' which will eventually control my natural instincts, especially the desire to be esteemed, and have me prove myself as an Ursuline — a true *lover* of God."[54]   Dorothy then lists her resolutions:

> *Means* of acquiring "Spirit of Prayer":
> 1. Recollection: walking in the Divine Presence. *Recall* this by looking at your crucifix.
> 2. Putting effort into meditation by thinking about truths of God rather than of self. Make *resolve* personal so it can be applied throughout the day.
> 3. Be attentive at community prayer.
> 4. Practice mortification especially by obeying the Rule and observances (*silence*).[55]

Another retreat resolution Dorothy wrote during the years of her initial religious formation focuses on prayer: "to practice the art of prayer — learn to develop a *loving* conversation with Him."[56]

Shortly after Dorothy moved to Sacred Heart Academy in August 1965, she kept a written record of her prayer life for several days before she began to teach. In most of the entries, she lists each of her prayer practices and briefly evaluates her participation in them. The evaluations, such as the one dated August 27, 1965, exhibit Dorothy's desire to improve the quality of her prayer:

> 1. Morning Office: distracted, drowsy
> 2. Mass: half awake
> 3. Examen:[57] not pinpointed
> 4. Office: carelessly said
> 5. Stations [of the Cross]: too fast
> 6. Recollection Through Day: poor — very distracted today![58]

Her entry for August 29 is similar but slightly more positive:

> 1. Office: half-concentrated
> 2. Mass: fair

3. Holy Hour: *first* actual one since I arrived; much fervor — thanks to the mercy of God
4. Examen: better than yesterday; if I can but become more conscious of all I should be striving to perfect myself in.[59]

On September 1 Dorothy made a resolution regarding prayer:

For the past two days there has been great negligence to prayer life. Those that get said are done carelessly; others are eliminated. This month I will aim to get prayers said *early* so that they will not be neglected. Help me, please, Mary.[60]

Two days later Dorothy expresses some satisfaction regarding her practice of prayer but feels that she still has not been as attentive to her prayers as she should be:

Today — *finally* — the opportunity to get prayers said was given. What will it be like throughout the year?? Thank you for this opportunity, dear Jesus — if only I could have concentrated more it might have been more profitable.[61]

Journal entries in which Dorothy refers to her practice of prayer do not appear again until the summer of 1973. At the end of a retreat she made from June 10-17, she composed several resolutions: "to make an avid study of Christ through reading scripture daily *so* that I may learn of His attitudes and make them my own; to do my half-hour meditation daily without failure."[62] The last resolution reads: "to remain *free* and *open* to the Spirit; to listen to what He speaks and then act on it."[63] Six years later, while attending a retreat in Guatemala from November 11-16, 1979, Dorothy wrote the following: "*Prayer of Perspective*: I am as present to my prayer as I am present to my life."[64] This comment on prayer is the final one that appears in Dorothy's personal written reflections.

Although Dorothy's prayer life was a hidden one in the sense that she refrained from discussing it with people, friends and co-workers certainly witnessed her attentiveness to prayer. "Dorothy was a very prayerful person,"[65] asserts Susan Mary Rathbun. She further explains:

Dorothy spent a lot of time in chapel. When I lived with her at Sacred Heart and at Beaumont, I know she used to pray a lot in her room. And on retreats she always made sure she had some "alone" time even though she was a very friendly person who liked to see everybody.[66]

When Dorothy served in El Salvador, "especially in the later years," claims Martha Owen, "she took her Bible, and she meditated every single day."[67] Martha adds, "Dorothy always wanted to know God's will, and she always prayed about it. She never made decisions for herself without getting some input from her prayer."[68] While she was in El Salvador, Dorothy also faithfully said Night Prayer[69] as Christine Rody confirms: "She had this little Night Prayer booklet, and every night she would get into bed and pray it and then turn off her light."[70]

*   *   *   *   *   *   *   *   *

Dorothy's spirituality also manifested itself through her love of nature. Family picnics, outings to the verdant Ohio countryside, and trips to sites of scenic beauty such as Niagara Falls and the Grand Canyon early sparked Dorothy's attraction to nature. By the time she reached adulthood, however, her attraction to nature had evolved into a deep appreciation and fondness for it. "Dorothy was very nature-oriented,"[71] claims Donna Zaller, while reminiscing about her and Dorothy's novitiate and juniorate days at the Ursuline Motherhouse. "Whenever we were outside, she was just so enthralled by sunsets. Or she would get so excited when she found clumps of daisies growing in the field,"[72] recalls Donna. She further explains:

> Dorothy collected all kinds of things. On her windowsill in her cell,[73] where you weren't supposed to have anything, she had rocks, which she had painted. She also collected little pieces of driftwood. Dorothy was really into nature.[74]

Martha remembers that while Dorothy was in El Salvador, "She would walk for miles along the beach, picking up shells, star fish, and sand dollars."[75]

During the summer of 1969, when Dorothy taught Catholic doctrine to Native Americans of the Papago Tribe in Topawa, Arizona, she frequently alluded to the beauty of nature in her diary: "beautiful sunset!"[76] "rained — but beautiful red orange sunset — looked like pink rain!"[77] and "saw unusual rainbow-colored cloud above a thunderhead."[78] Dorothy also expressed her enjoyment of nature: "stayed in the monastery garden and enjoyed its beauty and the stars"[79] and *"rain — two rainbows — waded."*[80]

In her diary Dorothy also mentioned that she painted rocks, an activity that always gave her much pleasure. When she left Arizona by Greyhound bus, Dorothy brought with her all the rocks she had painted that summer as well as others she had collected because she thought they were unusual or pretty. Malvina recalls that when she saw Dorothy heaving a box filled with the rocks, she said to her, "My goodness, Dorothy, you mean you carried these *all* the way from Arizona?"[81] "But Mother, they're beautiful! Just look at them,"[82] she replied.

Dorothy's love of nature likewise included a great affection for animals. When she was a child, she had a dog that she named "Ko-Ko" because of his brown and white fur. While she was in the novitiate, Dorothy "collected caterpillars and kept them in jars in her cell because she wanted to have a butterfly come out,"[83] remembers Donna Zaller. During that time Dorothy also had a pet mouse, Donna states: "She cornered a mouse in our dorm and was feeding it. One night it got out of the novitiate and went into the juniorate. Somebody killed it, and Dorothy really felt bad."[84]

In El Salvador Dorothy had two pet cats named "Paja" and "Boogers." Christine Rody recalls that Dorothy often assisted in the birth of Paja's kittens. On one occasion one of the kittens underwent a breech birth, and Christine was a little surprised, she claims, that Dorothy knew what to do: "But she did. Paja was in terrible pain, and Dorothy helped the birth happen so that it would not be so painful and that the kitten would be okay."[85] Christine remembers another incident that well illustrated Dorothy's kindness to animals:

At about 2:00 one morning, while everybody was asleep, Boogers came in the house and started whimpering. He jumped on Dorothy's bed, and she reached out to touch him. Apparently he had fallen into some wet cement, for he was covered with it. So Dorothy got up and washed the cat. But she didn't wash him in cold water, which was the only kind we had. No, she heated water in our little ceramic coffee pot and gave Boogers a nice hot bath.[86]

In her tapes to her family and friends, Dorothy often told her own stories about the cats and other animals she had encountered in one way or another. Her anecdotes revealed her love for the animals, as well as their affection for her, depicted in the following examples.

In July of 1979, having just returned to Salvador from her vacation in the States, Dorothy described the greeting that she and her newly permed hair received from Paja and her four kittens: "They were really cute. . . . At night they'd run all over my body just hither, dither, and yon, and then they'd do these running leaps into my hair, thinking it was a haystack or something, and just having the best time."[87] About a year later, Jean's dog "Vista" made friends with Dorothy, as she related in a tape to her parents:

> Vista's five months old, and he's going to be a monster of a dog. . . . One night when Jean wasn't home, I went up to Zaragoza because I was going to stay overnight there, and I took the dog. Well, he sat on my lap — I was driving the pick-up truck — with his paws around my neck and his head on my shoulder all the way up.[88]

During Dorothy's final year and a half in El Salvador, her animal stories perhaps assured her family and friends that her life still retained some normalcy. They also offered comic relief as she sometimes interwove the animal anecdotes with the stories she told of the suffering Salvadoran people. For example, Dorothy included the following cat story on the same tape that contained her narration of Oscar Romero's assassination:

> This bat is in the house again. I also have Paja. . . . We have a little bat that comes into the house every now and then. He's now hanging from the ceiling, and Paja is beginning to jump from desk to desk, trying to catch it.
>
> We still have three kittens here with us, too. Paja had the two black ones and a striped one, and they are at the very playful stage . . . They keep dumping my wastebasket over, and it's rolling around right now, and there's one kitty in it. "Stripey" is on my bed, chewing on my fingers. I had a brown bag on this bed. I just bought some new batteries for the radio and stuff, and she was just inside the bag.[89]

Because of her love of animals, Dorothy went out of her way to avoid harming them in any way. Martha Owen relates an episode that occurred while she and Dorothy were driving along the countryside of El Salvador:

We were driving fast, and a dog was sleeping in the road. He got up when he saw us and started walking along the road. So Dorothy, who was driving, swerved in the direction opposite the dog. What does he then do but changes his direction and walks right in front of us! Rather than hit the dog, Dorothy swerved again. We were driving on two wheels and almost tipped over twice![90]

Martha also recalls another, similar episode: "Sometimes during the rainy season, frogs would come up on the road — hundreds of them at a time. To avoid hitting the frogs, Dorothy would swerve the jeep or van back and forth, back and forth."[91]

* * * * * * * * *

How do those who knew Dorothy fairly well characterize her spirituality? "The spirituality that I could see in Dorothy," states Kay O'Malley, "was the charity that she had for everybody and the love that she seemed to have for everybody."[92] Kathleen Cooney claims:

Dorothy didn't talk about the things that were really deep inside of her. So I think she was more of a counselor to other people who were in need, and she was a great supporter and listener. And that might be one way that her spirituality came out.[93]

To Anna Margaret Gilbride, Dorothy's spirituality "was one of joy."[94] She explains: "I felt that Dorothy had a relationship with God, but she was very joyful, and it overflowed into service of others."[95] Donna Zaller asserts:

Many times Dorothy didn't feel self-confident, and her self-esteem was not always the highest. And yet I think her spirituality grew from her vulnerabilities. I believe she thought, "I'm so weak. You're going to have to do it God because I can't. I'm just a little ship on the big sea, and I'm blowing every which way!"[96]

"Dorothy's joy and sincerity reflected her spirituality,"[97] declares Maddie Dorsey. "She lived out Gospel values in her life,"[98] Maddie adds.

*   *   *   *   *   *   *   *   *

Nobody other than Dorothy herself, however, could best describe her own spirituality, which she did through her writing. Retreat conference and spiritual-reading notes and personal reflections reveal the progress of Dorothy's spirituality as a Christian as well as an Ursuline Sister. And although Dorothy did most of this writing prior to her departure for El Salvador in 1974, it does offer insight into issues about which she was concerned until her death.

Dorothy's retreat conference notes, of which there is an ample supply,[99] provide a first-hand account of her initial religious formation and the early influences on the development of her spiritual life. Notes she recorded during retreats from 1961 through 1966 reflect a pre-Vatican II spirituality of religious life. Main topics covered are aiming for perfection and practicing mortification: "vows and rules: means of perfection";[100] "We want to fulfill God's will in a perfect way — not an ordinary way";[101] "exterior mortification: silence, modesty, self-denial; interior mortification: discipline of mind, will, imagination, and control over passions";[102] and "To come closer to Christ, ask for sorrow, anguish, and interior pain."[103]   Other subjects included death to the world and to the self and a scrupulous following of the Rule of the congregation: "On entering the convent there is a 'pinch' of death, for we die to the world and gradually take on the means of a happy eternity";[104] "Offer *now* your death to God!"[105] "*Joy* follows death to self!"[106] "Your *Rule* is to help you control your emotions and bring you to God";[107] and "duties in our state of life: *Rule!*"[108]

Various notations from Dorothy's 1961-66 collection of retreat conference notes, however, reveal universal themes of spirituality for the religious life. And although her descriptions have a pre-Vatican II flavor, the themes themselves were ones that she deemed important to her own spiritual development throughout her life. Evidence of this fact appears later in her written personal reflections.

Some timeless themes apparent in Dorothy's 1961-66 journals are conformity to God's will, love as the greatest of the virtues, and God as the focal point in the life of a religious: "Don't be an *ordinary* religious — be *extra-ordinary* — be perfect by following God's will to a 'T!'";[109] "habitual attitude: whatever God wants, I *want!*"[110] "*Learn love* and *love alone counts!*"[111] "primary purpose of religious life: *to grow in love*, sanctity";[112] "Realize the *presence* of God in *every* thing";[113] and "God must be the *beginning* and *end* of all we do."[114]   References to the meaning of religious vows are also present: [poverty] "Evaluate the things in view of eternity — will it be necessary there? Will it help me love God more?"[115] [chastity] "*love* fulfills a person, and this we do not give up!"[116] and [obedience] "unites us more closely to God; enables us to keep our will in conformity with God."[117]

During the summer of 1967, Dorothy made a retreat that had a profound effect on her spirituality. In the Catholic Church at the time, the teachings of the Second Vatican Council had secured a foothold. The Church was emphasizing the complete Paschal Mystery of Christ's life, death, and Resurrection rather than simply his death; it was also encouraging an "openness to the modern world"[118] rather than a separation from it. Some of Dorothy's retreat conference notes, like the following, illustrated this dramatic shift in spirituality:

A real Christian is
- dominated by the presence of the Risen Christ (knows that the living Christ is here; knows that the living Christ is real)
- a person with a mission to the world of 1967: loves the world; is caught up with the world; must be equipped with solid learning and mature love; makes use of natural history and philosophy of our time; listens with an open heart
- a person who lives in the *here* and *now*. *Listen* to others — don't think about what you will answer.[119]

Other notes included: "Live *constantly* under the inspiration and influence of the Holy Spirit";[120] "Christ wants you to be an Incarnation, a flesh-and-blood person for Him";[121] "The Church is *people*, *Christ alive!*"[122] and "*Resurrection: Easter* — true meaning of life; grow; rise in glory."[123] Dorothy's notes referring to religious life also reflect a Vatican II Spirituality: "Vows are a prophecy: [they] foretell the resurrection of Christ born in the Word";[124] "*purpose* of religious life: show Christ to the world!"[125] and "By poverty you show your real interest in others — *not* yourself."[126]

One of the last notes Dorothy took during her retreat of the summer of 1967 was "Be a living Alleluia!"[127] She seemed to take this precept to heart as evidenced by a statement she made the following year. During an ecumenical retreat weekend in East Cleveland that Dorothy attended, the group leader asked her what she would like engraved on her tombstone. Dorothy replied, "I want to be remembered as an

Alleluia because 'a Christian should be an Alleluia from head to foot.'"[128]   Her comment is reminiscent of Anna Margaret Gilbride's description of Dorothy's spirituality: "Hers was a spirituality of joy."[129]

*   *   *   *   *   *   *   *   *

The bulk of Dorothy's surviving spiritual-reading notes were written during her initial few years in the convent. These notes are similar in subject matter to her retreat conference notes and therefore also reveal early influences on the development of her spiritual life. And like those from her retreat conferences, the notes Dorothy took from her spiritual reading echo themes which became for her life-long concerns in terms of her own spirituality: the importance of love, openness to God's will, and union with God.

Dorothy's spiritual-reading notes present a wide array of spiritual writers from classical through contemporary times. The most often-quoted classical writer is Saint Augustine. Scattered throughout Dorothy's notes are quotations by Saint Augustine like the following: "*Love* and do what you like";[130] "Strive to find God in *all* things!"[131] and "The love of truth seeks holy leisure; the necessity of love takes righteous action."[132]

Another classical spiritual writer Dorothy quoted quite a bit was John Henry Cardinal Newman. In her journals are maxims Newman wrote as well as prayers he composed. One of his prayers in particular Dorothy liked and apparently said every day. She had typed the prayer on a heavy piece of paper and wrote above it, "Every morning, Jesus invites anew: 'Dorothy, come follow me!'" Underneath the title of the prayer, which is "Radiating Christ," Dorothy had typed "Mother Teresa's favorite prayer." The prayer, as follows, was found in Dorothy's Christian Prayer Book:

> Dear Jesus, help me to spread Thy fragrance everywhere I go. Flood my soul with Thy spirit and life. Penetrate and possess my whole being so utterly that all my life may only be a radiance of Thine. Shine through me, and be so in me that every soul I come in contact with may feel Thy presence in my soul. Let them look up and see no longer me but only Jesus! Stay with me, and then I shall begin to shine as Thou shinest, so to shine as to be a light to others; the light, Oh Jesus, will be all from Thee: none of it will be mine; it will be Thou shining on others through me. Let me thus praise Thee in the way Thou dost love

best by shining on those around me. Let me preach Thee without preaching, not by words but by my example, by the catching force of the sympathetic influence of what I do, the evident fullness of the love my heart bears to Thee.

Into her Bible and some of her spiritual-reading books, Dorothy had inserted copies of "Pastoral Meditation," also by Newman. Some of her friends claim that this meditation was Dorothy's favorite:

God has created me to do Him some definite service: He has committed some work to me which He has not committed to another. I have my mission — I may never know it in this life, but I shall be told it in the next.

I am a link in a chain, a bond of connection between persons. He has not created me for naught. I shall do good — I shall do His work. I shall be an angel of peace, a preacher of truth in my own place, while not intending it — if I do but keep His commandments.

Therefore I will trust Him. Whatever, wherever I am. I can never be thrown away. If I am in sickness, my sickness may serve him; in perplexity, my perplexity may serve Him; if I am in sorrow, my sorrow may serve Him. He does nothing in vain. He knows what He is about. He may take away my friends; He may throw me among strangers. He may make me feel desolate, make my spirits sink, hide my future from me — still He knows what He is about.

Dorothy quoted other classical spiritual writers in her notes, including Meister Eckhart, from whom Dorothy took, "What a man takes in by contemplation, he pours out in love,"[133] and Saint John of the Cross: "In the evening of life, we shall be judged on *love*!"[134] Another writer Dorothy quoted was Saint Catherine of Siena:

Let Jesus be in your heart,
Eternity in your mind,
The world under your feet,
God's will in all your acts,
And above all,
May the love of God light you in all things![135]

A more contemporary spiritual writer Dorothy held in high esteem was Teilhard de Chardin, S.J. Quotations from his works on the spiritual life appeared quite frequently in her notes. Some examples are: "Lord, that in every creature I may discover you";[136] "Love is the only strength which makes things one without destroying them"; and

> Lord, lock me up in the deepest depths of your heart; and then holding me there, burn me, purify me, set me on fire, sublimate me, until I become utterly what You would have me be, through the utter annihilation of my ego.[137]

Other contemporary spiritual writers Dorothy quoted are Louis Evely[138] and Carlo Carretto.[139] During the summer of her final profession, Dorothy wrote the following prayer by Evely in her journal:

> Lord, I believe, come to the help of my unbelief. Lord, you can heal me. Lord, I know that I do not know anything. But I know also that you are Father, that you are able to create your Son in me. I know that I do not deserve anything — but that you will give me everything if only I trust you.[140]

About a year before she left for El Salvador, Dorothy quoted this particular reading of Carretto's:

> Love transforms me slowly into God.
> But sin is still there, resisting this transformation, knowing how to, and actually saying "no" to love.
> Living in our selfishness means stopping at human limits and preventing our transformation into Divine Love. And until I am transformed, sharing the life of God, through love, I shall be of "this earth" and not of "that heaven." Baptism has raised me to the supernatural state, but we must grow in this state, and the purpose of life is precisely that growth. And charity, or rather God's love, is what transforms us.[141]

Among Dorothy's spiritual-reading notes are small pieces of paper on which she wrote or typed anonymous passages and sayings. She had the habit of tucking these "courage builders" into her journals and prayer books. The following passage was found in Dorothy's Christian

Prayer Book. Because this anonymous quotation must have been of some importance to her, it merits mention:

> You cannot understand how hard it is for one to be practical who hopes for tenderness behind every face; how hard it is for one to be severe and profound who believes herself to be living a story that is glorious and true. Others can be impersonal, but not one who believes that she is on an eminently personal adventure. Others can be important, but not one who is so small that she wonders why anyone save the infinitely kind God should be good to her. Others can be sensible, but not one who knows in her heart how few things really matter. Others can be sober and restrained, but not one who is mad with the loveliness of life and almost blind with its beauty. So others can live with the wise and important, while I must always presume on those who are kind enough to forgive and weak enough to understand.

Examples of other anonymous aphorisms recovered from Dorothy's spiritual-reading notes include: "To hit the mark, you have to aim higher";[142] "You can't do good to everyone, but to everyone you can show kindness";[143] and "Genuine love ultimately leads to crucifixion."[144]

*   *   *   *   *   *   *   *   *

The amount of personal writing Dorothy did is meager in comparison to her retreat-conference and spiritual-reading notes. However, her personal writing in the form of retreat resolutions and journal entries is the most revelatory in terms of goals to which she had aspired in her spiritual life as well as the struggles she underwent. And to a certain extent Dorothy's personal reflections echoed thoughts and opinions to which she had been exposed on retreats and through her spiritual reading.

Retreat resolutions Dorothy wrote during many of her years as an Ursuline Sister present a fairly good indication of her spiritual goals. The earliest of the resolutions appeared in February 1962. Dorothy entitled them "Perfection Through Love":

> With God's grace I desire to learn to truly *love* Him. This can be done by observing and practicing the qualities of love

enumerated by St. Paul and applying them to all I may come in contact, most especially my fellow Sisters.

1. Love is patient: bears with one another and with self.
2. Love is kind: courtesy, respect, reverence.
3. Love feels no envy or jealousy.
4. Love is never perverse or proud, never insolent.
5. Love does not claim its rights: no selfish aims.
6. Love is not provoked to anger.
7. Love does not brood over an injury.
8. Love takes no pleasure in wrong-doing: avoids sin.[145]

Shortly before she made her first vows in August 1963, Dorothy wrote the following:

Motto:
I am an Ursuline. This is the *root* of me. *Everything* else is secondary because I am an Ursuline. Therefore there can be *no mediocrity*!
What is an Ursuline?
A woman in love; a Sister dedicated to the work of *solely* loving God through daily praise, reverence, and service.[146]
Two years later Dorothy's main resolution was, "To learn to *love God As God*."[147] She explains:
1. I recognize myself as a creature and instrument of God. If He wants me to "act" in a certain situation, *He* will determine it — *not me*. I am *not* indispensable (pride)!
2. To practice the art of prayer — learn to develop a *loving* conversation with Him.
3. I will daily re-consecrate myself to God through my vows and *not* take back, piece by piece, what I promised Him. *His love for me* is the standard on which I shall judge acts.[148]

Although Dorothy's retreat resolutions for the next several years retained their spiritual quality, they also gave evidence of her emotional growth. In her resolutions of 1966, for example, Dorothy claimed:

I must learn to *love* others fully:
1. be willing to be "transparent"

2. be willing to be involved with all
3. be willing to "encounter" those whom He wishes you to

I must love supernaturally *and* naturally. I must have true Christian love for all — this must be *affective*, *warm*, and *personal*. I must see each person as an individual and treat him or her as someone *special*. Each has God living within him or her; therefore this *is* necessary. Courage of conviction is needed. Therefore I will pray for *fortitude* — strength of soul (*intellect* and *will*).[149]

Before her final profession in August 1968, Dorothy wrote:

I accept the fact that I *am human* and with this human nature strive to become as perfect and loving a *woman*, Christian, and religious that I can be.

Teach me, dear Jesus, to accept my femininity and my womanhood. Help me to realize that this is what I have to work with to become the religious I was meant to be. Help me, too, to realize that it is all good for it is a *gift* from you — one that cannot be denied, but one that must be accepted if I am to become a real, genuine woman, Christian, and religious.

Help me, too, to accept the fact that I *need* others. Give me the grace to let others know I need them. And let me never forget to always remain open to others — open so that they may realize You through me, for of myself I am nothing.[150]

Four years later Dorothy resolved "to make an effort to 'share' [her]self with others."[151] She also wrote:

- *Listen* to what He is saying. He wants you to do something special. Leadership is needed in our Community.
- Develop memory.
- Fight my sensual self; rid distractions immediately. Change them to prayers.[152]

Besides her retreat resolutions, Dorothy's personal written reflections also described the goals of her spiritual life. Unlike her retreat resolutions, though, Dorothy's personal reflections, which she recorded from August 1965[153] through July 1974,[154] present a multi-faceted portrait of her spirituality. And although the entries are sporadic, there exist some common threads that bind them together: Dorothy's experience of accomplishment and setbacks; her expression of her desires and fears; and her feelings of elation and desolation.

Several of Dorothy's personal journal entries offer insight into the development of her spirituality at various points in her religious life. During the summer of 1968, before she made her final vows, Dorothy wrote a summary of her own spiritual and emotional growth of the previous eight years. She stated:

> *First Three Years*:
> - Don [Kollenborn] and Dad
> - learned to love the community, the people, God
> - loved praying and becoming acquainted with spiritual things
> - slowly learned what *love* is about
> - developed deep love of people — much empathy
> - went through stages of love
> - somewhat independent
> - dragged down self
> *Juniorate*:
> - emerged; stood on two feet
> - first year out: difficult
> - second year out: learned to slowly love all; my fears slowly broke down; *not* afraid to give or receive affection now.
> *Now:*
> - standing on two feet
> - not afraid to love
> - feel secure here
> - *afraid* to lose this security[155]

Two years later Dorothy wrote a list of her fears, followed by ways in which she believed she could overcome them. Most of her fears were spiritual in nature; a few related to her own emotional growth:

> Overcome *fear* of . . .
> - going into deep waters: Be courageous, open.
> - going into the depths of the Word: Meditate in the morning.

- living the crucified, disciplined life: Accept sufferings graciously, willingly.
- submitting to one another: *Listen*, be open.
- laying down my life in very service to others: Rid selfish tendencies — think first of others.
- letting the cross of Christ cut into my very soul: Love the cross — accept it totally — it is *He*.
- dying to my flesh: Rid sensuousness, pleasure.[156]

While on retreat in the summer of 1973, Dorothy described her spiritual growth of the past year in the mode of an answer to a question she had asked herself. The question is "What has God done for me?"[157] and her reply is the following:

- brought me closer to Him
- freed me from my selfish possessiveness
- brought new people into my life
- has let me be His instrument
- has changed my heart
- has made me more aware of who *He* is and how much I need Him[158]

Dorothy's personal reflections also provide evidence of the inadequacies she felt in terms of her spirituality as well as her desire to make God the center of her life. These elements are present in her journal entries of the early 1970s, apparently a difficult period for her. The first is from May of 1970. Here Dorothy likewise expresses a wish to follow God's will, a main concern of hers throughout her religious life:

Where are you, Lord? I need you now. I'm lost again. Make me like unto you, Lord. Let me be able to say — I must be about my Father's business — I have come to do the will of my Father. You are my model, Lord — it is you who have set the example for me. Open my eyes that I might see how you lived so that I might live that way too.

I am supposed to be a professed follower of you — and yet, Lord, I am not totally converted — I have yet to be healed of many sins. Change my selfish heart into a totally loving heart

— melt me, Lord, I am a stone. I cannot be you, I cannot share you, Jesus, when I am filled with self. Heal me, Lord — *love* me — so that I'm "twirling" in your care. Remove my fears, Lord, of all that I might have to "surrender" so that I might become lost in you. You are my God — what should I fear — You have made me and fashioned me — why would I not trust you — Please Jesus — melt me now — purge out my evil ways — make me one with you — make me loving in your sight, for I am such a miserable soul. Free me from myself. . . . Be with me — cleanse me — keep me. I need constant encouragement — I am weak. Strengthen me continually lest I falter.[159]

Several months later Dorothy wrote a reflection similar to the one above:

Jesus, I am a weak and sinful human creature who so often gives in to her own whims, fancies, and desires. I am selfish — I want things for myself and am often reluctant to share them with others. I am proud — I want others to see me and recognize me for the supposed great person that I am and believe I have made all by myself.

Yet how wrong this is. Of myself I can do nothing, and this I have proven over and over again. Only with you can all things be accomplished. As soon as things get a little "rosy," and all is going well, I forget this because I forget you. Only when I am down in the dregs and much evil and affliction is upon me do I really see how weak I am. Jesus, I beg of you to help me realize that I am a sinner and that I, too, need to ask forgiveness. Maybe if I realize that I need *you* in my life because I am weak of myself, I may help others to do this also and thus relieve some of the evil in the world.[160]

Dorothy repeated her concerns about her weaknesses and her need to be strengthened by God in a journal entry three years later. She prayed:

Heavenly Father, I place myself in your hands. Lavish your love on me as I need to be strengthened. I am weak — I need you. . . . I feel empty — void. Fill up this chasm with *you*.

Speak to me, Lord — I am straining to listen. Lord, that I may be one *with* you and *in* you. Pull me together, Lord. I cannot hear — open my heart to you. . . . Help me not to falter into unbelief, especially in little things. Open my eyes, my ears — all my senses — so they may draw you in so that I may more and more become *you*. Rid me of myself, Lord — it is not an asset, for it often gets in the way of you. Purify me — make me single-minded — all for thee.[161]

A journal Dorothy kept from January through April of 1974 is probably the most revealing of all her journals because of the many aspects of her spiritual life that she described. At the beginning of the journal, Dorothy expressed delight, for example, in God's goodness: "After supper a quick, refreshing ice skate with Martha [Mooney, O.S.U.] — sun setting, beautiful full moon — all was perfect. Your goodness overwhelms me, Lord!"[162] In another entry that has a similar, light tone, Dorothy claimed:

The more you love Jesus and the more open you are with Him — the more lovable and beautiful all the rest of mankind becomes. Praise you, Jesus, for showing yourself so vividly and openly. I love *you* more because of all the love I experience in people.[163]

Just as she conveys the high points of her spiritual life in her journal, so, too, does Dorothy mention the low ones: "Woke up feeling 'unimportant'";[164] "I am shallow, Lord. I need rejuvenation; I need depth";[165] and "Jesus, I am desolate and in need of you."[166] Dorothy inevitably turned to Christ during her melancholy moments, though, and was refreshed: "Thank you for the beautiful day, Jesus — for restoring my sense of worth. You always come through when I give myself back to you and stay open to you. Grant me the grace to always be able to do this."[167]

On the title page of the journal under where she had printed "1974," Dorothy wrote, "I have come to do your will, Lord."[168] This avowal seemed to be her theme for the year as it appeared in several other entries in the journal: "'I come to do your will, Lord.' Please keep me attuned to it. Do not let me overpower it through selfish wants and desires."[169] On the feast of the Annunciation of the Lord,

Dorothy again wrote, "Here I am, Lord, I come to do your will."[170]

Several months later, though, on June 24, 1974, Dorothy indicates that she is in conflict with God's will for her and her own will:

> Jesus, I am fighting you again. I am fighting "dying to self."
> I am fighting "stripping myself of my own willful pleasures."
> Jesus, I am sick at the pit of my stomach. Give me the peace
> to know I am doing your will and the joy that goes with it.
> Help me overcome my selfish whims and desires. Jesus, I
> believe you will do this and handle the whole situation.[171]

        *   *   *   *   *   *   *   *   *

Dorothy's written reflections often revealed her desire to unite herself more completely with God. In her 1974 journal she described her desire metaphorically, but perhaps more than anything she wrote, this entry best represents Dorothy's spirituality:

> I keep watching these two wooden pieces, Jesus. My theory
> did not seem to hold true — they did not burst into a flaming
> holocaust for you. No, they slowly, quietly became filled with
> the heat and burned through the center. Maybe that's more
> real, Lord. Maybe we just slowly become filled with you, and
> when it reaches the core of our being, and there is no more we
> can absorb, we transcend to another being: to another way of
> unity; to the way for which we are longing to be with you; to
> the way for which we came into being. Praise you, Jesus, and
> thank you for such a total consuming love. Envelope me in it
> now. Make me one with you.[172]

5

A Woman of Dedication:
Dorothy's Missionary Ministry

Before I entered, I traveled to the West Coast four times. It was then that I was first impressed with the Spanish and Indian people. I wanted to stay, get to know them, and help them. . . .

Letter, November 4, 1967

On February 4, 1980, for Mother Bartholomew McCaffrey, General Superior of the Cleveland Ursulines at the time, Dorothy completed a congregational questionnaire on personal ministry choice.[1] The form asked for information regarding the past ministry experiences of an individual Sister as well as her preferences for future ministry assignments. In response to the statement, "Place a check next to areas in which you have worked," Dorothy indicated, "disadvantaged, sacramental preparation, individualized program, Parish School of Religion,[2] special education, deaf, etc., adult education, and renewal programs."[3] In response to the question, "In which of the areas mentioned would you like to work or continue to work?"[4] Dorothy answered "disadvantaged."[5]

That Dorothy desired to work with disadvantaged people is no surprise to those familiar with her ministry as a Cleveland Ursuline Sister. However, her first association with the disadvantaged came before she joined the Ursuline Congregation. When Dorothy taught the third grade at St. Robert Bellarmine School in Euclid, three-fourths of the school's student body consisted of children from a housing project located a short distance from the school. Margaret La Ganke, who taught with Dorothy at that time, further explains: "They were children from large families living in a crowded area. Economically, many of them were poor, but some also came from homes with one or more alcoholic parents."[6] So, quite possibly, Dorothy may have first considered working with the disadvantaged as a result of her experience at St. Robert Bellarmine School.

Dorothy's next teaching assignment was at Sacred Heart Academy, which was located in the poorest area of the three high schools sponsored by the Cleveland Ursulines. According to Susan Mary Rathbun, who taught with Dorothy for seven years at the school, "We probably saw the poor more than some of the other Sisters did."[7] During her years at Sacred Heart, Dorothy taught business, typing, and secretarial courses. As early as her second year at the school, however, she began to move beyond the boundaries of her high school ministry to persons who were physically challenged or who were marginalized by poverty or race. From 1966 through 1969, in addition to doing classroom teaching, Dorothy worked with deaf children, served the city's poor at the Martin de Porres Center, and taught Catholic doctrine to Native Americans of the Papago Tribe in Topawa, Arizona. In 1970 she started work on a Master's Degree in guidance and counseling so that she could minister to yet another group of the marginalized.

From 1972-74 Dorothy served in the guidance department at Beaumont School for Girls, a college-preparatory high school in Cleveland Heights. Although most of the girls she counseled were from middle and upper-middle-class economic levels,[8] and therefore not materially poor, they had their own set of unique problems that included drug and alcohol abuse and difficult family situations.[9] Martha Mooney describes Dorothy's ability to minister to some of the troubled students at Beaumont:

> As a guidance counselor Dorothy was able to talk to kids from all different kinds of situations. And the kids who had problems went to her right away . . . she got right into the drug situation which was very problematic at the time and was trying to get kids into treatment and trying to get parents to accept the fact that their kid needed treatment. So, she was knee-deep into the problems that existed among the students, and the waifs just flocked to her and loved her.[10]

Because of Dorothy's compassion, understanding, and natural ability to deal with young people, many of these girls turned to her for direction at all hours of the day and night. In the journal she kept from January through April of 1974, Dorothy frequently mentioned the girls with whom she was working and also prayed about them: "Jesus, please keep our girls in your loving care. They want you and need you!"[11] and "Last night — session until 4:00 a.m.; admitted truth. Jesus, help this girl. . . . Touch her — she is in pain."[12]

When she was not counseling the Beaumont students, Dorothy volunteered her services at the city jail in Warrensville Heights, known then as the "Workhouse," and at Sunny Acres Skilled Nursing Facility, a hospital for chronically ill patients. She referred to these experiences in her 1974 journal: "went to Workhouse; more wonderful people — in a different way; learned lots; Touch their hearts, Lord";[13] "went to Sunny Acres and Workhouse; beautiful people! Thank you, Jesus!"[14] and "Workhouse has new girls; atmosphere is different. Thank you for making us grow, Jesus!"[15] Although Dorothy was a fine classroom teacher at both Sacred Heart Academy and Beaumont School for Girls, "working with the disadvantaged and the disenfranchised just seemed very easy for her."[16]

* * * * * * * * *

If "it is not geography that makes one missionary but the response to the call to 'love one another as I have loved you,'"[17] then Dorothy's ministry to the marginalized during her ten years as a teacher and counselor certainly qualified as missionary service. Apparently, though, Dorothy thought about being a *foreign* missionary long before she chose the vocation of teaching or religious life, as she explained in the letter she wrote in which she volunteered for the Cleveland Latin American Mission Team. Dated November 4, 1967, this letter is addressed to Mother Annunciata Witz. In the opening paragraphs Dorothy explained why she wanted to be a missionary and why she would especially like to serve in Latin America:

> In a way this deciding whether or not you are qualified for a position can be a very humbling experience. It really makes you stop and take inventory of what you are, what you have, and what you can give to others. Mother, I have always been of the nature of a person eager to be on the move — to go to new places, to meet new people, to learn to understand these people, and to help them. Before I entered, I traveled to the West Coast four times. It was then that I was first impressed with the Spanish and Indian people. I wanted to stay, get to know them, and help them. I had even "day dreamed" that my parents would disown me and leave me there. Then I entered. As a junior Sister I attended Ursuline College. While at the

College, I took a course about Latin America, and since then I have even more earnestly had the desire to go there. The countries and people hold a very special appeal for me. It may sound strange — I am eager to go anywhere — but if we had opened a mission in Africa rather than Latin America, I am sure I would be "less" inclined to want to go. My preference is Latin America, although, as I say, I would be willing to go anywhere.[18]

Dorothy then listed her qualifications that she claimed "may be of some value:"[19]

1. I am presently 28 years old and consider myself as mature as I should be at this time.
2. I have had a year's experience in teaching elementary school (third grade, St. Robert Bellarmine School) which I did enjoy very much.
3. I have been trained in the "practical arts" of the business field and have had some experience in managing the books for our institute. I have also had the opportunity of shopping for groceries and fulfilling the immediate and necessary needs of our sisters. I have also been attempting to instruct others in these "practical arts."
4. I have short term experience in working with the deaf — instructing them in our faith. This past summer at the workshop in Detroit, I was able to pick up some sign language and information on the psychology of the deaf and how to teach them. This also may be beneficial.
5. My actual experience in teaching religion is very limited as I have just begun to teach high school girls this subject this year. I believe that teaching religion, doing catechetical work, showing your interest and love for people through home visits, etc., is a vital part of religious life. I have been eager to do this kind of work, but up until now have not had too much of an opportunity. I enjoy this work, for through it I am working with the "whole" person and not just one part of him or her. While teaching skill subjects, I have gotten a very limited picture; the opportunity to get to know the "whole" person is not as

great through subjects such as these. Because I have been interested in catechetical work and wanted the chance to attempt teaching religion, I became engaged in teaching CCD [Confraternity of Christian Doctrine] to the deaf. This, too, has taught me much and opened my vision and made me more aware of other people and their needs.[20]

Dorothy concluded her letter by reiterating her aspiration to serve Spanish and Indian people and the important role she believed pastoral work plays in religious life:

Mother, I don't know how coherent this letter is. My two main points that I am trying to get across are 1) that I have a sincere love for and desire to help people — and for some reason the Spanish and Indian people do have a special appeal for me, and 2) I believe that catechetical work is an important part of religious life — one so important that I would venture to say that maybe religious life should revolve more closely around it.

Mother, please understand that I do see and realize the need we have for missionaries right here in Cleveland — and I am very happy to be a part of this work right now. If this is where you think I am most effective, I shall be very happy to continue on as such.[21]

In the years between her initial declaration of her wish to engage in missionary work and her actual appointment to El Salvador in the spring of 1974, Dorothy wrote no more about why she felt called to be a foreign missionary. Several weeks before she left for El Salvador on July 29, 1974, however, she wrote an entry in her journal that offers a reason for her desire to do foreign missionary work. The reason, actually a conjecture, is similar to one Dorothy expressed in her 1967 letter, "the opportunity to get to know the 'whole' person."[22] On July 4, 1974, she wrote:

I attended a beautiful Mass this morning. Alice [Brickman, O.S.U.][23] gave beautiful introduction — makes me realize my narrowness and how I have to grow into awareness of universal humanity. Maybe that is what El Salvador is all about — expanding my narrow vision. Do with me, Lord, what you will.[24]

That Dorothy retained as one of her motivations for doing foreign missionary work the intention to grow in awareness of universality is confirmed by Sheila Marie Tobbe, a friend of Dorothy's who later also served on the CLAM Team. After Dorothy had spent a few years in El Salvador, and while Sheila was thinking about foreign missionary work herself, she and Dorothy occasionally discussed their mutual "sense of call to mission life."[25]   Sheila remembers that she and Dorothy both decided "that something was calling us to experience beyond our own world."[26]

Less than two months before she was murdered, Dorothy again wrote about why she wanted to continue doing foreign missionary work. This time, however, she expressed her views in a letter to Mercy Sister Theresa Kane who had been the main focus of an article in the September 5, 1980, issue of the *National Catholic Reporter*. The article contains segments of Theresa's final address to the Leadership Conference of Women Religious (LCWR). She had been its president for that year. And because Dorothy referred in her letter to some of Theresa's comments, quotation of these comments is necessary for clarity.

In her address Theresa condemned the Catholic Church for its exclusion of women from the Church as institution and discussed the ramifications of this exclusion:

> The exclusion of women from the Church as a system is a root evil and a social sin which must be eradicated if women are to be engaged in the institutional church. I am concerned for the growing number of women who have left the Roman Catholic Church and for those among us, both Sisters and lay women, who can no longer enter into the sacramental life of the Church because of the sin of sexism.
>
> The Church preaches a message of dignity, reverence, and equality of all persons to people and governments of the world, but it has yet to recognize the injustices it imposes on women. Until the institutional Catholic Church undertakes a serious, critical examination of its modes of acting toward women, it cannot, it will not, give witness to justice in the world. The

challenge for women in the 1980s is to confront and eradicate the systematic evils of sexism, clericalism, and paternalism.[27]

Later in her address, Theresa also discussed "the institutionalized and middle-class nature of U.S. nuns' work."[28] She claimed:

> The intention of our predecessors was not to erect buildings solely, but to do whatever was essential for the missionary service. Today, when two-thirds of the world's population live below subsistence level, women are again being challenged by the overwhelming needs of the poor and the oppressed to respond anew. Today we who are women religious need to de-institutionalize ourselves and become missionaries once again.
>
> The concentration of women religious in the United States, and especially on the East Coast, is not a witness to a global consciousness; it is not a witness to the overwhelming needs of the poor and the oppressed in the Third and Fourth Worlds. There needs to be a redistribution of woman power if we are to be in solidarity with the poor and the marginated of our society. This call may even cause many to step outside of the established systems to eventually withdraw from traditional-based ministries such as Catholic schools and health systems.[29]

In her letter to Theresa, Dorothy commended her for her address: "It truly was impressive — and hopeful — as well as challenging."[30] Having been particularly struck by Theresa's views concerning the middle-class nature of U.S. nuns' work, Dorothy related them to her own ministry:

> I was especially impressed with what you had to say about the "middle-class nature of U.S. nuns' work" — and how important it is to serve the poor and oppressed. I believe that wholeheartedly — that's why I'm here in El Salvador. I should be coming back to the States next year. It will be then that I face a greater challenge. I hope to continue working with the poor and oppressed. Just *how* is where the challenge will come in.[31]

Dorothy concluded her letter to Theresa with the following remarks:

Within this past year I had been fortunate to meet women theologians like Barbara Doherty [C.D.P.] and Sandra Schneiders [I.H.M.]. They — along with the little I've actually read about you — do give me the hope that the Reign of God is making headway. And for this I am grateful. Do continue to be Spirit-filled and challenging. Please keep the people of Salvador before the Lord as we are literally living in time of persecution. We need His strength.

Thank you for being freed up enough to speak the truth so clearly and publicly. God love you.[32]

Whatever Dorothy's reasons were for wanting to be a foreign missionary and working with the poor, her choice to do so may seem a radical one to some people. For Dorothy, however, such a choice was one she needed to make, as Kathleen Cooney explains:

When Dorothy decided to enter the convent, her decision was a radical choice for her because the man she was engaged to had become a Catholic, and she was concerned that anything would happen to him because of her choice — that he might do something that would be harmful or hurtful to him. But I think that radical decision made her see religious life as a radical option for God and that later on she just had to do more: it wasn't just doing the daily tasks inside a classroom — that there was a call to something more for her. And perhaps this explanation might answer questions regarding the missionary dimension of Dorothy's call.[33]

*   *   *   *   *   *   *   *   *

As a foreign missionary Dorothy engaged primarily in pastoral or parish ministry. In the letters and tapes she composed during her years in El Salvador, Dorothy's description of the team's parish activities were in many ways "very much like work at home," as she claimed at various times.[34] However, Dorothy also made it a point to describe how the team's pastoral work was very different from the kind performed in the United States. For example, early in her missionary experience, she explained the following in a tape to her parents:

What we have been doing mostly this past week is distributing these 10,000 bulletins . . . We had these bulletins made up about the church — it's just a simple, little bulletin telling when the Masses are scheduled and how to participate at Mass, and there's a calendar on the last page.

We decided to print these bulletins so that we'd have an opportunity to go door-to-door and meet people, let them get to know who we are, etc., and that we're interested in them. So, we have been tramping around. We went through the whole city last week, and this week we started on the mountains: [the town of] Conchagua. . . . They're just so glad to have you visit their house. That's another very important thing — just the fact that we take time to even pass the bulletins out. To stop and visit the people makes them feel important.[35]

Several months later, also in a tape to her parents, Dorothy mentioned another team pastoral activity: the training of lay catechists. She then explained the role the catechists played in the parish:

Yesterday we had a catechists' day here. The catechists are the people who are in the cantones — who live there — and they are the ones who work for us. They are like the priests' replacement in the canton because the priest can only get to some of these places once a month or sometimes once every other month to celebrate Mass and administer the sacraments. So, during the rest of the time, the catechist is responsible for having celebrations of The Word with the people or classes in marriage instruction or pre-baptismal talks.[36]

A letter Dorothy wrote to the Sisters at Beaumont Convent on May 10, 1976, particularly gave an informative account of her work at that time. At the beginning of the letter, she again described "pastoral work" Salvadoran style:

We're sure most of you know we live in a city (La Union just got daily water in April!), but we also work in small farm villages. Perhaps most of our working time is spent at the latter in a basic doctrine program we bring to the farmers. We also work closely with the priests helping them form community and celebrating the sacraments in these small cantones. There is also a large group of teenagers we meet with regularly and a group of women leaders for whom we are responsible. We also serve as links between the priests and the catechists conveying messages and getting needed materials. First Communion in the city is probably as big as any place back home and will be June 20 this year. There are also the continual jobs of learning new songs, working with the choir, cleaning the house (we have help, but with the dust the work never seems to be done), cooking once a week, weekly and monthly meetings, etc.[37]

Dorothy then reported on five projects she and the other missionaries have begun in La Union. The first one, Dorothy explained, "is a vocation program for girls that we've been planning for almost six months now. We think we are sure of three vocations for the native communities right now."[38] The other four projects were made possible by the Cleveland Ursuline Silver Jubilarians of 1975, who donated their gift money to Dorothy and Martha Owen. Dorothy consequently referred to these four projects as "Projecto Plata," or "Silver Project," and described them in great detail in her letter:

For project two we were able to purchase 96 books with $200 of their [Silver Jubilarians'] money for our traveling library. On discounts we saved $30 which we used to buy carrying cases and plastic bags (it rains inside these houses). We have six cases ready to go for one month to a canton. All are catalogued (our own system). At the end of the month the cases will rotate. We're very excited and the people are very anxious for us to begin.

Project three is probably our biggest: it deals with $1,000 that we put into the parish lending cooperative. Not only will the money be lent to buy fertilizer, but we have purchased the fertilizer at a reduced price as an additional savings to the campesino. We have renounced any dividends we might gain in the cooperative and have instructed that they be divided among the members. Thus the 2% interest will be divided among the members of the cooperative who are the same borrowers and our catechists. They gain in all ways. We also are praying that with good growing weather, they will be able to turn their investment into food and money worth ten times the original investment. We'll try to get sample figures as the growing season progresses.

Project four deals with a reading and writing program called "Alfalit." We are going to use $100 as support money for the program, mostly as aid to the volunteer teachers who give the classes.

And finally, project five will help our Promoters of Health in the cantones. We will try to equip them with a limited supply of basic first-aid necessities which are impossible to get up in the mountains: band aids, aspirin, worm pills, vitamins, burn ointment, etc. The final $100 of the $1400 will be used for this project.[39]

In the conclusion to this lengthy letter, Dorothy related even more of her experiences as a missionary in El Salvador:

And so we continue, living through earthquakes, eating beans and tortillas in the cantones, taking attempted suicide victims to the hospital, walking in dust or water up to our ankles (depends on the season), removing knifed victims from the main streets, building houses, demolishing and rebuilding churches, enduring the heat and mosquitoes, fighting malaria and dysentery and just generally having a great time in the name of the Ursulines and The Christ who is Lord! God Love You All![40]

The vocation program Dorothy mentioned in her May 10, 1976, letter she later wrote about in the *Universe Bulletin*, Cleveland's Catholic diocesan newspaper. In an article entitled, "First Stirrings of Religious Life," Dorothy reported on the progress of the vocation program:

We now have a group of fifteen girls with whom we are in contact. We have a private conference with each girl once a month as well as a general reunion each fourth Sunday. During these times we have been inviting religious from various congregations here in Salvador to speak to our girls so they can learn about their communities and get to know some of the native Sisters.

The Sisters, in turn, have been inviting our girls to visit with them in their convents and schools. Seeing as we are a three-hour drive away from the capital where most of them are located, it is difficult to get our girls there to visit — but slowly but surely, things are working out.

The native communities have been very responsive to us and our girls. At first they were not able to understand why we weren't sending the girls to our own communities. But when you are working in a country like El Salvador where the number of native priests in our diocese of San Miguel is sixteen, and the number of native women religious is twenty-five, and you have a population of 500,000 people, you realize the great need that is here.[41]

A program in which Dorothy consistently took part throughout her years in El Salvador was the Caritas Program. In a letter she wrote to the Diocese of Cleveland in June of 1977, Dorothy clearly explained this program and its origins:

Many times we hear the word *Caritas*, and we immediately think "love." Actually, that's what it's all about! We use that word down here for the name of an organization — Caritas de El Salvador. Fundamentally it is an extension of the love of other people in other countries for the poor here in El Salvador.

Caritas was founded on December 30, 1960, and has been working in the five dioceses since then, offering programs of community development and social assistance to the needy. In collaboration with the Government of this Republic, international organizations such as Catholic Relief Service (CRS) and the Agency for International Development (AID) have voluntarily helped to make this program a reality.

What does that mean for our three parishes today? It means that through this organization we can help fight against the prevalent malnutrition and lack of education. In each of the parishes, we have a Mother-Child Care Program which brings food (flour, corn meal, oil, and powdered milk) into the homes of children six years old and younger as well as to expectant mothers. These significant supplements to their regular diet of tortillas, rice, and beans are received monthly for twenty-four cents per child and mother receiving the food. This accents the fact that it is not just a "handout" and helps them to safeguard their self-respect.

The women also must come to an educational program once a month. Here they receive information on food preparation, house care, nutrition, child care, health, etc. Occasionally there are times of fiesta. Mother's Day is very important here, so we in La Union planned a party for 500 women (!!!). Since our Casa Comunal [Community House or Center] holds only about 300 comfortably, it was quite a "wall-to-wall-people" party. But they loved it — especially the entertainment: twenty-four amateur acts! Their treat of ice cream in a plastic dixie cup was special as they each then had a little something extra to take home if they did not win a door prize.

"Sightseeing" is also part of the educational program. Sister Loretta [Schulte, C.S.J.] in La Libertad has just begun the Caritas Program there. In order to have her ladies understand the practical points of the program, she brought them to Chirilagua (a two-and-a-half hour trip) to see how the ladies there maintain their program under the direction of Rosemary Smith. Well, this was quite a treat for the women as they had never visited this part of their country. And when they had to cross the Rio Lempa — over a very big and long bridge — they were just "oohing" and "aahing" as it was the first time they had ever seen it!

Therefore, if you think "love" when you hear the word caritas, you're thinking right. Love *does* make the world go 'round — and also helps to make it a better place to live in. So we would like to thank you once again for all the love *you* continue to shower on us here in El Salvador. Truly your love for your neighbor down here makes life a little easier for them to live. God love you for this![42]

Several years later Dorothy wrote the last CLAM Team letter she would ever write. In this letter, dated November 1980, she informed the Cleveland Diocese of feasts and sacramental celebrations that will take place in La Libertad and Chirilagua during the month of December. The letter is informative and descriptive, but it assumes a particular poignancy when the reader realizes that the activities Dorothy described are ones in which she will never take part.

Dorothy began her letter with a question: "What does December bring for us here in El Salvador?"[43] She then answered her own question with an account of the programs she and the other missionaries will coordinate during the month:

> First of all, it will bring us the Advent season — a time of waiting, a time of hoping, a time of yearning. Yet in the midst of this, we will also be in celebration as the feast of the Immaculate Conception is the patronal feast in the Port of La Libertad, and the Feast of Our Lady of Guadalupe is the patronal feast in Chirilagua. When celebrating the feast in the Port, we try to include everyone so on the First Friday in December we have a Mass for the anointing of the sick. This means that we take our jeep, pick-up, and minibus and go up and down the hillsides picking up the sick and bringing them to the celebration in the church. It is something they appreciate and look forward to. On Sunday, December 7, we will have another special celebration — a Mass for group marriages. Some may just be beginning married life, but the majority are those who have been living together for years and are now ready to reconcile themselves with the Lord. This way they are able to do it without "fuss and fanfare" and spending money unnecessarily.[44]

At the conclusion of her letter, Dorothy thanked the people of the Diocese of Cleveland for their continued support of the mission in El Salvador and asked them to pray for the Salvadoran people. She adds, "They are the Lord's 'little people' struggling to survive — to make it alive through another day — and needing His daily loving help to do it.[45]

*   *   *   *   *   *   *   *   *

What was Dorothy's philosophy of working with the poor of El Salvador? That is, what did she hope to accomplish? According to Christine Rody, Dorothy "didn't talk about it; she just did it."[46] On only one occasion in her surviving letters did Dorothy mention the goals that she and her co-workers hoped to fulfill through their ministry to the poor. In her letter of May 10, 1976, to the Sisters of Beaumont Convent, she claimed:

> We know perhaps better than any Ursuline how important these contributions [gift money from the Ursuline Silver Jubilarians

of 1975] are to the lives of our 51,000 parishioners whom we are trying to help realize their full dignity as persons, new persons capable of reaching full development through their ability to read and write. This will make accessible to them the ways of learning and the rich possession of truth, both human and divine, that we enjoy. We hope to help them become people who can "rule the earth," that is to say, people who are able to tame the land and put it at the service of humanity.[47]

Persons who spent time with Dorothy in El Salvador and observed her interaction with the people there can make judgements about her philosophy of working with the poor. Christine believes that Dorothy's philosophy was apparent in "her attitude of respect for the people."[48] She explains:

Dorothy was very respectful of people just in simple ways. For example, she would pick up a campesino on the road who was going wherever we were going. And when the person got into the jeep, she made sure that she had a place to put his machete. If he was carrying grain or something, she would help him put it in the back of the jeep.[49]

Dorothy expressed her respectful, caring attitude towards those she served through numerous other small acts — ones that the Salvadoran people readily recall years after her death because she had made them feel special or had empowered them in some way. For example, Maria del Rosario de Heron of Zaragoza recalls that Dorothy gave her dress material in her favorite color on her birthday every year.[50] Andres Piñeda of La Libertad remembers how Dorothy helped him develop self-confidence as a lay catechist:

She taught us how to celebrate The Word of God and how to give pre-baptismal talks. . . . She wanted us then to give talks with her, but we felt insecure. So, she helped us to overcome our fear. . . . At one time we used to celebrate The Word by just reading the prayers. Madre Dorothea told us that it would be better for us to speak to the people without reading from the paper. . . . In 1978 the archdiocese started a family program in San Salvador. She got together a group from here to go there.

It was called the "Family Office" and was just for parents: how husband and wife should respect each other and live together. These are the kinds of things Madre Dorothea taught us, and we were then supposed to go and teach others. . . . She visited our homes, too. She wrote down all our names and where we lived. These are the kinds of things I remember that she did with us. Most of all, she helped us get over our fear — to make us more free with all the people.[51]

Another person Dorothy empowered was Maria Rosa Rivera, also from La Libertad. When Dorothy noticed that Maria was struggling to support her nine children on the meager salary she earned selling produce in the marketplace, she got Maria the job of sacristan in the Immaculate Concepción Church in La Libertad, a job Maria holds to this day. Because this position had traditionally been held by a man, some of the people in the Port criticized Maria for accepting the job. When Maria told Dorothy about the criticism, she replied, "There's nothing wrong about a woman being a sacristan. The people will just have to get accustomed to some new things." Maria also fondly recalls how Dorothy would always bring her something — a pack of crackers or some little thing--when she returned from trips outside of La Libertad.[52]

A sense of accompaniment, of being with the poor through their pain, struggles, and trials and being one with them, is how Sheila Marie Tobbe[53] and Maddie Dorsey describe Dorothy's missionary work. Sheila states, "Dorothy really was with the people and accompanying the people, and they felt that presence and the importance of that presence. I think they felt her spirituality also."[54] "She accompanied them," Maddie agrees, "And she shared their faith. But Dorothy was also inspired by their living of the Gospel."[55] Terry Alexander believes that Dorothy "certainly worked for the liberation of the people, to teach them how to better their lives."[56]

*   *   *   *   *   *   *   *   *

That Dorothy remained in El Salvador when the political situation of the country was becoming increasingly chaotic and violent may be difficult for some people to understand. She, however, *chose* to stay and states this fact very clearly in a letter she wrote to Martha Owen on October 3, 1979. This letter, better than any others, serves as the legacy of Dorothy's desire to accompany the people of El Salvador even to the point of her own death:

I do want to say something to you — I think you will understand. We talked quite a bit today about what happens *if* something begins. And most of us feel we would want to stay here. Now this depends on *what* happens — if there is a way we can help — like run a refugee center or something. We wouldn't want to just run out on the people. Anyway, Al [Winters] thinks people we love should understand how we feel — in case something happens . . . I thought I should say this to you because I don't want to say it to anyone else because I don't think they would understand. Anyway, my beloved friend, just know how I feel and "treasure it in your heart." If a day comes when others will have to understand, please explain it for me.[57]

Epilogue: The Significance of a Death

You cannot understand how hard it is for one to be practical
who hopes for tenderness behind every face. . . . Others can
be important but not one who is so small that she wonders why
anyone save the infinitely kind God should be good to her.
Others can be sensible but not one who knows in her heart
how few things really matter. . . .

Found in Dorothy's Christian Prayer Book,
Author Unknown

From the very beginning, the murder of the four Churchwomen has been inextricably tied to questions of American military and economic aid to El Salvador and the role of high-ranking Salvadoran officials in the deaths.

On the day after the bodies of the women were found, December 5, 1980, the United States announced that it was suspending military and economic assistance pending clarification of the circumstances of the killings of the women. From December 6-9 a Special Presidential Commission, headed by William D. Rogers, a former official in the Administration of President Gerald Ford, and William G. Bowdler, a State Department official, conducted an investigation of the crime in El Salvador. They found no direct evidence of the crime, nor any evidence implicating the Salvadoran authorities, but they concluded that the operation had involved a cover-up of the murders.[1] They also suggested that autopsies be performed on the bodies of the women for the purpose of firearms identification[2] and that the Federal Bureau of Investigation (FBI) should play an active role in the murder investigation.[3]

Several days after the Rogers-Bowdler Mission, a new Salvadoran Government Junta was established, and a civilian, José Napoleon Duarte, was named President. Considering this a positive step, the United States resumed its economic assistance to El Salvador on December 17.[4] The Salvadoran Government Junta then named Colonel Roberto Monterrosa to head an official investigation of the case. Colonel Carlos Eugenio Vides Casanova, Director-General of the National Guard, put Major Lizandro Zepeda Velasco in charge of another investigation. Neither official took the case seriously, and in fact, covered up for the members of the National Guard who had committed the crime. Learning from Zepeda that Luis Antonio Colindres Alemán was responsible for the execution of the women, Monterrosa failed to submit Colindres' fingerprints to the United States Embassy. Zepeda personally took charge of covering up for the murderers by ordering them to exchange their rifles for a different set of arms and to remain loyal to the National Guard by suppressing the facts.[5]

In April 1981 the United States Embassy provided the Salvadoran authorities with evidence incriminating Colindres and his men. Despite the existence of this evidence, such as fingerprints taken from the women's van, neither Colindres nor his subordinates were charged with any crime.[6]

Five months later in September 1981, the United States Senate passed a bill requiring President Reagan to certify twice a year that the Salvadoran government was making improvements in the area of human rights and political reforms as a condition for receiving further economic aid from the United States. That progress also be made in the investigation of the murders of the Churchwomen and two American labor advisors was clearly stated in the bill.[7]

In December of 1981, Colonel Vides Casanova commissioned Major José Adolfo Medrano to carry out a new investigation. On February 8, 1982, one of the men involved in the murders confessed his guilt and implicated the others, including Colindres.[8] All of them were charged with the deaths of the women. Two days later President Duarte in a televised message informed the public that the case had been solved. He also gave the public to understand that Colindres and his men acted independently and had not received any orders from a superior.[9]

For over a year the judicial investigation made no additional progress over what had been accomplished by the Medrano team. Nevertheless, under questioning by the FBI, Sergeant Dagoberto Martínez, who, at the time of the crime was Colindres' immediate superior, admitted that he had been notified by Colindres about the Churchwomen's murders and about his direct role in them. On that occasion Martínez advised Colindres not to say anything unless his superiors asked him about it. Martínez also said that he had not been aware that orders had been given by a superior.[10]

Since it did not seem apparent that the Salvadoran government was serious about prosecuting the five guilty guardsmen, in May of 1983, Deputy Assistant Secretary of State for Inter-American Affairs

James H. Michel appointed Judge Harold R. Tyler, Jr., to conduct another investigation. On December 2, 1983, Judge Tyler completed a lengthy report on his investigation in which he claimed "that Colindres acted on his own initiative,"[11] and "the evidence of lack of higher involvement is persuasive and the evidence to the contrary largely, if not entirely, speculative."[12]

On May 23-24, 1984, a trial was held in Zacatecoluca, El Salvador, and Deputy Sergeant Luis Antonio Colindres Alemán and National Guard members Daniel Canales Ramírez, Carlos Joaquín Contreras Palacios, Francisco Orlando Contreras Recinos, and José Roberto Moreno Canjura were found guilty of murder and sentenced to thirty years imprisonment. Despite ambiguous statements by some of its official representatives, the United States Government conditioned its economic and military support to El Salvador on the resolution of this case.[13]

In March of 1993, the United Nations Report of the Truth Commission for El Salvador, *From Madness to Hope: The 12-Year War in El Salvador*, published the following conclusions:

1. There is sufficient evidence that:
   a) The arrest of the Churchwomen at the airport was planned prior to their arrival.
   b) In arresting and executing the four women, Deputy Sergeant Luis Antonio Colindres Alemán was acting on orders of a superior.
2. There is substantial evidence that:
   a) Then Colonel Carlos Eugenio Vides Casanova, Director-General of the National Guard, Lieutenant Colonel Oscar Edgardo Casanova Vejar, Commander of the Zacatecoluca military detachment, Colonel Roberto Monterrosa, Major Lizandro Zapeda Velasco, and Sergeant Dagoberto Martínez, among other officers, knew that members of the National Guard had committed the murders, and through their actions, these officers facilitated the cover-up of the facts which obstructed the judicial investigation.
   b) The Minister of Defense at the time, General José Guillermo García, made no serious effort to conduct a thorough investigation of responsibility for the murders of the Churchwomen.

    c) Local Commissioner José Dolores Meléndez also knew of the murders and covered up for the members of the security forces who committed them.

3. The State of El Salvador failed in its obligation under international rights law to investigate the case, to bring to trial those responsible for ordering and carrying out the executions, and finally, to compensate the victims' relatives.[14]

       *   *   *   *   *   *   *   *   *

In the sixteen years since they have died, the four Churchwomen live in the consciousness of many. Those who remember the shocking events of early December 1980 also surely remember that the deaths of Dorothy and her companions brought the tiny country of El Salvador and its problems to the attention of the entire world and prompted the United States Government to suspend for almost two weeks the military aid that Dorothy had claimed was contributing to the deaths of so many innocent Salvadoran people. Those who followed the murder case to its trial in May of 1984 may also recall that the trial marked the first time in Salvadoran history that a member of the armed forces was convicted of murder by a judge.[15]

Dorothy, Jean, Maura, and Ita, however, continue to live today for reasons that reach beyond the factual — reasons why each year on the anniversary of their deaths, countless communities of all faiths around the world celebrate their memory. For people today — those who remember December 2, 1980, or not — the four women have become symbols of hope and healing in a world fraught with violence, injustice, and poverty. Their courageous and moving testimony of what it means to fully live the Gospel has motivated thousands of North Americans to commit themselves to work for peace and justice either individually, through direct service to the poor and oppressed, or collectively, through membership in the various local and national peace and justice organizations which have formed in the past sixteen years.

For the Salvadoran people and the Cleveland Ursuline Sisters, however, Dorothy's death has taken on a special significance. Maria Imelda Hernandez who knew Dorothy in La Libertad, believes that Dorothy's martyrdom "is a sign that God loves us and is with us every moment."[16] For Jaime Eduardo Alvarez Burgos of Zaragoza, Dorothy's death is significant because she "helped the poorest of the poor."[17] Teresa Arias de Gutierrez, who first met Dorothy in La Union, says that Dorothy's death teaches "what it truly means to be a human being."[18]   The late Arturo Rivera y Damas," archbishop of San Salvador at the time of the women's deaths, believes that their deaths revealed the power of love: "They were from another country and yet they loved and identified with my people so much that they were able to give their lives for them in heroic sacrifice.[19]

Finally, Dorothy's death has had and continues to have a profound effect on her own Cleveland Ursuline Congregation. During one recent celebration of Dorothy's martyrdom, some Cleveland Ursulines offered these reflections on the witness value of her death:

[Her death] made me aware of our congregation's universal mission in the Church. Being a local congregation in the diocese for so long tends to give one a limited vision. Dorothy's death with its international aftermath enlarged my view of one person's effect in today's complicated world.

M. Benedict Badzik

Her death has affected me personally in a number of ways — not the least of which is an openness to a ministry with and among the poor.

Dorothy Bondi

Dorothy's death continues to gradually awaken Ursulines to new depths of reality as individuals, as a religious congregation, and as global Church.

Joanne Therese Buckman

Her death helped me to break out of institutionalized structures, to live life fully right now, to make real decisions, and to be at peace with who I am.

Barbara Eppich

Dorothy's death has caused me to reflect deeply on the meaning of giving my life in "service of the Church." Dorothy's death and life continue to challenge me to give more fully of myself.

Gale Marn

Dorothy is a real person, someone I knew who suffered persecution and death for the sake of the Kingdom. Her death ranks with those of the early Christian martyrs of the Church.

Donna Mikula

Her death significantly changed my life. . . . I have taken more time to renew my commitment to prayer and ministry during the past years and pray that through her intercession I, too, may remain faithful.

Name Withheld

As someone who shared the same religious formation with Dorothy, I was and continue to be aware of what God can do and does in the lives of those open to Him. Dorothy's "red" martyrdom is for me a public demonstration of the "white" martyrdom, the daily "yes," which we commit ourselves to. Her courage gives me courage and hope.

Anne Marie Diederich

Adelante![20]
for Ita, Maura, Dorothy, and Jean

Do not remember us then,
violated, blood darkening
an earth strewn with bodies,
broken egg shells, discarded,
silent as Victor Jara's lost fingers.
Listen to the wind
shaking these fields,
the poor's voices whispering
into North American ears,
"We are dying while
you are our assassins."
Bearing this voice, act
to hold back the hand that fires.
Remember us then as ones
the people taught courage.

Remember us when
they sing again.
Sing of innocence
soaring like doves
against the night fire,
silver cracks of rifle shots.
The death each morning when
mothers dig their children's graves.
Sing of the insolence
of the dead, brushing
the stars above Chalatenango,
when we gringas
stayed with the people
until we broke with them,
like fingers from a hand.
Then sing compañeras,
sing with the people,
Adelante!

Renny Golden

Notes

Preface

[1] A postulant is a candidate for religious life. The postulancy, or time before the formal reception into the novitiate, can be six months to a year. The length of time differs with each religious congregation.

[2] The main house of a religious congregation is called a "motherhouse" because traditionally it is where the congregation's General Superior or President, who was called "Mother," resides. The congregation's administrative and business offices are also usually located in the motherhouse, and the congregation's retired sisters may also live there.

[3] The modified habit Dorothy was wearing in my dream was the one the Cleveland Ursulines were wearing at the time of her departure for El Salvador in 1974: a knee-length black dress with long or three-quarter length sleeves and a headdress with a white cloth band and a short black veil.

[4] The first tape is dated July 31, 1974, two days after Dorothy's arrival in El Salvador, and the last tape is dated November 14, 1980, eighteen days before her death. Dorothy's parents saved most of these tapes, as well as most of the other surviving letters, and had stored them in the attic of their house.

[5] Virginia Woolf, "The New Biography," Collected Essays, vol. 4 (New York: Harcourt, 1967) 229.

Introduction: The Significance of a Life

[1] Christian Prayer is The Liturgy of the Hours, the daily public prayer of the Church which priests, religious, and some clerics have an obligation to recite.

[2] Dorothy's baptismal name.

[3] Dorothy's religious name, that is, the name she was given when she received the Ursuline religious habit.

[4] These initials, which an Ursuline Sister usually writes after her name, mean "Order of Saint Ursula." The initials after a Catholic sister's name identify her religious congregation.

[5] This was Dorothy's title when she served as a missionary in El Salvador. The translation is, literally, "Mother Dorothy." The Salvadoran people address missionary sisters as "Madre" rather than the more familiar "Sister."

[6] T.A. Carroll, R.S.M., as quoted in Kathleen Cooney, O.S.U., "Reasons for Staying in a Religious Congregation from the Viewpoint of Women Who Entered Between 1945 and 1975," diss., Case Western Reserve University, 1988, 6.

[7] Cooney 6.

[8] John Carmody, "Vatican II Spirituality," The Westminster Dictionary of Christian Spirituality, ed. Gordon S. Wakefield (Philadelphia: Westminster, 1983) 384.

[9] Transformative Elements for Religious Life in the Future (Louisville: Joint CMSM/LCWR Assembly, 1989) 2.

[10] Transformative Elements 3.

[11] Maria Augusta Neal, S.N.D. de Namur, From Nuns to Sisters: An Expanding Vocation (Mystic: Twenty-Third, 1990) 39.

[12]Pamela Seracino, "Her Passion Perseveres," *Catholic Peace Voice* Summer 1996: 7. On June 28, 1996, the Intelligence Oversight Board released a fifty-three-page study of CIA abuses in Guatemala, and although this report is another significant step toward the declassification of documents relating to human rights abuses in Guatemala, it is not expected to clear up details of individual cases like that of Sister Dianna Ortiz.

[13]Elisabeth Young-Bruehl, as quoted in Gail Porter Mandell, *Life Into Art: Conversations with Seven Contemporary Biographers* (Fayetteville: U of Arkansas P, 1991) 190-91.

[14] Virginia Woolf, "The Art of Biography," *Collected Essays*, vol. 4 (New York: Harcourt, 1967) 227.

[15] Frances Harbert, personal interview, 10 July 1991.

[16] Barbara Jean Sever, O.S.U., personal interview, 5 Sept. 1991.

[17] Russell Smith, phone interview, 5 Sept. 1991.

[18] Anna Margaret Gilbride, O.S.U., personal interview, 12 Oct. 1990.

[19] Donald Kollenborn, phone interview, 17 Sept. 1991.

[20] Maria Imelda Hernandez, personal interview, 21 June 1992.

[21] Christine Rody, V.S.C., personal interview, 11 July 1991.

[22] Teresa de Jesus Portillo de Flores, personal interview, 19 June 1992.

[23] Rev. Paul Schindler, personal interview, 15 Nov. 1994.

[24] Andres Pineda, personal interview, 21 June 1992.

[25] Martina S. Horner, foreward, *Simone Weil: A Modern Pilgrimage*, by Robert Coles (Reading: Addison-Wesley, 1987) ix.

1. A Record of Life

[1] The Lithuanian neighborhood to which Malvina and her family moved when she was a child was located in Downtown Cleveland in and around the 30s block of Superior Avenue. The Kazlauskas family lived on Oregon Avenue, which was in the area of the present East 18th Street. In the early 1920s, as the business section of Downtown Cleveland began to expand, the Lithuanian colony moved eastward and settled between East 65th and East 82nd streets. Malvina and her family followed this migration, and throughout the remaining years of her childhood, her adolescence, and into her young adulthood, rented a succession of apartments in the area.

[2] Malvina Kazel, personal interview, 12 Feb. 1991.

[3] "Kazlauskas" is a common Lithuanian name. Since their parents were from different parts of Lithuania, it was by sheer coincidence that Joseph and Malvina shared this surname.

[4] Lucy Marie Kazlauskas, O.S.F., telephone interview, 16 Sept. 1991.

[5] St. George Catholic Church, founded to meet the needs of the Lithuanian people of Cleveland, also moved eastward from the downtown area of the city with the Lithuanian colony in the early 1920s. It relocated from Oregon Avenue to East 67th Street and Superior Avenue in 1921. From this location St. George Church continues to serve the Lithuanian people but has expanded its parish boundaries to include parishioners from as far east as Ashtabula County and as far west as Lorain and Summit counties. It also claims registered parishioners from the East 185th Street section of Cleveland, Bratenahl, Brecksville, Seven Hills, Parma, Parma Heights, and Geauga County.

[6] Malvina Kazel, personal interview, 15 Oct. 1990.

[7] Malvina Kazel, personal interview, 15 Oct. 1990.

[8] Malvina Kazel, personal interview, 15 Oct. 1990. "Dottie" and "Dot" were Dorothy's nicknames until she began high school.

[9] Joe's parents, Andrew and Magdalene Kazlauskas, lived in the downstairs home of the duplex on Addison Road, and Joe and Malvina and their children lived upstairs. Joseph Kazlauskas, Malvina's father, who was a widower, moved in with Joe and Malvina after they married and lived with them until his death.

[10] Malvina Kazel, telephone interview, 14 Oct. 1991.

[11] Malvina Kazel, Kazel Family Photograph Album, 1951, Archives of the Ursuline Sisters of Cleveland (hereafter cited as USCA).

[12] Frances Harbert, personal interview, 10 July 1991. Fran, a close friend of Dorothy's who also grew up with her, comments on the role drinking played in the social activities of their parents' generation: "It just seemed to be part of the lifestyle of the parents who came of age in the Depression and got married. They would socialize by going to different taverns or farms in Burton and Geneva and drinking a lot."

[13] Ann Marie Lostoski, O.S.F., personal interview, 19 Oct. 1991.

[14] Joseph Chapon, Sylvia Greer, Edward Anderson, and Marie Closky, respectively, as quoted in Dorothy Kazel's Autograph Book, 16 May 1950, ms., USCA.

[15] Elementary School Report Cards, St. George School, Cleveland, 1948-51, ms., USCA. Dorothy's report cards from the fourth, fifth, and sixth grades only survive.

[16] M. Helene Balciunas, O.S.F., personal interview, 19 Oct. 1991. Agnes Kathryn Wilson, O.S.F., telephone interview, 23 Oct. 1991. The late Sister Mary Helene taught Dorothy in the first grade (1945-46), and Sister Agnes Kathryn taught her in the eighth grade (1952-53).

[17] Mary Anne Metalonis, O.S.F., personal interview, 19 Oct. 1991. Sister Mary Anne taught Dorothy in the third grade (1947-48).

[18] Mary Anne Metalonis, O.S.F., personal interview, 19 Oct. 1991.

[19] When she danced the traditional Lithuanian dances at school and parish functions, Dorothy wore her paternal grandmother's costume, which her grandmother had brought with her when she came to America from Lithuania.

[20] The St. George Sodality, like many others of its time, promoted devotion to the Blessed Virgin Mary. It encouraged its members or sodalists to attend Mass and pray the rosary daily and to recite novenas, nine consecutive days of private or public prayer, in honor of the Blessed Virgin. Sodalists also attended Marian devotions, like the May crowning of the Blessed Virgin, as a group.

[21] Because of the changing neighborhood and consequent drop in enrollment, Notre Dame Academy moved to 13000 Auburn Road, Chardon, Ohio, in 1963. In 1988 it merged with Cathedral Latin High School, and today it is known as "Notre Dame-Cathedral Latin School."

[22] Notre Dame Academy acquired the nickname "the castle on Ansel" because of its huge square shape, punctuated at its four corners by towers.

[23] Eileen Best, telephone interview, 8 Nov. 1991. Eileen was Dorothy's freshman homeroom teacher and was moderator of the Athletic Association, to which Dorothy belonged. At the time, 1953-54, Eileen was a member of the congregation of the Sisters of Notre Dame and was known as Sister Mary Georgemarie. She also taught

English, religion, and history at the Academy.

[24] Frances Harbert, personal interview, 10 July 1991.

[25] Permanent Record, Notre Dame Academy, Cleveland, 1953-57, ts., USCA, 1 (hereafter cited as NDAPR).

[26] In an article in the October 21, 1955, issue of *The Tower*, Notre Dame's school newspaper, the Living Rosary devotion is described: "Encircling the chapel as a giant rosary, sodalists will participate in the living rosary ceremony, October 31. Representative sodalists from each homeroom will walk to Mary's altar, say an Ave [a Hail Mary] and offer her a rose . . ." (1).

[27] The Summer School of Catholic Action (SSCA), whose purpose was to train young Catholic leaders, was a week-long "convention" on Catholicism held each August in a different American city. Officers of high school organizations and sodalities were chosen to participate. The SSCA program included daily Mass, classes on Catholic leadership, the Queenship of Mary, and marriage, as well as various social activities.

[28] The Mission Club sponsored activities to raise money for the foreign missions, particularly the Notre Dame mission in India, which the Notre Dame Sisters had started just a few years before Dorothy began attending the Academy.

[29] Notre Dame Day was an event that promoted school spirit. It occurred each year in October on the day when the students switched from their light blue cotton uniforms to their navy blue jumpers. The class periods were shortened in order to accommodate special events such as a movie, a special food treat in the cafeteria, and an all-school parade. The students also made construction paper hats which they wore all day and asked their friends to autograph.

[30] The parties were initially held in Dorothy's large home on Addison Road and later at 24730 Shoreview Avenue in Euclid where she and her family moved in July of 1955. Euclid is the first suburb immediately east of Cleveland and is located on the shoreline of Lake Erie.

[31] Frances Harbert, personal interview, 10 July 1991. The memorable pajama party was a surprise party for Fran on her sixteenth birthday.

[32] Two photograph albums from Dorothy's adolescence survive. The first contains photos of Dorothy's graduation from St. George School in June 1953 and photographs of parties, school activities, and other events until December 1955. This album also includes undated earlier pictures and several from Dorothy's First Communion, which occurred on May 23, 1948. The second photograph album holds pictures of events from December 1955 through April 1956. Photographs of Fran Harbert's sixteenth birthday party are included in this second album. The albums are in the archives of the Ursuline Sisters of Cleveland.

[33] Russell Smith, telephone interview, 5 Sept. 1991.

[34] Blue was Dorothy's favorite color.

[35] Frances Harbert, personal interview, 10 July 1991.

[36] Dorothy Kazel, High School Diary, 1956, ms., USCA, 6 Jan. 1956 (hereafter cited as HSD).

[37] HSD, 9 Sept. 1956.

[38] HSD, 21 Sept. 1956.

[39] HSD, 16 Jan. 1956.

[40] HSD, 10 Jan. 1956.

[41] HSD, 17 Jan. 1956.

[42] M.Owen Kleinhenz, S.N.D., personal interview, 3 Oct. 1991.

[43] Marilyn Friga, telephone interview, 26 Sept. 1991.

[44] *Rolla-Revels of 1955*, 29-31 Jan. 1955, USCA.

[45] HSD, 11 Jan. 1956.

[46] HSD, 13 Jan. 1956.

[47] HSD, 28 Jan. 1956.

[48] HSD, 29 Jan. 1956.

[49] Marilyn Friga, telephone interview, 26 Sept. 1991.

[50] Malvina Kazel, telephone interview, 14 Oct. 1991.

[51] The Carnegie Institute, formerly located at 4707 Euclid Avenue, Cleveland, Ohio, was a training school for medical receptionists, office assistants, and technicians. It closed in the 1960s.

[52] NDAPR, 2.

[53] Dorothy purchased four paperback manuals for her courses at the Carnegie Institute. Each manual is a section of the medical secretary course offered by the school. The title of the course that appears on each manual is *A Training Program in Personal Development and Medical Procedure for Medical Receptionists, Assistants, and Technicians*. In order, the sections of the course are Personality, Atmosphere, Responsibilities, and Medical Records (A): Recording and Filing. The manuals are in the archives of the Ursuline Sisters of Cleveland.

[54] The Carnegie Institute in Troy, Michigan, which received the records of the Carnegie Institute, Cleveland, when it closed, has no financial or academic records for Dorothy. She, therefore, never actually took any courses at the school.

[55] NDAPR, 2.

[56] Donald Kollenborn, telephone interview, 17 Sept. 1991.

[57] Donald Kollenborn, telephone interview, 17 Sept. 1991.

[58] Donald Kollenborn, telephone interview, 17 Sept. 1991.

[59] Record of Study, St. John College, Cleveland, 1957-60, ts., 1, USCA.

[60] Mercita Thailing, telephone interview, 24 Sept. 1991.

[61] Donald Kollenborn, telephone interview, 17 Sept. 1991.

[62] Donald Kollenborn, telephone interview, 17 Sept. 1991.

[63] Mercita Thailing, telephone interview, 24 Sept. 1991.

[64] Russell Smith, telephone interview, 5 Sept. 1991.

[65] Donald Kollenborn, telephone interview, 17 Sept. 1991.

[66] Russell Smith, telephone interview, 5 Sept. 1991.

[67] Malvina Kazel, personal interview, 12 Feb. 1991.

[68] Malvina Kazel, personal interview, 12 Feb. 1991.

[69] Ursuline Sisters taught at St. John College, and some were students there as well.

[70] Donald Kollenborn, telephone interview, 17 Sept. 1991.

[71] Donald Kollenborn, telephone interview, 17 Sept. 1991.

[72] Donald Kollenborn, telephone interview, 17 Sept. 1991.

[73] Donald Kollenborn, telephone interview, 26 Feb. 1992. Dorothy had requested a pearl engagement ring because, according to Donald, "she was not taken with diamonds at all."

[74] Margaret LaGanke, telephone interview, 25 June 1996. Margaret taught with Dorothy at St. Robert School.

[75] A retreat is, literally, a retreat from everyday activities in order to have time for prayer and reflection. The length of a retreat could be one day to a week or even a month. Aside from praying privately and participating in group prayer and discussions, retreatants usually attend Mass.

[76] Donald Kollenborn, telephone interview, 17 Sept. 1991.

[77] Donald Kollenborn, letter to Dorothy Kazel, Feb. 1960, USCA.

[78] Donald Kollenborn, telephone interview, 17 1991.

[79] Donald Kollenborn, telephone interview, 17 Sept. 1991.

[80] Margaret La Ganke, telephone interview, 25 June 1996.

[81] Rev. Joseph Wagner, letter to Mother Marie Sands, O.S.U., 23 May 1960, USCA.

[82] Dorothy Kazel, "Ursuline Sisters of Cleveland: Application Form," 29 June 1960, ms., USCA (hereinafter cited as USCAF).

[83] Donald Kollenborn, telephone interview, 17 Sept. 1991.

[84] Donald Kollenborn, telephone interview, 17 Sept. 1991.

[85] Lucy Marie Kazlauskas, O.S.F., telephone interview, 16 Sept. 1991.

[86] Lucy Marie Kazlauskas, O.S.F., telephone interview, 16 Sept. 1991.

[87] Lucy Marie Kazlauskas, O.S.F. telephone interview, 16 Sept. 1991.

[88] Two letters survive: one is dated August 6, 1960, and the other is dated August 19, 1960.

[89] Donald Kollenborn, letter to Dorothy Kazel, 19 Aug. 1960, USCA.

[90] Donald Kollenborn, letter to Dorothy Kazel, 19 Aug. 1960, USCA.

[91] Donald Kollenborn, telephone interview, 26 Feb. 1992.

[92] Marilyn Friga, telephone interview, 26 Sept. 1991.

[93] Mercita Thailing, personal interview, 5 Oct. 1991.

[94] Marilyn Friga, telephone interview, 26 Sept. 1991.

[95] September 8 is the birthday of the Blessed Virgin Mary. In the past, young women usually entered the novitiate of the Ursuline Congregation on a feastday of Mary. Another popular entrance date was September 12, the Holy Name of Mary.

[96] The novitiate is the first stage of religious life. During this period postulants and novices are acquainted with religious life, test their suitability for it, and are likewise tested by the congregation. As a group the postulants and novices were also called "the novitiate."

[97] A novice, as the term implies, is a "beginner" in religious life. She wears the religious habit of the congregation but is not under vows. The length of time one spends as a novice varies from congregation to congregation. Some congregations require that only one year be spent as a novice. In the Cleveland Ursuline Congregation, a sister is a novice for two years.

[98] A junior professed sister is one who has taken temporary vows. That is, she has taken vows for a period of one, two, or three years.

[99] The Ursuline Sisters of Cleveland have traditionally referred to a group of women who enter the novitiate on the same date as a "set."

[100] The Little Office of the Blessed Virgin Mary is a brief office in honor of the Blessed Virgin Mary modeled on the Divine Office. The Morning Hours of the Little Office are called Lauds.

[101] The Midday Hours of the Little Office are Prime, Terse, Sext, and None and were said as a unit.

[102] During recreation time the postulants and novices would engage in sports, such as baseball and basketball, work in the garden, play table games, take walks, and participate in group singing.

[103] The postulants and novices drove the sisters who taught them to and from Ursuline College each day. Ursuline College is now located on the same property as the motherhouse in Pepper Pike, Ohio.

[104] Transcript, Ursuline College, Cleveland, 1960-65, ts., USCA, 1 (hereafter cited as UCT).

[105] The Clothing and Profession of Vows ceremonies usually took place around August 8, the date on which the first Ursuline Sisters arrived in Cleveland from France in 1850.

[106] A white veil signifies that the Sister has not yet taken vows.

[107] As part of the traditional Ursuline habit, the guimpe was a rectangular piece of stiff cloth, creased in the middle, that covered the Sister's neck and upper body. The bandeau, a wide band constructed of the same cloth as the guimpe, was worn around the head, covering the forehead.

[108] In many congregations Sisters traditionally assumed the name "Mary" in honor of the Blessed Virgin Mary. Often they would simply write "M." before their religious names.

[109] "The Ursuline Martyrs of Valenciennes," *Ursuline Mission Services* Nov.-Dec. 1974: 3-4. Sister M. Laurentine Prin belonged to the Ursuline Congregation that had been established at Valenciennes, France, in 1654. This group of Ursulines devoted themselves mainly to the education of poor children. The Sisters' "excellent methods, self-forgetfulness, and their efficiency made them popular, and their fervent religious life was a fitting preparation for the ordeal that awaited them."

During the Reign of Terror in the summer of 1794, the eleven Ursulines of Valenciennes were imprisoned for two months, first in their convent, and then in the public prison. On October 19 five of the Ursulines, including Sister Laurentine, were condemned to death. As they walked to the scaffold of the guillotine, they joyfully sang the Magnificat. Four days later, the remaining six Ursulines were also executed. The eleven Ursuline Martyrs of Valenciennes were beatified by Pope Benedict XV on June 13, 1920.

[110] Mary Jo Lackamp, personal interview, 14 Nov. 1991. Mary Jo remembers how these words echoed in her memory on the day Dorothy's murder was announced.

Around the time of Dorothy's Clothing, Father Eldon Reichert, one of her confessors, also made an ironic comment, although indirectly, regarding her religious name. Eldon could not attend the reception because he was in Dayton, Ohio, but he called Dorothy and left the following message: "Congratulations. Pray you will be worthy of your saintly name." Dorothy saved the message and had inserted it into an album of hers that contained photographs of her as a postulant, novice, and junior.

[111] Donald Kollenborn, telephone interview, 26 Feb. 1992.

[112] Donald Kollenborn, telephone interview, 26 Feb. 1992. After waiting for Dorothy for two years, Donald married in 1962 and during the following year heard from Dorothy for the first time since she had entered the convent. At this particular time in his life, Donald was experiencing a tremendous amount of turmoil. Dorothy, of course, did not know this because they had been out of touch for three years. But she must have sensed something was wrong because she wrote him a note in which she told him that she had been thinking about him — she could not get him off her mind, actually — and asked him if everything was alright. She enclosed her address. Donald wrote back and told Dorothy her suspicions were correct but that he was dealing with his difficulties.

[113] Canonical Year is a year of intense formation in spirituality and the rules of the congregation. The Canonical novice also gives service in various capacities to the congregation. When Dorothy was in the Ursuline novitiate in the early 1960s, Canonical Year was designated for first-year novices. Currently, in the Ursuline Congregation, novices can complete their Canonical year during their first *or* second year as a novice.

[114] The Rule Dorothy studied and followed was the one that had been revised in 1949. It consisted of the following chapters: "Of the End and Spirit of the Institute," "Of Union and Mutual Conformity," "Of Poverty," "Of Prayer," "Of Fasting and Refection," "Of Modesty and Decorum," "Of Fraternal Correction and Religious Humility," "Of Clothing and Cleanliness," "Of the Care of the Sick and the Wants of the Sisterhood," "Of Peace and Reconciliation," and "Of the Reciprocal Duty of the Superioress Towards the Sisters, and the Sisters Towards the Superioress."

[115] The Constitutions Dorothy likewise studied and followed were the 1949 revision. They were comprised of three main parts: "The End for Which the Ursuline Order Was Established," "The Admission, the Vows, the Community Life and Exercises," and "The Government of the Institute."

[116] M. Kenan Dulzer, O.S.U., personal interview, 29 July 1991.

[117] UCT, 1.

[118] Dorothy's obedience for June 1963 read, "My Dear Sister, Your obedience for this year is to study at Ursuline College. May the grace of this obedience bring you many blessings throughout the year. Lovingly, Mother." Although a record of the yearly appointments is kept in the archives of the Ursuline Sisters, Dorothy saved twelve of the handwritten obediences she received from General Superiors during her twenty years in the congregation.

[119] The three high schools owned and operated by the Ursuline Sisters at the time were Sacred Heart Academy, Villa Angela Academy, and Beaumont School for Girls.

[120] M. Kenan Dulzer, O.S.U., personal interview, 29 July 1991.

[121] According to *The Broad Highway: A History of the Ursuline Nuns in the Diocese of Cleveland, 1850-1950*, by M. Michael Francis Hearon, O.S.U., the Ursulines of the Congregation of Paris, France, decided to take a fourth vow, the Vow of Instruction, on June 13, 1632 (29). The adoption of the Fourth Vow "distinguished the Congregation of Paris and the houses founded by it from all other Ursuline Communities (29)." Since the congregation of the Ursuline Sisters of Cleveland was founded from the monastery of Bologne-sur-Mer, a community of the Congregation of Paris, it, too, adopted the Fourth Vow of Instruction. In the early 1960s the Fourth Vow was called the "Instruction of Youth." The Ursuline Sisters of Cleveland continue to take a fourth vow, but it is presently called the vow of "Christian Education."

[122] The vow formula at the time read: In the name of Our Lord Jesus Christ and in honor of His most holy Mother, of our Holy Father, Saint Augustine, of Saint Ursula, our patroness, and of Saint Angela, our Foundress, I, Dorothea Kazel, in Religion, Sister Mary Laurentine, do vow and promise to God for three years Poverty, Chastity, Obedience, and to employ myself in the Instruction of Youth, according to the Rule of our Holy Father, Saint Augustine, and the Constitutions of this Institute of Saint Ursula, in conformity with the requirements of Canon Law and the Bull of our Holy Father, Paul V, into the hands of the Reverend Mother, Marie Sands, in Religion, Mother Marie, General Superior of this Institute of Saint Ursula, in the year of our salvation, one thousand nine hundred sixty-three this thirteenth day of August.

[123] UCT, 2.

[124] Kathleen Cooney, O.S.U., personal interview, 13 Oct. 1990.

[125] Mary Catherine Cummins, O.S.U., personal interview, 23 Feb. 1995.

[126] M. Kenan Dulzer, O.S.U., personal interview, 29 July 1991.

[127] Ann Letitia Kostiha, O.S.U., personal interview, 23 Feb. 1995.

[128] M. Kenan Dulzer, O.S.U., personal interview, 28 July 1991.

[129] M. Kenan Dulzer, O.S.U., personal interview, 28 July 1991.

[130] Susan Mary Rathbun, O.S.U., personal interview, 15 Oct. 1990.

[131] Kathleen Cooney, O.S.U., personal interview, 13 Oct. 1990.

[132] Anna Margaret Gilbride, O.S.U., personal interview, 12 Oct. 1990.

[133] Mary Jo Lackamp, personal interview, 14 Nov. 1991.

[134] Mary Jo Lackamp, personal interview, 14 Nov. 1991.

[135] M. Kenan Dulzer, O.S.U., personal interview, 28 July 1991.

[136] The Generalate, the administration of the Cleveland Ursuline Congregation, consists of the General Superior and her four councilors.

[137] Anna Margaret Gilbride, O.S.U., personal interview, 12 Oct. 1990.

[138] M. Kenan Dulzer, O.S.U., personal interview, 28 July 1991.

[139] Mary Jo Lackamp, personal interview, 14 Nov. 1991.

[140] M. Kenan Dulzer, O.S.U., personal interview, 29 July 1991.

[141] M. Michael Francis Hearon, O.S.U., *Look to This Day: Ursuline Frontiers and Horizons, 1950-75* (Cleveland: Western, 1975) 38.

[142] *Chronicle*, Sacred Heart Academy, East Cleveland, Aug. 1965-Aug. 1969, ts., USCA, 17 Jan. 1966 (hereafter cited as SHAC).

[143] M. Vincent de Paul Witchner, O.S.U., "Sister Dorothy Kazel," Reflection at the Eucharistic Celebration of the Fifth Anniversary of the Martyrdom of Dorothy Kazel, O.S.U., Ursuline Motherhouse, Cleveland, Ohio, 2 Dec. 1985, 1.

[144] Witchner 2.

[145] Witchner 2.

[146] Russell Smith, telephone interview, 5 Sept. 1991. Another memorable meeting between Russell and Dorothy occurred when he was working with the ambulance unit of the police department. He and another officer were sent to Sacred Heart Convent to rush one of the Sisters to the hospital. They arrived to discover that the sick Sister was Dorothy. Russell describes this incident as "another shock situation."

[147] Patricia Maresco, telephone interview, 24 June 1996.

[148] Elizabeth Thomas, letter to Joseph and Malvina Kazel, 12 Dec. 1980, USCA.

[149] Pauletta A. Melago, letter to Joseph and Malvina Kazel, 5 Dec. 1980, USCA.

[150] Susan Freeman Topich, letter to Joseph and Malvina Kazel, 5 Dec. 1980.

[151] Kathleen Cooney, O.S.U., personal interview, 13 Oct. 1990.

[152] Barbara Jean Sever, O.S.U., personal interview, 11 July 1991.

[153] Dorothy Kazel, O.S.U., letter to Mary Annunciata Witz, O.S.U., 4 Nov. 1967, USCA (hereafter cited as L1).

[154] Established by the Cleveland Diocese in 1967, Martin de Porres Center is a multi-service agency that ministers to the poor in the Glenville area of Cleveland.

[155] From 1962-65 The Second Vatican Council of the Roman Catholic Church was convened at the request of Pope John XXIII. According to *The Oxford Dictionary of the Christian Church*, Pope John XXIII "defined its [the-Council's] immediate task as renewing the religious life of the Church and bringing up to date its teaching, discipline, and organization, with the unity of all Christians as the ultimate goal" (1428). An area included in the renewal was that of the religious state of life. In *The Documents of Vatican II: All Sixteen Official Texts Promulgated by the Ecumenical Council, 1963-65*, the "Decree on the Appropriate Renewal of the Religious Life (Perfectae Caritatis)," states that the members of religious congregations "have handed over their entire lives to God's service in an act of special consecration [the profession of the evangelical counsels or religious vows] which is deeply rooted in their baptismal consecration and which provides an ampler manifestation of it" (470). In other words, the "Decree on the Appropriate Renewal of the Religious Life" put more emphasis on the religious life as a state of living out one's baptismal commitment and less of an emphasis on it as a state of dying to the world. After The Second Vatican Council, therefore, members of religious congregations were given the option of returning to the use of their baptismal name. The taking of a religious name had signified the pre-Vatican II notion of death to the former self as well as to the world.

The "Decree on the Appropriate Renewal of the Religious Life" also directed that "religious habits should be simple and modest, at once poor and becoming. They should meet the requirements of health and be suited to the circumstances of time and place as well as to the services required by those who wear them" (478). From 1967 to 1969, the Ursuline Sisters of Cleveland modified their traditional Ursuline habit. In 1967 they began wearing a one-piece visor-like headdress and round white collar in place of the guimpe and bandeau; in 1969 they switched from the long habit to a dress, which had a jewel neckline and three-quarter length sleeves and whose hem measured right below the knees.

[156] In 1955, at the request of Pope Pius XII, the Latin American bishops established an organization to address concerns of the Catholic Church in Latin American. Various political upheavals in Latin American countries had resulted in the loss of many members or in nominal membership. Papal concern for the need to re-evangelize people nominally Catholic continued in 1961 with a letter of Pope John XXIII, delivered at a conference of Major Superiors at Notre Dame University. The letter asked the superiors to send ten per cent of their membership to Latin America by 1971.

Although the response of the North American Catholic Church and ultimately that of the diocese of Cleveland to the plight of the Latin American Church came as the consequence of papal pleas, it can also be attributed to the bishops of the United States. In 1959 they formed a committee, and as the result of meeting with the Latin American bishops, agreed to help re-evangelize the countries of Latin America by assistance through personnel, funding, and ongoing communication. A Latin American Bureau was founded in 1964 to coordinate activities, raise funds, and educate people. The final step in responding to papal requests for aid to the Latin American Church was the recruitment of diocesan priests through some organized system by diocesan bishops.

[157] M. Annunciata Witz, O.S.U., personal interview, 9 July 1991.

[158] Susan Mary Rathbun, O.S.U., personal interview, 15 Oct. 1990.

[159] Susan Mary Rathbun, O.S.U., personal interview, 15 Oct. 1990. Sister Susan Mary recalls how Dorothy questioned her when she returned from a summer of study in 1967 at the University of Arizona: Dorothy wanted to know if Susan Mary had had contact with any Native Americans, and could she suggest reservations to which she could write.

[160] Mary Jane Mertens, S.C.C., letter to Mary Eileen Boyle, O.S.U., 26 Sept. 1992.

[161] Dorothy Kazel, O.S.U., Papago Mission Diary, 15 June-8 Aug. 1969, ms., USCA, 19 June 1969 (hereafter cited as PMD).

[162] PMD, 21 June 1969.

[163] PMD, 27 June 1969.

[164] PMD, 23 June 1969.

[165] Mary Jane Mertens, S.C.C., letter to Mary Eileen Boyle, O.S.U., 26 Sept. 1992.

[166] PMD, 30 June 1969.

[167] PMD, 25 July 1969.

[168] Mary Jane Mertens, S.C.C., letter to Mary Eileen Boyle, O.S.U., 26 Sept. 1992.

[169] Hearon, *Look to This Day* 39.

[170] Hearon, *Look to This Day* 39.

[171] Hearon, *Look to This Day* 39.

[172] SHAC, 12 Feb. 1969.

[173] Kathleen Cooney, O.S.U., personal interview, 13 Oct. 1990.

[174] Hearon, *Look to This Day* 39.

[175] Witchner 3.

[176] Because Beaumont School for Girls is a college-preparatory high school, there is no business track. In the personal typing course, students learn the typing skills necessary for the preparation of papers for college.

[177] Susan Mary Rathbun, O.S.U., personal interview, 15 Oct. 1990.

[178] Rev. Kenneth Myers, personal interview, 26 June 1992. Ken had been appointed to Immaculate Concepcion Parish in La Libertad, but because he had to remain at his assigned parish in Cleveland until another diocesan priest could replace him, he did not arrive in La Libertad until September 3, 1974. Later that month he went to Antigua, Guatemala, for three months to study Spanish. Until he returned to La Libertad in mid-December 1974, Father Denis St. Marie worked with Father Paul Schindler who was also stationed in La Libertad.

[179] A casario is a little group (ten-fifteen) of houses.

[180] Dorothy Kazel, O.S.U., audiocassette to Joseph and Malvina Kazel, 31 July-2 Aug. 1974, USCA, 31 July 1974 (hereafter cited as T1).

[181] T1, 31 July 1974.

[182] T1, 31 July 1974.

[183] Dorothy Kazel, O.S.U., El Salvador Diary, 29 July-23 Aug. 1974, ms., USCA, 29 July 1974 (hereafter cited as ESD).

[184] Founded in 1960 in collaboration with the government of El Salvador and agencies such as the Catholic Relief Service (CRS) and the Agency for International Development (AID), Caritas (Latin for "love") is a food assistance and educational program operating in five dioceses of El Salvador. Through this organization food is distributed to families with expectant mothers and with children six years of age and younger. Mothers who receive the food must also attend an educational program once a month where they learn about food preparation, nutrition, child care, and health.

[185] ESD, 31 July 1974.

[186] ESD, 1 Aug. 1974.

[187] ESD, 6 Aug. 1974.

[188] Dorothy Kazel, O.S.U., letter to Joseph and Malvina Kazel, 30 July 1974, USCA.

[189] T1, 1 Aug. 1974.

[190] Dorothy Kazel, O.S.U., Costa Rica Diary, 24 Aug.-24 Nov. 1974, ms., USCA, 26 Aug. 1974 (hereafter cited as CRD).

[191] CRD, 30 Aug. 1974.

[192] CRD, 25 Oct. 1974.

[193] CRD, 9 Nov. 1974.

[194] The diary Dorothy kept of her experiences in Costa Rica is the last surviving diary of her years as a missionary in El Salvador. Martha Owen claims that Dorothy was keeping a personal journal up until her death. The journal was probably lost, however, in the transference of Dorothy's personal belongings from El Salvador to the United States after her murder.

[195] The Cleveland Diocese accepts lay women for its mission team. Rosemary Smith was the first lay woman to join the team. She arrived in El Salvador shortly after the first priests were sent there by the diocese in 1964.

[196] The CLAM Team members decided among themselves who would accompany whom to a particular area of the parish. That group would then serve the same area so that they could get to know the parishioners and the parishioners them.

[197] The term canton means "outpost." The villages and casarios were cantones or outposts of the larger towns and cities.

[198] Martha Owen, O.S.U., telephone interview, 5 Jan. 1992.

[199] Martha Owen, O.S.U., telephone interview, 5 Jan. 1992.

[200] In order to qualify as a catechist, the native lay person had to know how to read and had to be willing to commit himself or herself to the community in his or her village or casario.

[201] A cursillo is a "small course."

[202] The large training center for catechists was El Castaño, Queen of Peace Center, which was near Chirilagua. Team members would also hold large meetings of catechists in the hall of the main church of a parish. Because of increased acts of violence against the Church by the government, however, the CLAM Team discontinued large-group instruction of lay catechists around 1977 or 1978. During the war El Castaño was occupied by soldiers and gutted. With the help of funds donated by Cleveland parishes, El Castaño is presently undergoing reconstruction.

[203] The people of a village or casario who had the Eucharist built a chapel in which to house it. One of the CLAM Team's goals was to make each village or casario a Eucharistic Community.

[204] At a communion service the readings of the day (Epistle and Gospel) are read and the parts of the Mass are recited, but there is no consecration of the bread. Toward the end of the service, bread that had been previously consecrated by a priest is distributed to the community.

[205] Rev. James Kenny, letter from the Cleveland Latin American Mission Team to the Diocese of Cleveland, Apr. 1980, USCA.

[206] The readings read and reflected upon at the Liturgy of the Word were usually the readings of the day.

[207] Martha Owen, O.S.U., telephone interview, 5 Jan. 1992.

[208] Dorothy Kazel, O.S.U., audiocassette to Joseph and Malvina Kazel, 12, 14-15, 17 Apr. 1975, USCA, 12 Apr. 1975 (hereafter cited as T2).

[209] T2, 12 Apr. 1975.

[210] T2, 12 Apr. 1975.

[211] In March of 1977, Rutilio Grande, a Salvadoran Jesuit priest was murdered by the Salvadoran military, and in the spring of that year, the first professional death squads were formed. A detailed explanation of El Salvador's political situation is contained in chapter 2, "A Record of a Death."

[212] Dorothy Kazel, O.S.U., audiocassette to Joseph and Malvina Kazel, 4, 7-8, 11-12 Dec. 1976, USCA, 11 Dec. 1976.

[213] Rev. Paul Schindler, personal interview, 15 Nov. 1994.

[214] Dorothy Kazel, O.S.U., audiocassette to Joseph and Malvina Kazel, 15, 17, 19 Oct. 1978, USCA, 15 Oct. 1978.

[215] Dorothy Kazel, O.S.U., audiocassette to James and Dorothy Kazel, 17, 21 Feb. 1979, USCA, 21 Feb. 1979.

[216] Martha Owen, O.S.U., personal interview, 15 Oct. 1990.

[217] Dorothy Kazel, O.S.U., audiocassette to Joseph and Malvina Kazel, 16-17 July 1979, USCA, 16 July 1979 (hereafter cited as T6).

2. A Record of a Death

[1] John McFadden and Ruth Warner, trans., translators' preface, *Archbishop Romero: Martyr of Salvador*, by Placido Erdozain (Costa Rica: Departamento Ecumenico de Investigaciones, 1980; New York: Orbis Books, 1981) xxi.

[2] Daniel Santiago, O.Carm., "The Peace Progress in El Salvador (A Hermeneutic of Suspicion)," *America* 11 Jan. 1992: 15.

[3] Santiago 15. In his article, "The Peace Process in El Salvador (A Hermeneutic of Suspicion)," Daniel Santiago, O.Carm., describes the Indians' traditional system of communal lands:

Nuclear families kept gardens close to home for fresh fruits and vegetables. Large, extended families used fields for common grazing, cultivation of staples and some crops for sale. The extended families adopted a saint as protector and used the saint's feast day as an annual celebration and opportunity to review communal leadership. (15)

[4] Santiago 15.

[5] The "famous fourteen families" consisted of the original Spanish families who settled in the area of El Salvador after the conquest and other European and North American adventurers who came to El Salvador in the mid-nineteenth century.

[6] Santiago 16.

[7] Santiago 16.

[8] Santiago 16.

[9] Ana Carrigan, *Salvador Witness: The Life and Calling of Jean Donovan* (New York: Simon and Schuster, 1984) 80.

[10] Carrigan 80.

[11] Carrigan 81.

[12] The left-wing opposition groups that emerged during the first half of the 1970s were the guerrillas (extreme left) and the popular organizations. The guerrilla groups include the Popular Liberation Forces (FPL), the Revolutionary Army of the People (ERP), the Armed Forces of National Resistance (FARN), and the Revolutionary Party of Central American Workers (PRTC).

The popular organizations of the time were the United Popular Action Front (FAPU) and the Popular Revolutionary Bloc (BPR), which had been the largest mass organization in El Salvador. Rural and urban trade unions and the Social Democratic Party, which was the democratic opposition to the government, were the political allies of these popular organizations.

[13] The devotion of the Latin American Catholic Church to the poor has its roots in a conference of all Latin American bishops that was held in Medellin, Columbia, in 1968. According to Ana Carrigan in *Salvador Witness: The Life and Calling of Jean Donovan*, at the Medellin Conference

> the Latin American Church, bastion of the status quo and ideological force behind the conquest and enslavement of the native people, dramatically switched its allegiance from the oppressor to the oppressed. . . . The bishops signed a series of documents that would provide a Magna Carta for a new, socially active "Church of the Poor," committed to the transformation of the Latin societies. (82-83)

The Medellin Conference gave birth to a "Theology of Liberation," which Carrigan defines as "liberation from sin, but also from the consequences of sin, which the bishops defined in terms of the social evils around them: hunger, infant mortality, injustice, torture, arbitrary arrest, and the absence of any political rights for the vast majority" (83-84).

[14] Carrigan 81-82.

[15] Involvement in the politics of El Salvador has never been the intention of the CLAM Team. In a letter written to the Diocese of Cleveland in November 1979, the team states its mission role after briefly describing the ramifications of the military coup of October 15:

> To announce the Good News of Jesus and to denounce sin and injustice which cause human misery. We feel that our presence here is more important than ever, as the people in our parishes struggle to discover the road out of confusion and poverty toward lasting peace and justice.

Of special note in the missioners' explanation of their role is the phrase, "as the *people* (emphasis added) . . . struggle to discover." When I interviewed former CLAM Team member Christine Rody, V.S.C., on 11 July 1991, she reiterated the idea that the Salvadoran people must be their own agents in effecting structural changes in the government:

We would never talk about politics with the people because, first of all, we were the outsiders, and we were very much respectful of the fact that if they were going to make changes, they had to make them. They couldn't be instigated by us. We would get thrown out of the country, too, if we would get involved in it. So how can you help them if you're not there?

Non-participation in political activities is also an unspoken policy among the Cleveland missionaries. It goes without saying, however, that because their parishioners are the poor, with whom the oligarchy wishes to maintain a "patron" or father-child relationship, the missionaries' efforts to educate the poor to realize their worth and dignity as human beings could be, and unfortunately, were interpreted as political or "subversive" acts by the Salvadoran government.

[16] Carrigan 77-78.

[17] Carrigan 77.

[18] Carrigan 78.

[19] In *Archbishop Romero: Martyr of Salvador*, John McFadden and Ruth Warner define campesino as

someone who lives from the land, the fields; a landworker. In Latin America poor campesinos own very little land and so are unable to support themselves and their families from their own holdings. They are thus totally dependent on nearby landowners, in one or another arrangement that almost invariably drives them deeper and deeper into deprivation, indebtedness, desperation, and readiness for change. (xxiii)

[20] Carrigan 89.

[21] A junta, generally speaking, is an assembly, meeting, or gathering. In terms of Salvadoran politics, junta means the government or group of men in power.

[22] Carrigan 122-23.

[23] Regarding the Christian Democratic Party, Ana Carrigan claims:

From the moment the Christian Democrats had elected to remain in the government [9 March 1980], the foreign press had in large measure adopted the image assiduously promoted by the U.S. State Department, of the Salvadoran regime as a centrist government dedicated to reform. The only dissenting voice willing to clarify the confusion was raised by Archbishop Romero. (156)

[24] Carrigan 132.

[25] Carrigan 132. Glaring examples of violence committed by security forces soon after the formation of the second junta include the following: on 22 January 1980 the popular organizations and their political allies marched in the streets of San Salvador to commemorate the uprising of 1932 and were shot down by the National Guard and the police; on 17 February members of the BPR occupied the cathedral in San Salvador to protest full-scale military operations against striking harvest workers across the countryside; on March 6 the government announced the first phase of its Agrarian Reform Program, but in the weeks that followed, peasant leaders were murdered, revealing a pattern linking the reforms to the repression of peasant organizations.

[26] Although a lone, young man in street clothes, who was probably a hired assassin, had actually pulled the trigger, former military officer Major Roberto D'Aubuisson

ordered the assassination. D'Aubuisson had been an intelligence officer for the National Guard until the first junta when he left the military. Army Captain Eduardo Avila, former Captain Alvaro Saravia, and Fernando Sagrera played an active role in the assassination. At Romero's funeral on March 30, 1980, where thirty people were killed, witnesses claimed shots fired into the crowd originated from the second floor of the National Palace.

Since the murder of Rutilio Grande, S.J., Romero had publicly spoken out against the military forces and its repression of the poor as well as its domination of the government. In the month before his own murder, Romero appealed to the Christian Democrats to withdraw from the government because "at the international level [their] presence serve[d] to mask the repressive character of this regime" (qtd. in Carrigan 146). During his homily at Mass on the day before he was killed, Romero pleaded with the members of the National Guard and the police to stop murdering their own people. He claimed:

> The Church, defender of the rights of God . . . cannot remain silent in the presence of such abominations. . . . The government must understand that reforms, steeped in so much blood, are worthless. In the name of God, in the name of our tormented people whose cries rise up to heaven, I beseech you, I command you, *stop the repression*! (qtd. in Carrigan 157)

[27] Carrigan 181.

[28] Carrigan 169.

[29] Carrigan 169.

[30] Carrigan 217.

[31] Carrigan 217.

[32] Dorothy Kazel, O.S.U., and Rev. Paul Schindler, audiocassette to Martha Owen, O.S.U., 9-10 Aug. 1979, USCA, 9 Aug. 1979.

[33] Martha had sent the articles with Christine Rody who was returning to El Salvador after her yearly month-long vacation in the States. The missionaries never sent articles, letters, etc., that contained references to politics through the mail because their letters were often confiscated by the Salvadoran government.

[34] Dorothy Kazel, O.S.U. , audiocassette to Martha Owen, O.S.U., 29 Aug. 1979, USCA (hereafter cited as T8).

[35] T8.

[36] T8.

[37] Carrigan 100.

[38] Carrigan 110.

[39] The Nicaraguan Civil War broke out in 1978 when the guerrilla group, the Frente Sandinista de Liberacion Nacional ("Sandinistas") attempted to overthrow the military-dictatorship of Anastasio Somoza Debayle. They were successful, and on July 17, 1979, Somoza fled Nicaragua.

[40] Judith M. Noone, M.M., *The Same Fate as the Poor*, rev. ed. (New York: Orbis, 1995) 80.

[41] Dorothy Kazel, O.S.U., letter to M. Bartholomew McCaffrey, O.S.U., Nov. 1979, USCA.

[42] Dorothy Kazel, O.S.U., letter to family and friends, 20-30 Jan. 1980, USCA.

[43] After the first junta had collapsed on January 3, 1980, a second junta composed of Christian Democrats and the military was formed on January 9, 1980.

[44] On January 14, 1980, Cleveland diocesan priest John F. Loya and Vincentian Sister of Charity Elizabeth Kochik arrived in El Salvador. Ursuline Sister Therese Mary Osborne came on January 27.

[45] Dorothy Kazel, O.S.U., letter to M. Bartholomew McCaffrey, O.S.U., 15 Feb. 1980, USCA (hereafter cited as L4).

[46] L4.

[47] L4.

[48] Archbishop Oscar A. Romero, letter to President Jimmy Carter, trans. Cleveland Latin American Mission Team, 17 Feb. 1980, USCA.

[49] United States Catholic Missionaries, letter to President Jimmy Carter, 20 Feb. 1980, USCA.

[50] Carrigan 154.

[51] Rev. Paul Schindler, personal interview, 15 Nov. 1994. The airport Dorothy is referring to is the Comalapa International Airport which is located near the southern border of the country about a half-hour's drive east of La Libertad. At the time the airport had been newly built. Father Schindler explains why so many police were around the airport: "The military were trying to make it safe around the airport. They were fearful that since it was out in the middle of nowhere, it would be a prime area the left would attack. So, the military was trying to make sure that there were no leftists around the airport. The police had a lot of bases around there, and of course, the whole command post for the security in that area was in [nearby city of] Zacatecoluca."

[52] The University where Dorothy and Paul took the young man and his wife was the Jesuit-sponsored University of Central America (UCA). Earlier in her tape, Dorothy explains why they would not take shooting victims to one of the hospitals in San Salvador: "We took them to the University to be taken care of because you can't take them to the hospital because if they've been shot, they may never come out of the hospital again."

[53] Dorothy Kazel, O.S.U., audiocassette to Martha Owen, O.S.U., 28, 30 Mar. 1980, USCA, 28 Mar. 1980 (hereafter cited as T9).

[54] Rev. James R. Brockman, S.J., *Romero: A Life* (New York: Orbis, 1989) 245.

[55] T9, 28 Mar. 1980. For an accurate version of this section of Romero's homily of March 23, 1980, see note 26.

[56] T9, 30 Mar. 1980.

[57] T9, 30 Mar. 1980.

[58] Martha Owen, O.S.U., personal interview, 15 Oct. 1990.

[59] M. Bartholomew McCaffrey, O.S.U., telephone interview, 21 Jan. 1992.

[60] M. Bartholomew McCaffrey, O.S.U., telephone interview, 21 Jan. 1992.

[61] Noone 102-104.

[62] Dorothy Kazel, O.S.U., audiocassette to Joseph and Malvina Kazel, 3-5 June 1980, USCA, 4 June 1980 (hereafter cited as T10).

[63] Rev. Paul Schindler, personal interview, 15 Nov. 1994. Paul adds: "About a week before the women were killed, Urioste preached at the fiesta [November 21, 1980] in Tamanique. Dorothy and Jean picked him up and brought him to the fiesta. He said to me, 'I feel so safe. I got an American blonde on my right and one on my left.'"

[64] Dorothy Kazel, O.S.U., audiocassette to Martha Owen, O.S.U., 1-2, 4-5 June 1980, USCA, 1 June 1980 (hereafter cited as T11).

[65] T11, 1 June 1980.

[66] T11, 2 June 1980.

[67] The Guardia was suspicious that the missionaries were helping the people to organize themselves.

[68] T11, 2 June 1980.

[69] T11, 4 June 1980.

[70] T11, 4 June 1980.

[71] Desiring more independence, Jean moved out of the house in Zaragoza, where she had lived with Dorothy and Christine, to her own apartment above the parochial school in La Libertad during January 1980.

[72] Rev. Paul Schindler, as quoted in Carrigan 186.

[73] Carrigan 187.

[74] Noone 104.

[75] Noone 117.

[76] In *The Same Fate as the Poor*, Judith Noone, M.M., states that the colonel at the army base would occasionally release a prisoner to Church personnel (120). Ita believed that he released prisoners to them "perhaps to save face" (qtd. in Noone 120).

[77] Paul Schindler, letter from the Cleveland Latin American Mission Team to the Diocese of Cleveland, Sept., 1980, USCA.

[78] That is, the letter was delivered personally — not sent through the mail.

[79] Dorothy Kazel, O.S.U., letter to Martha Owen, O.S.U., 5 Sept. 1980, USCA (hereafter cited as L5).

[80] L5.

[81] Dorothy Kazel, O.S.U., letter to President Jimmy Carter, 23 Sept. 1980, USCA.

[82] In an interview I conducted with Christine Rody, V.S.C., on 11 July 1991, she explained how fearful she and the other CLAM Team members felt regarding the violence in El Salvador, especially during the late 1970s and 1980:

> Jean, Dorothy, and I had some serious discussions about torture because we were all afraid of torture — I mean, *really* afraid of torture! We used to laugh and say, "We don't care if they kill us, but just don't torture us!" What was so interesting was that after the summer of 1980, when we [team members] all got back from vacation and retreat, we had a team meeting and got into a conversation and learned that we had all considered death as a part of our retreat experience because we knew that it was a real possibility.

[83] Jean Donovan, as quoted in Carrigan 213.

[84] Dorothy Kazel, O.S.U., audiocassette to Joseph and Malvina Kazel, 24, 26 Oct. 1980, USCA, 24 Oct. 1980.

[85] Often when referring to the unpredictable political situation — or just to life in general — in El Salvador, the CLAM Team members would say, "Ah, saber," to mean "Who knows?" Since saber is the infinitive form "to know," the missionaries would just say its literal translation in English — "Ah, to know" — since "who knows" is so hackneyed in Spanish.

[86] Dorothy Kazel, O.S.U., letter to Joseph and Malvina Kazel, 9 Oct. 1980, USCA.

[87] Dorothy Kazel, O.S.U., audiocassette to Martha Owen, O.S.U., 21, 23-24 Oct. 1980, USCA, 21 Oct. 1980 (hereafter cited as T13).

[88] T13, 21 Oct. 1980.

[89] T13, 21 Oct. 1980.

[90] T13, 21 Oct. 1980.

[91] T13, 24 Oct. 1980.

[92] Dorothy Kazel, O.S.U., letter to Joseph and Malvina Kazel, 30 Oct. 1980, USCA. At the party Dorothy took pictures of everyone in their Halloween costumes, and the pictures did come out quite well. They were found among Dorothy's personal belongings after she was murdered and are currently housed in the archives of the Ursuline Sisters of Cleveland.

[93] Dorothy Kazel, O.S.U., letter to Joseph and Malvina Kazel, 2 Nov. 1980, USCA (hereafter cited as L9).

[94] L9.

[95] Dorothy Kazel, O.S.U., letter to Martha Owen, O.S.U., 5 Nov. 1980, USCA.

[96] John D. Blacken, letter to Dorothy Kazel, O.S.U., 7 Nov. 1980, USCA.

[97] Carrigan 231.

[98] Dorothy's tape had been mailed from Washington, D.C., and it was postmarked "Dec. 2, 1980." Apparently, she had given it to someone to mail for her in the United States. Joseph and Malvina Kazel received the tape shortly after they had been notified of her death.

[99] Dorothy Kazel, O.S.U., audiocassette to Joseph and Malvina Kazel, 14-15 Nov. 1980, USCA, 14 Nov. 1980 (hereafter cited as T14).

[100] T14, 14 Nov. 1980.

[101] T14, 14 Nov. 1980.

[102] T14, 15 Nov. 1980.

[103] Rev. Paul Schindler, personal interview, 15 Nov. 1994. According to Paul, at the ecumenical prayer service, Jean told Robert White that she had seen American-made (Huey) helicopters flying over El Salvador and that she had taken photographs of them. White's reply was, "We don't have those here." When Jean insisted that the helicopters were American — she had recognized them because at one time her father had manufactured them — White said, "We've got to talk more about this. They're not supposed to be in this country." And that was when he invited the missionaries to his residence for dinner the following Monday.

The helicopters Jean had seen really were American-made, as Paul explains: "They were coming in from Honduras which the United States Government was using as a base to ship American advisors — more than the fifty-five permitted by congressional law — into El Salvador. The government would base the advisors in Honduras, and then fly them to Salvador for a few days. So, we had many more American advisors in the country than people were aware of, and it was the helicopters that were bringing them back and forth."

Robert White had no knowledge that the additional advisors were coming into the country. Apparently, at that time he had already been informed that his tenure as ambassador to El Salvador would soon end. Higher-ranking United States Government officials were bringing the advisors into El Salvador without White's permission.

[104] Dorothy Kazel, O.S.U., letter to Martha Owen, O.S.U., 28 Nov. 1980, USCA. This letter is probably the last one Dorothy wrote before she was murdered.

[105] Robert White, personal interview, 4 June 1993.

[106] Philip Warburg and James Zorn, *Justice in El Salvador: A Case Study, A Report on the Investigation into the Killing of Four U.S. Churchwomen in El Salvador* (New York: The Lawyers Committee for International Human Rights, 20 July 1982) 22.

[107] Teresa Alexander, M.M., "Sister Dorothy Kazel, O.S.U.," Tenth-Anniversary Celebration of the Martyrdom of Dorothy Kazel, O.S.U., Ursuline College, Pepper Pike, 5 Dec. 1990.

[108] Alexander.

[109] Noone 1.

[110] Alexander.

[111] Paul Carroll, *A Report on the Investigation into the Killing of Four American Churchwomen in El Salvador* (New York: The Lawyers Committee for International Human Rights, Sept. 1981) 3.

[112] The women were killed in a cow pasture on the San Francisco Hacienda.

[113] Judge Harold Tyler, Jr., *The Churchwomen Murders: A Report to the Secretary of State* (New York: n.p., 2 Dec. 1983) 35.

[114] The facts of the case are still unknown, sixteen years later, because only one of the five guardsmen who murdered the women, Carlos Joaquin Contreras Palacios, ever confessed to the crime and gave some details of it. The other four guardsmen as well as Salvadoran military officers who knew of the murders and those who had ordered them have never given information about the sequence of events of the crime. What is presently known about the crime had been revealed from investigations conducted by the United States and the testimonies of a few eye witnesses.

[115] This witness as well as the others who talked with Paul would only give him information on the condition that their names would not be disclosed.

[116] According to *Justice in El Salvador*, 20 July 1982, at the time Dorothy and Jean picked up Maddie and Terry from the airport, a radio transmission was intercepted between military units nearby and the airport forces (23). Warburg and Zorn in *Justice in El Salvador* claim that a witness, a high-ranking politician, later reported to the U.S. Embassy that he had overheard the radio transmission, and it contained the following: "No, she didn't arrive on the flight. We'll have to wait for the next" (23). Evidence of such a message would surely suggest that the National Guard was awaiting the arrival of Maura and Ita from Nicaragua — particularly Ita, as later believed — and that a prearranged plot was in effect.

[117] Rev. Paul Schindler, personal interview, 15 Nov. 1994. Paul's theory does confirm the facts given about the murders of the North American Churchwomen in *From Madness to Hope: The Twelve-Year War in El Salvador*, the United Nations Truth Commission Report, March 1993. After the report states that Deputy Sergeant Luis Antonio Colindres Alemàn "had given orders to five of his subordinates that they should detain some people coming from Nicaragua," it continues:

> Then Colindres proceeded to the base at San Luis Talpa to notify the commandante that he should refrain from any action if he heard disturbing noises, since these noises would be resulting from an operation that he, Colindres, and his men would be engaged in. (3)

The town of San Luis Talpa is closer to the airport and Santiago Nonualco than Zacatecoluca is. The women most likely were taken to the barracks at the base located there. Also a possibility is that the guardsmen had been ordered to question the women *only*, but the situation got out of control, they raped the women, and then decided or were told to kill them.

[118] Rev. Paul Schindler, personal interview, 15 Nov. 1994. These witnesses confirm information contained in reports from several investigations conducted at the time of the murders.

[119] That is, the women were shot at close range in the back of the head. Dorothy, however, was also shot in the right shoulder. One of the five guardsmen later made a statement, as quoted in *The Churchwomen Murders: A Report to the Secretary of State* by Judge Harold S. Tyler, Jr., that explains why she was shot twice: "Jose Roberto Moreno Canjura stated that while in prison [he] had admitted that after the women were shot, he saw that one of them was still alive and that he had used his own rifle to kill her" (41).

[120] In other words the men drove in the opposite direction from the murder site.

[121] From the white van the men removed women's clothing (blouses, skirts, and dresses), a tire and jack, a shovel, papers, several sealed cardboard boxes, a tape recorder, rings, women's watches, and eyeglasses. Three days after the murder, the men burned the women's clothing in a cement tube near the Command Post Headquarters at the airport.

[122] Tyler 14-19. In his report Tyler refutes Paul Schindler's theory about the location of the women's abduction (77).

[123] As the branches measure about two inches in diameter, and the cross itself stands about three feet, the campesinos apparently meant the cross to serve as a marker. The cross is now housed in the archives of the Ursuline Sisters.

[124] Robert White, personal interview, 4 June 1993. Garcia's first response to White when he called him was, "Were they wearing habits?" His question immediately evoked a "bad feeling" for White because, as he explains, "That's the kind of standard defense that they [Salvadoran military] make — this arbitrary sharp distinction between traditional Church and new Church." White continues: "When Garcia gave me such an unusual response, I thought, 'He already knows something.'"

[125] Christine Rody, V.S.C., telephone interview, 1 Feb. 1992.

[126] Christine Rody, V.S.C., telephone interview, 1 Feb. 1992.

[127] Note especially that a villager — not the local police, military, or government officials — informed church authorities of the women's deaths and of the burial site. In April 1981 when officials of the United States Embassy identified the killers through their own investigation, they also learned that the identities of the killers were known to officials of the Salvadoran National Guard within days of the murders. The officials included the then Major Lizandro Zepeda Velasco, the National Guard officer in charge of the Guard's internal investigation, Sergeant Dagoberto Martinez, Colindres' immediate superior, Colonel Roberto Monterrosa, head of the government's official investigation of the crime, and Lieutenant Colonel Carlos Eugenio Vides Casanova, the then Director-General of the National Guard. The Truth Commission Report confirmed these findings.

In *The Churchwomen Murders: A Report to the Secretary of State* by Judge Harold R. Tyler, Jr., several days after the murders, Colindres approached Sergeant Dagoberto Martinez and reported that "the problem regarding the nuns is me" (23). Dagoberto and the other officials responded to Colindres' confession by concealing it from the outside world and ordering the transfer of the killers from their airport posts and the switching of their weapons to make detection more difficult. Immediately following the crime, Martinez retired from the National Guard and moved to Los Angeles, California.

[128] The sandals were further proof that the located bodies were those of foreigners because few Salvadoran women own a pair of sandals.

[129] Rev. Paul Schindler, personal interview, 15 Nov. 1994.

[130] Rev. Paul Schindler, personal interview, 15 Nov. 1994.

[131] Rev. John Spain, M.M., personal interview, 23 June 1992.

[132] Because they had determined that the women had been killed by the military, the doctors, fearing for their own safety, would not perform the autopsies.

[133] Rev. Paul Schindler, personal interview, 15 Nov. 1994.

[134] Carlos Cuellar Ortiz, M.D., Autopsy Report, ts., trans. Martha Owen, O.S.U. (San Salvador: 4 Dec. 1980). Note that the report does not say that Dorothy's wounds were gunshot wounds.

[135] Dorothy Kazel, O.S.U., letter from the Cleveland Latin American Mission Team to the Diocese of Cleveland, Nov. 1980, USCA. (hereafter cited as L10).

[136] D. Kazel, L10.

3. A Woman of Dimensions: Dorothy's Personality

[1] Muriel Petrasek, S.N.D., personal interview, 7 Sept. 1991.

[2] Donna Zaller, telephone interview, 1 Nov. 1991.

[3] Rev. Eldon Reichert, S.M., personal interview, 12 Sept. 1991.

[4] Eugene Best, telephone interview, 8 Nov. 1991.

[5] Lucy Marie Kazlauskas, O.S.F., telephone interview, 16 Sept. 1991.

[6] Patricia Healey, telephone interview, 29 Oct. 1991.

[7] Donald Kollenborn, telephone interview, 17 Sept. 1991.

[8] Donald Kollenborn, telephone interview, 17 Sept. 1991.

[9] Marilyn Friga, telephone interview, 26 Sept. 1991.

[10] Frances Harbert, personal interview, 10 July 1991.

[11] M. Helene Balciunas, O.S.F., personal interview, 19 Oct. 1991.

[12] M. Helene Balciunas, O.S.F., personal interview, 19 Oct. 1991.

[13] Catherine O'Malley, S.N.D., personal interview, 9 July 1991.

[14] Eileen Best, telephone interview, 8 Nov. 1991.

[15] Muriel Petrasek, S.N.D., personal interview, 7 Sept. 1991.

[16] Anna Margaret Gilbride, O.S.U., personal interview, 12 Oct. 1990.

[17] Kathleen Cooney, O.S.U., personal interview, 13 Oct. 1990.

[18] Barbara Jean Sever, O.S.U., personal interview, 11 July 1991.

[19] Christine Rody, V.S.C., personal interview, 11 July 1991.

[20] John F. Loya, *Gifts from the Poor* (Nashville: Winston-Derek, 1990) 37-38.

[21] Donald Kollenborn, telephone interview, 17 Sept. 1992.

[22] Marilyn Friga, telephone interview, 26 Sept. 1991.

[23] Marilyn Friga, telephone interview, 26 Sept. 1991.

[24] Frances Harbert, personal interview, 10 July 1991.

[25] Frances Harbert, personal interview, 10 July 1991.

[26] Martha Owen, O.S.U. personal interview, 15 Oct. 1990.

[27] Frances Harbert, personal interview, 10 July 1991.

[28] Dolores R. Leckey, introduction, *Women and Creativity*, by Leckey (Mahwah: Paulist, 1991) 1.

[29] A picture of the "Madonna of the Street" (Blessed Virgin Mary) in a white 2 1/2" by 2 3/4" plastic frame edged in gold was the award Dorothy received for being chosen the Valentine Queen of her sixth grade class. The small framed picture is still in its cardboard gift box on which is hand-printed "Valentine Queen, St. George School, sixth grade, Dorothy Kazel."

[30] Dorothy's prayer books and those that relate to her life as an Ursuline Sister include two Bibles (one in English and one in Spanish); a copy of the New Testament of the Jerusalem Bible; *Christian Prayer: The Liturgy of the Hours; Growth in the Knowledge of Our Lord: Meditations for Every Day*, Vol. I, by Mother M. Fidelis (used in the novitiate); *Ursulines in Training: A Study Based Upon the Counsels of Saint Angela Merici* by M.Gertrude Ftechschulte, O.S.U.; *The Rule of Our Holy Father Saint Augustine and The Constitutions of The Institute of the Ursuline Nuns of Cleveland, Ohio; The Writings of Saint Angela Merici; The Counsels of Saint Angela: A Meditative Approach Prepared by the Ursuline Nuns of Cleveland; Look to This Day: Ursuline Frontiers and Horizons, 1950-75* by M. Michael Francis Hearon, O.S.U., and *The Saint Joseph Daily Missal*.

[31] At their third hemispheric conference in Puebla, Mexico, in October 1978, the organization of the bishops of twenty-three Latin American countries, the Consejo Episcopal Latinamericano (CELAM), discussed evangelization in Latin America and reaffirmed their preferential option for the poor and their commitment to human rights. The four sections of their report are entitled, "Pastoral Vision of Latin American Reality," "God's Design upon the Reality of Latin America, " "Evangelization in the Latin American Church: Communion and Participation," and "The Missionary Church at the Service of Evangelization in Latin America."

[32] Photographs developed from the film found in Dorothy's camera at the time of her death include those of Jean Donovan holding her guitar at a parish Mass, Dorothy, Teresa Alexander, M.M., and Monsignor Ricardo Urioste, vicar general of the archdiocese, in front of the church in Tamanique on November 21, 1980, Maura Clarke, M.M., and Ita Ford, M.M., at the airport before leaving for Managua, Nicaragua, on November 24, 1980, and American ambassador Robert White and his wife Mary Anne at their American Embassy residence on December 1, 1980.

[33] HSD, 13 Jan. 1956.

[34] HSD, 18 Jan. 1956.

[35] The Passion Play is an enactment of the Passion and Death of Jesus Christ and is usually performed during Lent.

[36] HSD, 18 Mar. 1956.

[37] HSD, 20 Jan. 1956.

[38] Dorothy was suspended from her office of Senior Class President and Marilyn Friga from her office of secretary of the Student Council.

[39] HSD, 11 Jan. 1957. Dorothy kept a record of the first eleven days of 1957 by writing in the blank spaces of her 1956 diary under the appropriate dates.

[40] "SSCA Leads Teenagers to Catholic Activeness," *The Tower* 18 Oct. 1956: 3.

[41] The Timber Wolves were a reunion group from World War II.

[42] The "big" chaperone Dorothy mentions here was the chaperone of this particular meeting of the Summer School of Catholic Action.

[43] HSD, 31 Aug. 1956.

[44] HSD, 31 Dec. 1955.

[45] Malvina Kazel, personal interview, 12 Feb. 1991.

[46] Marilyn Friga, telephone interview, 26 Sept. 1991.

[47] Dorothy Kazel, O.S.U., Photograph Album, June 1953-Dec. 1955, ms., USCA, 11 Oct. 1953 (hereafter cited as PA).

[48] PA, 7 May 1955.

[49] PA, 11 Oct. 1953.

[50] PA, 10-17 July 1954.

[51] PA, 10-17 July 1954.

[52] Christine Rody, personal interview, 11 July 1991.

[53] Christine Rody, personal interview, 11 July 1991.

[54] Christine Rody, personal interview, 11 July 1991.

[55] Christine Rody, personal interview, 11 July 1991.

[56] Christine Rody, personal interview, 11 July 1991.

[57] T1, 2 Aug. 1974.

[58] The correct Spanish word for name is "llama."

[59] Dorothy Kazel, O.S.U., audiocassette to the Sisters of Beaumont Convent, 5, 10-11 Aug. 1974, USCA, 5 Aug. 1974.

[60] T6, 16 July 1979.

[61] Joan Mury, M.M. letter to Joseph and Malvina Kazel, 25 Jan. 1981, USCA.

[62] Mercita Thailing, personal interview, 5 Oct. 1991.

[63] Mercita Thailing, personal interview, 5 Oct. 1991.

[64] Malvina Kazel, personal interview, 12 Feb. 1991.

[65] Rev. Eldon Reichert, S.M., personal interview, 12 Sept. 1991.

[66] Rev. Eldon Reichert, S.M., personal interview, 12 Sept. 1991.

[67] Donald Kollenborn, telephone interview, 17 Sept. 1991.

[68] Marilyn Friga, telephone interview, 26 Sept. 1991.

[69] Mercita Thailing, personal interview, 5 Oct. 1991.

[70] Mercita Thailing, personal interview, 5 Oct. 1991.

[71] Barbara Jean Sever, O.S.U., personal interview, 11 July 1991.

[72] Marilyn Friga, telephone interview, 26 Sept. 1991.

[73] Marilyn Friga, telephone interview, 26 Sept. 1991.

[74] Marilyn Friga, telephone interview, 26 Sept. 1991.

[75] Dorothy Kazel, O.S.U., Journal 4, Jan. 1965-Aug. 1967, ms., USCA, 15 Jan. 1967.

[76] Dorothy Kazel, O.S.U., Journal 5, July 1968-June 1972, ms., USCA, 11 Aug. 1968 (hereafter cited as J5). Making resolutions at the end of an annual retreat is a common practice among religious women.

[77] Donna Zaller, telephone interview, 1 Nov. 1991.

[78] J5, 28 June 1972.

[79] Donald Kollenborn, telephone interview, 17 Sept. 1991.

[80] Donna Zaller, telephone interview, 1 Nov. 1991.

[81] Donna Zaller, telephone interview, 1 Nov. 1991.

[82] Donald Kollenborn, telephone interview, 17 Sept. 1991.

[83] Donald Kollenborn, telephone interview, 17 Sept. 1991.

[84] Donna Zaller, telephone interview, 1 Nov. 1991.

[85] Donna Zaller, telephone interview, 1 Nov. 1991.

[86] Donald Kollenborn, telephone interview, 17 Sept. 1991.

[87] J5, 11 Aug. 1968.

[88] J5, 1 Jan. 1969.

[89] Dorothy Kazel, O.S.U., Journal 8, Jan. 1974-Apr. 1974, ms., USCA, 4 Jan. 1974 (hereafter cited as J8).

[90] J8, 4 Jan. 1974.

[91] J8, 5 Jan. 1974.

[92] J8, 5 Jan. 1974.

[93] J8, 5 Jan. 1974.

[94] Dorothy Kazel, O.S.U., Journal 9, June 1974, ms., USCA, n.d.

[95] Dorothy Kazel, O.S.U., Journal 6, 10-17 June 1973, ms., USCA, 10 June 1973 (hereafter cited as J6).

[96] J6, 10 June 1973.

[97] Martha Owen, O.S.U., personal interview, 15 Oct. 1990.

[98] Martha Owen, O.S.U., personal interview, 15 Oct. 1990.

[99] Christine Rody, V.S.C., personal interview, 11 July 1991.

[100] Christine Rody, V.S.C., personal interview, 11 July 1991.

[101] Christine Rody, V.S.C., personal interview, 11 July 1991.

[102] Patricia Murray, M.M., personal interview, 8 June 1993.

[103] Donna Zaller left the congregation of the Ursuline Sisters of Cleveland in 1972 and was working In Washington D.C. in 1980.

[104] Donna Zaller, telephone interview, 1 Nov. 1991.

[105] Donna Zaller, telephone interview, 1 Nov. 1991.

[106] Donna Zaller, telephone interview, 1 Nov. 1991.

[107] Donna Zaller, telephone interview, 1 Nov. 1991.

[108] Donna Zaller, telephone interview, 1 Nov. 1991.

[109] Marilyn Friga, telephone interview, 26 Sept. 1991.

[110] Lucy Marie Kazlauskas, O.S.F., personal interview, 19 Oct. 1991.

[111] Frances Harbert, personal interview, 10 July 1991.

[112] Donald Kollenborn, telephone interview, 17 Sept. 1991.

[113] Donald Kollenborn, telephone interview, 17 Sept. 1991.

[114] Barbara Jean Sever, O.S.U., personal interview, 11 July 1991.

[115] T7, 9 Aug. 1979.

[116] Anna Margaret Gilbride, O.S.U., personal interview, 12 Oct. 1990.

[117] Anita Whitely, O.S.U., personal interview, 23 Feb. 1995.

[118] Angelita Zawada, O.S.U., personal interview, 23 Feb. 1995.

[119] Marilyn Friga, telephone interview, 26 Sept. 1991.

[120] Mercita Thailing, telephone interview, 24 Sept. 1991.

[121] Rev. Ernest Hepner, personal interview, 18 Nov. 1994.

[122] Rev. Ernest Hepner, personal interview, 18 Nov. 1994.

[123] Dorothy had been experiencing nausea and an upset stomach.

[124] Rev. Ernest Hepner, personal interview, 18 Nov. 1994.

[125] Dorothy Kazel, O.S.U., "Final Profession Summer," unbound journal entry, 13 June 1968, ms., USCA (hereafter cited as UJE3).

[126] UJE3.

[127] Donna Zaller, telephone interview, 1 Nov. 1991.

[128] Donna Zaller, telephone interview, 1 Nov. 1991.

[129] Donna Zaller, telephone interview, 1 Nov. 1991.

[130] Donna Zaller, telephone interview, 1 Nov. 1991.

[131] Ellen Roonan, telegram to Dorothy Kazel, O.S.U., 13 Aug. 1968, USCA.

[132] Christine Rody, V.S.C., personal interview, 11 July 1991. Priests and Sisters from congregations other than Maryknoll and diocesan priests can serve for a period up to six years in Maryknoll-sponsored missions as Maryknoll Associates.

[133] T8, 29 Aug. 1979.

[134] At this time Dorothy had planned to return home for good in June of 1980. After the assassination of Archbishop Oscar Romero on March 24, 1980, she was asked to serve on the CLAM Team an additional year. She then scheduled her final return to Cleveland for May 1981.

[135] Because of her work with the poor, Dorothy might have been wondering how the Ursulines incorporate the spirit of poverty of St. Francis of Assisi into their lives and ministry.

[136] Dorothy apparently believed that the Cleveland Ursulines were too provincial and needed to develop relationships with other Ursuline Congregations in the United States and Canada. One way such relationships could be fostered was through the Ursuline Institutes, annual meetings in which members from all the North American Ursuline Congregations shared their ideas regarding the vision of St. Angela Merici, foundress of the Ursulines, and various angles of contemporary religious life. Dorothy was very interested in the Ursuline Institutes, and in fact, planned to attend the one scheduled for the summer of 1981.
    In a tape to Martha Owen on January 6, 1980, Dorothy claims, "I would love to get involved with them [Ursuline Institutes] when I get home. . . . It sounds interesting — all the insights about Angela and what our charism [a congregation's distinctive way of living out religious life] is, and that really is exciting to me." She then adds, "I don't know how much we'll ever grow as Cleveland Ursulines, but there certainly are other Ursuline groups that sound very enticing."

[137] Among the Maryknoll Sisters who served in Nicaragua, Dorothy sensed a bond of deep friendship as well as a good working relationship. She got to know some of these Maryknoll Sisters quite well in the few years before her death.

[138] A member of the CLAM Team, Denny, Father Denis St. Marie, was serving at the parish of Chirilagua in 1979. He had been one of the first two priests sent by the Cleveland Diocese to El Salvador in 1964 to open a mission in the Diocese of San Miguel.

[139] Dorothy Kazel, O.S.U., Journal 11, Oct. 1976-Nov. 1979, ms., USCA, 12 Nov. 1979 (hereafter cited as Jll).

[140] Jll, 16 Nov. 1979.

[141] Dorothy Kazel, O.S.U., letter to Sheila Marie Tobbe, O.S.U., 2 Oct. 1979, USCA.

[142] Sheila Marie Tobbe, O.S.U., personal interview, 21 Sept. 1991.

[143] Sheila Marie Tobbe, O.S.U., personal interview, 21 Sept. 1991.

[144] During a religious congregation's chapter, a lengthy meeting convened every four years, elected delegates from the congregation determine goals for the upcoming four years, discuss relevant issues, and vote to change various regulations, such as those pertaining to dress.

[145] T8. In a tape she had sent to Martha earlier that month (August 9, 1979) Dorothy said, "This is probably the hardest time for vocation. . . . I get angry, upset, and impatient with where we're at or what we're doing but not in the sense that I want to leave our community. It's just that I get sick of being where we're at and not being someplace else."

[146] Beaumont's large community consisted of persons of diverse backgrounds and personalities. As problems do arise when such a mixed group lives together, Beaumont was no exception. Dorothy had obviously heard about some of the problems of the community.

[147] Dorothy Kazel, O.S.U., audiocassette to Martha Owen, O.S.U., 6, 10-11 Jan. 1980, USCA, Jan. 6, 1980 (hereafter cited as T18).

[148] T18.

[149] J5, 9 Feb. 1971.

4. A Woman of Depth: Dorothy's Spirituality

[1] Christine Rody, V.S.C., personal interview, 11 July 1991.

[2] Mercita Thailing, personal interview, 5 Oct. 1991.

[3] Frances Harbert, personal interview, 10 July 1991.

[4] Catherine O'Malley, S.N.D., personal interview, 9 July 1991.

[5] Frances Harbert, personal interview, 10 July 1991.

[6] Frances Harbert, personal interview, 10 July 1991.

[7] Catherine O'Malley, S.N.D., personal interview, 9 July 1991.

[8] Catherine O'Malley, S.N.D., personal interview, 9 July 1991.

[9] HSD, 31 Dec. 1955.

[10] HSD, 4 Mar. 1956.

[11] USCAF, 3. Two questions stated on the application form are "How often do you receive the Sacrament of Penance? Holy Communion?" Dorothy respectively answered the questions, "twice a month" and "daily."

[12] Anna Margaret Gilbride, O.S.U., personal interview, 12 Oct. 1990.

[13] Marilyn Friga, telephone interview, 26 Sept. 1991.

[14] Marilyn Friga, telephone interview, 26 Sept. 1991.

[15] Marilyn Friga, telephone interview, 26 Sept. 1991.

[16] Mercita Thailing, personal interview, 5 Oct. 1991.

[17] Mary Jo Lackamp, personal interview, 14 Nov. 1991.

[18] Kathleen Cooney, O.S.U., personal interview, 13, Oct. 1990.

[19] Donald Kollenborn, telephone interview, 17 Sept. 1991.

[20] Marilyn Friga, telephone interview, 26 Sept. 1991.

[21] Catherine O'Malley, S.N.D., personal interview, 9 July 1991.

[22] Aspirants were young women who desired to join the Roman Catholic Sisterhood. At Notre Dame Academy in the 1950s, students who sought to become Notre Dame Sisters became aspirants in the ninth grade, and during the second semester of their senior year, they formally entered the Notre Dame Congregation as postulants. Notre Dame aspirants took the regular high school course of study and participated in extra-curricular activities. They lived in the convent, which was located on the third and fourth floors of the Academy but were permitted to go home to their families during vacation periods.

[23] Catherine O'Malley, S.N.D., personal interview, 9 July 1991.

[24] Helen Marie Davidson, O.S.U., telephone interview, 29 Oct. 1991.

[25] Helen Marie Davidson, O.S.U., telephone interview, 29 Oct. 1991.

[26] Donald Kollenborn, telephone interview, 26 Feb. 1992.

[27] Malvina Kazel, personal interview, 15 Oct. 1990.

[28] Malvina Kazel, personal interview, 15 Oct. 1990.

[29] Malvina Kazel, personal interview, 15 Oct. 1990.

[30] USCAF, 4.

[31] Helen Marie Davidson, O.S.U., personal interview, 11 Nov. 1991.

[32] Helen Marie Davidson, O.S.U., personal interview, 11 Nov. 1991.

[33] Catherine O'Malley, S.N.D., personal interview, 9 July 1991.

[34] Mercita Thailing, telephone interview, 24 Sept. 1991.

[35] Helen Marie Davidson, O.S.U., personal interview, 11 Nov. 1991.

[36] Anna Margaret Gilbride, O.S.U., personal interview, 12 Oct. 1990.

[37] John F. Loya, *Gifts from the Poor* (Nashville: Winston-Derek, 1990) 39.

[38] Donald Kollenborn, telephone interview, 17 Sept. 1991.

[39] Donald Kollenborn, telephone interview, 17 Sept. 1991.

[40] Donna Zaller, telephone interview, 1 Nov. 1991.

[41] Malvina Kazel, personal interview, 15 Oct. 1990.

[42] Mercita Thailing, personal interview, 5 Oct. 1991.

[43] Mercita Thailing, personal interview, 5 Oct. 1991.

[44] Mercita Thailing, personal interview, 5 Oct. 1991.

[45] Donald Kollenborn, telephone interview, 26 Feb. 1992.

[46] Donald Kollenborn, telephone interview, 17 Sept. 1991.

[47] Donald Kollenborn, telephone interview, 17 Sept. 1991.

[48] Donald Kollenborn, telephone interview, 26 Feb. 1992.

[49] Donald Kollenborn, telephone interview, 26 Feb. 1992.

[50] Donna Zaller, telephone interview, 1 Nov. 1991.

[51] Dorothy Kazel, O.S.U., Journal 10, 14-19 June 1975, ms., USCA, 16 June 1975.

[52] Dorothy Kazel, O.S.U., "First Profession Retreat Resolutions," unbound journal entry, 7 Aug. 1963, ms., USCA (hereafter cited as UJEl).

[53] UJEl.

[54] UJEl.

[55] UJEl.

[56] Dorothy Kazel, O.S.U., "Juniorate Retreat Resolutions," unbound journal entry, 20 Jan. 1965, ms., Ursuline College Library, Pepper Pike (hereafter cited as UJE2).

[57] An examen is a mental examination of conscience, usually performed daily.

[58] Dorothy Kazel, O.S.U., "Sacred Heart Academy (A)," unbound journal entry, 27 Aug. 1965, ms., USCA.

[59] Dorothy Kazel, O.S.U., "Sacred Heart Academy (B)," unbound journal entry, 29 Aug. 1965, ms., USCA.

[60] Dorothy Kazel, O.S.U., "Sacred Heart Academy (C)," unbound journal entry, 1 Sept. 1965, ms., USCA.

[61] Dorothy Kazel, O.S.U., "Sacred Heart Academy (D)," unbound journal entry, 3 Sept. 1965, ms., USCA.

[62] J6, 16 June 1973.

[63] J6, 16 June 1973.

[64] J11, 11 Nov. 1979.

[65] Susan Mary Rathbun, O.S.U., personal interview, 15 Oct. 1990.

[66] Susan Mary Rathbun, O.S.U., personal interview, 15 Oct. 1990.

[67] Martha Owen, O.S.U., personal interview, 15 Oct. 1990.

[68] Martha Owen, O.S.U., personal interview, 15 Oct. 1990.

[69] Night Prayer in the Liturgy of the Hours is the last prayer of the day, said just before going to bed.

[70] Christine Rody, V.S.C., personal interview, 11 July 1991.

[71] Donna Zaller, telephone interview, 27 Nov. 1991.

[72] Donna Zaller, telephone interview, 27 Nov. 1991. Daisies were Dorothy's favorite flowers.

[73] Cell, a monastic term, is a nun's or a monk's bedroom.

[74] Donna Zaller, telephone interview, 27 Nov. 1991.

[75] Martha Owen, O.S.U., personal interview, 15 Oct. 1990.

[76] PMD, 29 July 1969.

[77] PMD, 31 July 1969.

[78] PMD, 3 Aug. 1969.

[79] PMD, 4 July 1969.

[80] PMD, 8 July 1969.

[81] Malvina Kazel, personal interview, 15 Oct. 1990.

[82] Malvina Kazel, personal interview, 15 Oct. 1990.

[83] Donna Zaller, telephone interview, 27 Nov. 1991.

[84] Donna Zaller, telephone interview, 27 Nov. 1991.

[85] Christine Rody, V.S.C., personal interview, 11 July 1991.

[86] Christine Rody, V.S.C., personal interview, 11 July 1991.

[87] T6, 17 July 1979.

[88] T10, 4 June 1980

[89] T9, 28 Mar. 1980.

[90] Martha Owen, O.S.U., personal interview, 15 Oct. 1990.

[91] Martha Owen, O.S.U., personal interview, 15 Oct. 1990.

[92] Catherine O'Malley, S.N.D., personal interview, 9 July 1991.

[93] Kathleen Cooney, O.S.U., personal interview, 13 Oct. 1990.

[94] Anna Margaret Gilbride, O.S.U., personal interview, 12 Oct. 1990.

[95] Anna Margaret Gilbride, O.S.U., personal interview, 12 Oct. 1990.

[96] Donna Zaller, telephone interview, 27 Nov. 1991.

[97] Madeline Dorsey, M.M., personal interview, 10 Oct. 1991.

[98] Madeline Dorsey, M.M., personal interview, 10 Oct. 1991.

[99] Dorothy saved notes of retreats she attended from 1961, her Clothing retreat, through 1968, her Final Profession retreat. Notes from retreats she made in 1972, 1973, 1975, 1976, and 1979 also survive.

[100] Dorothy Kazel, O.S.U., Journal 1, Aug. 1961-Feb. 1962, ms., USCA, 2 Aug. 1961 (hereafter cited as J1).

[101] J1, 2 Aug. 1961.

[102] J1, 3 Aug. 1961.

[103] J1, 7 Aug. 1961.

[104] J1, 3 Aug. 1961.

[105] Dorothy Kazel, O.S.U., Journal 2, Aug. 1963-Jan. 1964, ms., USCA, 3 Aug. 1963 (hereafter cited as J2).

[106] J2, 9 Aug. 1963.

[107] J4, 18 Jan. 1965.

[108] J4, 16 Jan. 1965.

[109] J1, 4 Aug. 1961.

[110] J1, 6 Aug. 1961.

[111] J2, 25 Jan. 1964.

[112] J1, 29 Jan. 1962.

[113] J2, 27 Jan. 1964.

[114] J2, 27 Jan. 1964.

[115] J1, 2 Feb. 1962.

[116] J2, 8 Aug. 1963.

[117] J2, 29 Jan. 1964.

[118] John Carmody, "Vatican II Spirituality," *The Westminster Dictionary of Christian Spirituality*, ed. Gordon S. Wakefield (Philadelphia: Westminster, 1983) 384.

[119] J4, 1 Aug. 1967.

[120] J4, 2 Aug. 1967.

[121] J4, 4 Aug. 1967.

[122] J4, 6 Aug. 1967.

[123] J4, 6 Aug. 1967.

[124] J4, 2 Aug. 1967.

[125] J4, 3 Aug. 1967. Note the extreme difference in meaning in this definition of the purpose of religious life from the one expressed in note 112.

[126] J4, 3 Aug. 1967.

[127] J4, 4 Aug. 1967.

[128] Dorothy is quoting Saint Augustine here.

[129] Anna Margaret Gilbride, O.S.U., personal interview, 12 Oct. 1990.

[130] Saint Augustine, as quoted in Dorothy Kazel, O.S.U., Journal 3, Jan. 1964-Mar. 1965, ms., USCA, 1964 (hereafter cited as J3).

[131] J3, 1964.

[132] Saint Augustine, as quoted in J3, 1965.

[133] J3, 1965.

[134] Saint John of the Cross, as quoted in Dorothy Kazel, O.S.U., Notebook of College Course Notes, Feb.-July 1963, ms., USCA, 27 June 1963.

[135] Saint Catherine of Siena, as quoted in J3

[136] Teilhard de Chardin, S.J., as quoted in Dorothy Kazel, O.S.U., Journal 7, 1973, ms., USCA, n.d. (hereafter cited as J7).

[137] Teilhard de Chardin, S.J., as quoted in J3, 1965.

[138] Louis Evely was a popular spiritual writer of the 1960s.

[139] Carlo Carretto wrote numerous spiritual books during the 1970s and 1980s and continues to write today.

[140] Louis Evely, as quoted in J5.

[141] Carlo Carretto, as quoted in J7, n.d.

[142] Dorothy Kazel, O.S.U., "Aphorism (A)," unbound journal entry, n.d, ms., USCA.

[143] Dorothy Kazel, O.S.U., "Aphorism (B)," unbound journal entry, n.d, ms., USCA.

[144] Dorothy Kazel, O.S.U., "Aphorism (C)," unbound journal entry, n.d., ms., USCA.

[145] Dorothy Kazel, O.S.U., "Canonical Retreat Resolutions," unbound journal entry, 3 Feb. 1962, ms., USCA.

[146] UJE1.

[147] UJE2.

[148] UJE2.

[149] J4, 10 Aug. 1966.

[150] J5, 11 Aug. 1968.

[151] J5, 28 June 1972.

[152] J5, 28 June 1972.

[153] These initial journal entries consist of the record of her prayer life that Dorothy kept for several days before she began to teach at Sacred Heart Academy. They are quoted in the text above.

[154] Except for some brief personal reflections Dorothy wrote while on retreat in Guatemala from November 11-16, 1979, no other personal writing from her years in El Salvador exists. Short diaries that she kept during her first few weeks in El Salvador and of her time at the Language Institute in Costa Rica only survive.

[155] UJE3.

[156] Dorothy Kazel, O.S.U., "Sacred Heart Academy (E)," unbound journal entry, 1 Nov. 1970, ms., USCA.

[157] J6, 10 June 1973.

[158] J6, 10 June 1973.

[159] Dorothy Kazel, O.S.U., "Sacred Heart Academy (F)," unbound journal entry, 9 May 1970, ms., USCA.

[160] Dorothy Kazel, O.S.U., "Sacred Heart Academy (G)," unbound journal entry, Sept. 1970, ms.,USCA.

[161] J7, n.d.

[162] J8, 7 Jan. 1974.

[163] J8, 20 Mar. 1974.

[164] J8, 14 Jan. 1974.

[165] J8, 19 Jan. 1974.

[166] J8, 22 Feb. 1974.

[167] J8, 14 Jan. 1974.

[168] J8, 1 Jan. 1974.

[169] J8, 19 Jan. 1974.

[170] J8, 25 Mar. 1974.

[171] Dorothy Kazel, O.S.U., "Beaumont School for Girls (A)," unbound journal entry, 24 June 1974, ms., USCA.

[172] J8, 19 Jan. 1974.

5. A Woman of Dedication: Dorothy's Missionary Ministry

[1] To get some input from the Sisters on their ministry preferences, Mother Bartholomew McCaffrey would send one of these questionnaires every other year to each Sister in the congregation.

[2] The Parish School of Religion (PSR) is the program of instruction of Catholic doctrine for the children of parishioners who do not attend the parish elementary school or a Catholic high school. In former years the program was called the Confraternity of Christian Doctrine (CCD) program.

[3] Dorothy Kazel, O.S.U., Ursuline Sisters of Cleveland: Ministry Preference Form, ms., USCA, 2 (hereafter cited as USCMPF). The official title of the renewal program is "Christ Renews His Parish," and its general purpose is to deepen the spirituality of the total parish.

[4] USCMPF, 2.

[5] USCMPF, 2.

[6] Margaret La Ganke, personal interview, 25 June 1996.

[7] Susan Mary Rathbun, O.S.U., personal interview, 15 Oct. 1990.

[8] North Central Association of Colleges and Secondary Schools, *Beaumont School for Girls Summary of 1974-76 Self-Study* (Ohio: North Central Association of Colleges and Secondary Schools, 2, 6-7 Dec. 1976) 9.

[9] Susan Mary Rathbun, O.S.U., personal interview, 15 Oct. 1990.

[10] Martha Mooney, O.S.U., personal interview, 14 Oct. 1994.

[11] J8, 3 Jan. 1974.

[12] J8, 16 Feb. 1974.

[13] J8, 8 Jan. 1974.

[14] J8, 15 Jan. 1974.

[15] J8, 29 Jan. 1974.

[16] Rev. Eldon Reichert, S.M., personal interview, 12 Sept. 1991.

[17] Catherine M. Harmer, *Religious Life in the 21st Century: A Contemporary Journey into Canaan* (Mystic: Twenty-Third, 1995) 102-103.

[18] L1.

[19] L1.

[20] L1.

[21] L1.

[22] L1.

[23] Alice Brickman, O.S.U., was one of the first two Ursuline Sisters to join the Cleveland Latin American Mission Team. She served in El Salvador from 1968-74.

[24] Dorothy Kazel, O.S.U., "Beaumont School for Girls (B)," unbound journal entry, 4 July 1974, ms., USCA.

[25] Sheila Marie Tobbe, O.S.U., personal interview, 21 Sept. 1991.

[26] Sheila Marie Tobbe, O.S.U., personal interview, 21 Sept. 1991.

[27] Theresa Kane, R.S.M., as quoted in Mary Badar Papa, "'Fight Sexism, Paternalism in Church' — Kane," *National Catholic Reporter* 5 Sept. 1980: 23.

[28] Theresa Kane, R.S.M., as quoted in Papa 23.

[29] Theresa Kane, R.S.M., as quoted in Papa 23.

[30] Dorothy Kazel, O.S.U., letter to Theresa Kane, R.S.M., 6 Oct. 1980, OSCA (hereafter cited as L12).

[31] L12.

[32] L12.

[33] Kathleen Cooney, O.S.U., personal interview, 13 Oct. 1990.

[34] Dorothy Kazel, O.S.U., letter to the Sisters of Beaumont Convent, 10 May 1976, OSCA (hereafter cited as L13).

[35] Dorothy Kazel, O.S.U., audiocassette to Joseph and Malvina Kazel, 11-12, 16 Dec. 1975, USCA, 11 Dec. 1975.

[36] Dorothy Kazel, O.S.U., audiocassette to Joseph and Malvina Kazel, 1,3,5 Mar. 1976, USCA, 1 Mar. 1976.

[37] L13.

[38] L13.

[39] L13.

[40] L13.

[41] Dorothy Kazel, O.S.U., "First Stirrings of Religious Life," *Universe Bulletin* 18 Mar. 1977: 9.

[42] Dorothy Kazel, O.S.U., letter from the Cleveland Latin American Mission Team to the Diocese of Cleveland, June 1977, USCA.

[43] L10.

[44] L10.

[45] L10.

[46] Christine Rody, V.S.C., personal interview, 11 July 1991.

[47] L13.

[48] Christine Rody, V.S.C., personal interview, 11 July 1991..

[49] Christine Rody, V.S.C., personal interview, 11 July 1991.

[50] Maria del Rosario Mendez de Heron, personal interview, 26 June 1991.

[51] Andres Pineda, personal interview, 21 June 1992.

[52] Maria Rosa Rivera, personal interview, 21 June 1992.

[53] Although Sheila Marie Tobbe, O.S.U., never worked with Dorothy in El Salvador, she visited her there for a few weeks in December 1979.

[54] Sheila Marie Tobbe, O.S.U., personal interview, 21 Sept. 1991..

[55] Madeline Dorsey, M.M., personal interview, 10 Oct. 1991.

[56] Teresa Alexander, M.M., personal interview, 10 Oct. 1991.

[57] Dorothy Kazel, O.S.U., letter to Martha Owen, O.S.U., 3 Oct. 1979, USCA.

Epilogue: The Significance of a Death

[1] William D. Rogers and William G. Bowdler, *Report to the President: Special Mission to El Salvador* (Washington D.C.: n.p., 12 Dec. 1980) 10.

[2] Dorothy's autopsy was conducted on December 23, 1980. According to FBI reports filed from March through May of 1981 and declassified in September of 1982, the bullet fragments removed from Dorothy's body matched a type of bullet manufactured by two separate West German firms. It was also determined that this type of bullet was used in a Heckler and Koch G3 (very powerful) assault rifle. The information that the FBI did not release, however, was whether the United States had supplied the Salvadoran military with these rifles and ammunition.

[3] Rogers and Bowdler 10.

[4] United States, Department of State, "Press Statement: El Salvador" (Washington D.C.: n.p., 17 Dec. 1980) 1-2.

[5] United Nations, Commission on the Truth for El Salvador, *From Madness to Hope: The 12-Year War in El Salvador* (New York: United Nations, 1993) 5.

[6] United Nations, Commission on the Truth for El Salvador 6.

[7] Carrigan 294.

[8] El Salvador, National Guard, *Preliminary Investigation*, trans. Department of State Language Services (San Salvador: n.p., 10 Feb. 1982) 69-73.

[9] United Nations, Commission on the Truth for El Salvador 6.

[10] United Nations, Commission on the Truth for El Salvador 7.

[11] Tyler 10.

[12] Tyler 63.

[13] United Nations, Commission on the Truth for El Salvador. The five guardsmen remain in prison today because the Salvadoran Supreme Court ruled that the killings of the women were *not* political, and therefore, not covered by the amnesty passed by the Salvadoran National Assembly in 1992.

[14] United Nations, Commission on the Truth for El Salvador 9-10.

[15] United Nations, Commission on the Truth for El Salvador 7.

[16] Maria Imelda Hernandez, personal interview, 21 June 1992.

[17] Jaime Eduardo Alvarez Burgos, personal interview, 24 June 1992.

[18] Teresa Arias de Gutierrez, personal interview, 18 June 1992.

[19] Archbishop Arturo Rivera y Damas, personal interview, 24 June 1992.

[20] "Adelante" means "to go forward," or to keep going.

Selected Sources

Primary

I. DOROTHY KAZEL PAPERS

The following papers are contained in the Sister Dorothy Kazel Collection which is housed in the archives of the Ursuline Sisters of Cleveland, Pepper Pike, Ohio. The collection also includes Sister Dorothy's personal belongings (childhood mementos, books, artifacts from El Salvador, and articles of clothing), condolences sent to the Kazel family and the Ursuline Sisters of Cleveland at the time of Sister Dorothy's death, letters, newspaper and periodical articles, and other documents relating to the murder of the four Churchwomen and its political implications, audio-visual and other materials on various topics connected to Sister Dorothy, El Salvador, and the events of December 2, 1980, and testimonies and tributes to Sister Dorothy.

Diaries
Costa Rica Diary. 24 Aug.-24 Nov. 1974.
El Salvador Diary. 29 July-23 Aug. 1974.
High School Diary. 1956.
Papago Mission Diary. 15 June-8 Aug. 1969.

Journals (Bound)
Journal 1. Aug. 1961-Feb. 1962.
Journal 2. Aug. 1963-Jan. 1964.
Journal 3. Jan. 1964-Mar. 1965.
Journal 4. Jan. 1965-Aug. 1967.
Journal 5. July 1968-June 1972.
Journal 6. 10-17 June 1973.
Journal 7. 1973.
Journal 8. Jan. 1974-Apr. 1974.
Journal 9. June 1974.
Journal 10. 14-19 June 1975.
Journal 11. Oct. 1976-Nov. 1979.

Journals (Unbound)
Aphorism (A). N.d.
Aphorism (B). N.d.
Aphorism (C). N.d.
Beaumont School for Girls (A). 24 June 1974.
Beaumont School for Girls (B). 4 July 1974.
Canonical Retreat Resolutions. 3 Feb. 1962.

Final Profession Summer. 13 June 1968.
First Profession Retreat Resolutions. 7 Aug. 1963.
Juniorate Retreat Resolutions. 20 Jan. 1965.
Sacred Heart Academy (A). 27 Aug. 1965.
Sacred Heart Academy (B). 29 Aug. 1965.
Sacred Heart Academy (C). 1 Sept. 1965.
Sacred Heart Academy (D). 3 Sept. 1965.
Sacred Heart Academy (E). 1 Nov. 1970.
Sacred Heart Academy (F). 9 May 1970.
Sacred Heart Academy (G). Sept. 1970.

Letters (Manuscript)*
Sisters of Beaumont Convent. 10 May 1976.
President Jimmy Carter. 23 Sept. 1980.
Diocese of Cleveland. 18 Mar. 1977.
Diocese of Cleveland. June 1977.
Diocese of Cleveland. Nov. 1980.
Family and Friends. 20-30 Jan. 1980.
Theresa Kane, R.S.M. 6 Oct. 1980.
James Kazel. Nov. 1980.
Joseph and Malvina Kazel. 30 July 1974.
Joseph and Malvina Kazel. 9 Oct. 1980.
Joseph and Malvina Kazel. 30 Oct. 1980.
Joseph and Malvina Kazel. 2 Nov. 1980.
M. Bartholomew McCaffrey, O.S.U. Nov. 1979.
M. Bartholomew McCaffrey, O.S.U. 15 Feb. 1980.
Martha Owen, O.S.U. 3 Oct. 1979.
Martha Owen, O.S.U. 5 Sept. 1980.
Martha Owen, O.S.U. 5 Nov. 1980.
Martha Owen, O.S.U. 28 Nov. 1980.
Sheila Marie Tobbe, O.S.U. 2 Oct. 1979.
M. Annunciata Witz, O.S.U. 4 Nov. 1967.
Ursuline Sisters of Cleveland: Application Form. 29 June 1960.
Ursuline Sisters of Cleveland: Ministry Preference Form. 4 Feb. 1980.
* Besides these listed, approximately another 115 letters survive.

Letters (Audiocassette)
Sisters of Beaumont Convent. Aug. 5,10-11. 1974.
James and Dorothy Kazel. 17, 21 Feb. 1979.
Joseph and Malvina Kazel. 31 July-2 Aug. 1974.
Joseph and Malvina Kazel. 12, 14-15, 17 Apr. 1975.
Joseph and Malvina Kazel. 11-12, 16 Dec. 1975.
Joseph and Malvina Kazel. 1, 3, 5 Mar. 1976.
Joseph and Malvina Kazel. 4, 7-8, 11-12 Dec. 1976.
Joseph and Malvina Kazel. 15, 17, 19 Oct. 1978.
Joseph and Malvina Kazel. 16-17 July 1979.

Joseph and Malvina Kazel. 3-5 June 1980.
Joseph and Malvina Kazel. 24, 26 Oct. 1980.
Joseph and Malvina Kazel. 14-15 Nov. 1980.
Martha Owen, O.S.U. 9-10 Aug. 1979.
Martha Owen, O.S.U. 29 Aug. 1979.
Martha Owen, O.S.U. 6, 10-11 Jan. 1980.
Martha Owen, O.S.U. 28, 30 Mar. 1980.
Martha Owen, O.S.U. 1-2, 4-5 June 1980.
Martha Owen, O.S.U. 21, 23-24 Oct. 1980.
*Besides these listed, approxomately another 25 audiocassettes survive.

Notebooks/Photograph Albums
Autograph Book. 16 May 1950.
Notebook of College Course Notes. Feb.-July 1963.
Photograph Album. June 1953-Dec. 1955.
Photograph Album. Dec. 1955-Apr. 1956.
Photograph Album. June 1969 (Topawa, Arizona)-June 1970
    (Cape Cod, Massachusetts)
Photograph Album. July 29-Aug. 23, 1974. (El Salvador); Aug. 24-Dec. 13, 1974
    (Costa Rica); Dec. 14-31, 1974 (El Salvador).
Photograph Album. Jan. 1975-Feb. 1976 (El Salvador).
Photograph Album. Feb. 1976-Nov.1976 (El Salvador and Guatemala).
Photograph Album. Nov. 1976-July 1977 (El Salvador and Guatemala).
Photograph Album. July 1977-May 1978 (El Salvador).
Photograph Album. Oct. 1977-Jan. 1978 (El Salvador, Costa Rica, Peru).
Photograph Album. Jan. 1978-July 1978 (El Salvador and Guatemala).
Photograph Album. July 1978-Oct. 1978 (El Salvador, Guatemala, New Orleans,
    Washington, D.C.).
Photograph Album. Dec. 1978-Jan. 1979 (El Salvador, Guatemala).
Photograph Album. May 18-June 3, 1979 (California, Washington, Oregon, Canada).
Photograph Album. Sept.-Nov. 1979 (El Salvador).
Photograph Album. Dec. 1979 (El Salvador).
Photograph Album. Feb.-Aug. 1980 (El Salvador, Belize, Guatemala, New York).

II. INTERVIEWS

Teresa Alexander, M.M., Jaime Eduardo Alvarez Burgos, Teresa Arias de Gutierrez, Rev. Josepe A. Bacevice, the late M. Helene Balciunas, O.S.F., Eileen Best, Eugene Best, Kathleen Burke, O.S.U., Maria Sofía Caceres, O.C.J., Maria Ermina Chaves Serrano, Victor Chicas, Kathleen Cooney, O.S.U., Mary Catherine Cummins, O.S.U., Helen Marie Davidson, O.S.U., Margaret Dillon, M.M., Madeline Dorsey, M.M., Cynthia Drennan, M. Kenan Dulzer, O.S.U., Marilyn Friga, Rev. John Garrity, Rev. William Gibbons, M.D., Anna Margaret Gilbride, O.S.U., Marie Michelle Gouttiere, O.S.U., Frances Harbert, Patricia Healey, Rev. Ernest Hepner, Ph.D., Maria Imelda Hernandez, James Cardinal Hickey, S.T.D., J.C.D., Rosemary Jackson, Dorothy

Chapon Kazel, James Kazel, Malvina Kazel, Lucy Marie Kazlauskas, O.S.F., M. Owen Kleinhenz, S.N.D., Donald Kollenborn, Ann Letitia Kostiha, O.S.U., Mary Jo Lackamp, Margaret La Ganke, José Alfredo Lopez, Ann Marie Lostoski, O.S.F., Patricia Maresco, Benita de Jesus Martínez de Ramos, Victoria Martínez de Melendez, M. Bartholomew McCaffrey, O.S.U., Rev. James McCreight, Darlene McNamara, Maria del Rosario Mendez de Heron, Mary Anne Metalonis, Julie Miller, M.M., Martha Mooney, O.S.U., Maria Moore, M.M., Patricia Murray, M.M., Rev. Kenneth Myers, Catherine O'Malley, S.N.D., Martha Owen, O.S.U., Muriel Petrasek, S.N.D., Andres Piñeda, Julio Cesar Pocasangre Iraheta, Teresa de Jesus Portillo de Flores, Natalie Radauskas, Susan Mary Rathbun, O.S.U., Manuel de Jesus Reyes, Teresa de Jesus Gonzalez Reyes, C.S.J., the late Archbishop Arturo Rivera y Damas, Maria Rosa Rivera, Marta Rodriguez, Rev. Eldon Reichert, S.M., Christine Rody, V.S.C., Rev. Denis St. Marie, Rev. Paul Schindler, Loretta Schulte, C.S.J., Barbara Jean Sever, O.S.U., Russell Smith, Rev. John Spain, M.M., Mary Tadsen, O.S.U., Mercita Thailing, Sheila Marie Tobbe, O.S.U., Robert E. White, Anita Whitely, O.S.U., Agnes Kathryn Wilson, O.S.F., Rev. Alfred Winters, Ann Winters, O.S.U., M. Annunciata Witz, O.S.U., Donna Zaller, Angelita Zawada, O.S.U.

III. OTHER

Alexander, Teresa. "Sister Dorothy Kazel, O.S.U." Tenth-Anniversary Celebration of the Martyrdom of Dorothy Kazel, O.S.U. Ursuline College, Pepper Pike, 5 Dec. 1990.

Blacken, John D. Letter to Dorothy Kazel, O.S.U. 7 Nov. 1980.

Carroll, Paul. *A Report on the Investigation into the Killing of Four American Churchwomen in El Salvador.* New York: The Lawyers Committee for International Human Rights, Sept. 1981.

Chronicle. Sacred Heart Academy, East Cleveland, Aug. 1965-Aug. 1969.

Cooney, Kathleen. "Reasons for Staying in a Religious Congregation from the Viewpoint of Women Who Entered Between 1945 and 1975." DAI 49 (1988): 952 A.

Cuellar, Carlos Ortiz. Autopsy Report, ts. Trans. Martha Owen, O.S.U. San Salvador: 4 Dec. 1980.

Elementary School Report Cards. St. George School, Cleveland, 1948-51.

El Salvador. National Guard. *Preliminary Investigation.* Trans. Department of State Language Services. San Salvador: n.p., 10 Feb. 1982.

Kazel, Malvina. Kazel Family Photograph Album. 1951.

Kenny, James. Letter to the Diocese of Cleveland. Apr. 1980.

Kollenborn, Donald. Letter to Dorothy Kazel. Feb. 1960.

—. Letter to Dorothy Kazel. 19 Aug. 1960.

Mertens, Mary Jane. Letter to Mary Eileen Boyle, O.S.U., 26 Sept. 1992.

Mury, Joan. Letter to Joseph and Malvina Kazel. 25 Jan. 1981.

North Central Association of Colleges and Secondary Schools, *Beaumont School for*

Girls Summary of 1974-76 Self-Study. Ohio: North Central Association of Colleges and Secondary Schools, 2, 6-7 Dec. 1976.

Permanent Record. Notre Dame Academy, Cleveland, 1953-57.

Record of Study. St. John College, Cleveland, 1957-60.

Rogers, William D., and William G. Bowdler. *Report to the President: Special Mission to El Salvador. Washington D.C.: n.p., 12 Dec. 1980.*

Rolla-Revels of 1955. 29-31 Jan. 1955.

Romero, Oscar A. Letter to President Jimmy Carter. Trans. Cleveland Latin American Mission Team. 17 Feb. 1980.

Roonan, Ellen. Telegram to Dorothy Kazel, O.S.U. 13 Aug. 1968.

Schindler, Paul. Letter to the Diocese of Cleveland. Sept. 1980.

Transcript. Ursuline College, Cleveland, 1960-65.

Tyler, Harold. *The Churchwomen Murders: A Report to the Secretary of State*. New York: n.p., 2 Dec. 1983.

United Nations. Commission on the Truth for El Salvador. *From Madness to Hope: The 12-Year War in El Salvador*. New York: United Nations, March 1993.

United States Catholic Missionaries. Letter to President Jimmy Carter. 20 Feb. 1980.

United States. Department of State. "Press Statement: El Salvador." Washington D.C.: n.p., 17 Dec. 1980.

Wagner, Joseph. Letter to Mother Marie Sands, O.S.U., 23 May 1960.

Warburg, Philip, and James Zorn. *Justice in El Salvador: A Case Study, A Report on the Investigation into the Killing of Four U.S. Churchwomen in El Salvador.* New York: The Lawyers Committee for International Human Rights, 20 July 1982.

Witchner, M. Vincent de Paul. "Sister Dorothy Kazel." Reflection at Eucharistic Celebration of the Fifth Anniversary of the Martyrdom of Dorothy Kazel, O.S.U. Ursuline Motherhouse, Pepper Pike, 2 Dec. 1985.

Secondary

Abbott, Walter M., ed. *The Documents of Vatican II: All Sixteen Official Texts Promulgated by the Ecumenical Council, 1963-65*. Trans. Very Rev. Msgr. Joseph Gallagher. New York: American, 1966.

Brockman, James R. *Romero: A Life*. New York: Orbis, 1989.

Carmody, John. "Vatican II Spirituality." *The Westminster Dictionary of Christian Spirituality*. Ed. Gordon S. Wakefield. Philadelphia: Westminster, 1983.

Carrigan, Ana. *Salvador Witness: The Life and Calling of Jean Donovan*. New York: Simon and Schuster, 1984.

"Final Day of October Set for Living Rosary Devotion." *The Tower* 21 Oct. 1955: 1.

Harmer, Catherine M. *Religious Life in the 21st Century: A Contemporary Journey into Canaan*. Mystic: Twenty-Third, 1995.

Hearon, M. Michael Francis. *The Broad Highway: A History of the Ursuline Nuns in The Diocese of Cleveland, 1850-1950*. Cleveland: The Ursuline Sisters, 1951.

—. Look to This Day: Ursuline Frontiers and Horizons, 1950-75. Cleveland: Western, 1975.

Horner, Martina S. Foreward. *Simone Weil: A Modern Pilgrimage.* By Robert Coles. Reading: Addison-Wesley, 1987. IX.

Leckey, Dolores R. Introduction. *Women and Creativity.* By Leckey. Mahwah: Paulist, 1991. 1-5.

Loya, John F. *Gifts from the Poor.* Nashville: Winston-Derek, 1990.

Mandell, Gail Porter. *Life into Art: Conversations with Seven Contemporary Biographers.* Fayettville: U. Of Arkansas P, 1991.

McFadden, John, and Ruth Warner, trans. Translators' Preface. *Archbishop Romero: Martyr of Salvador.* By Placido Erdozain. Costa Rica: Departmento Ecumenico de Investigaciones, 1980. New York: Orbis, 1981. xxi-xxiii.

Neal, Maria Augusta. *From Nuns to Sisters: An Expanding Vocation.* Mystic: Twenty-Third, 1990.

Noone, Judith M. *The Same Fate as the Poor.* Rev. ed. New York: Orbis, 1995.

Papa, Mary Badar. "'Fight Sexism, Paternalism in Church'—Kane." *National Catholic Reporter.* 5 Sept. 1980: 1, 23.

Santiago, Daniel. "The Peace Progress in El Salvador (A Hermeneutic of Suspicion)." *America* 11 Jan. 1992: 14-16, 20.

"Second Vatican Council." *The Oxford Dictionary of the Christian Church.* 2nd ed. 1990.

Seracino, Pamela. "Her Passion Perseveres." *Catholic Peace Voice* Summer 1996:7.

"SSCA Leads Teenagers to Catholic Activeness." *The Tower.* 18 Oct. 1956: 3.

Transformative Elements for Religious Life in the Future. Louisville: Joint CMSM/LCWR Assembly, 1989.

Ursuline Mission Services. Nov.-Dec. 1974: 3-4.

Woolf, Virginia. *Collected Essays.* Vol. 4. New York: Harcourt, 1967.

Acknowledgments

I am deeply grateful to the following people:

- Mrs. Malvina Kazel, James and Dorothy Kazel, Martha Owen, O.S.U., and Sheila Marie Tobbe, O.S.U. for their generous contributions of letters, photographs, and research materials;

- Martha Owen, O.S.U., Sheila Marie Tobbe, O.S.U., Fran Harbert, and Christine Rody, V.S.C., upon whom I called countless numbers of times for information and clarifications;

- Martha Owen, O.S.U., who served as my guide and translator when I traveled to El Salvador, and Kate O'Brien, O.S.U., and Jean Iffarth, O.S.U., who accompanied me in my research trips to various parts of the United States;

- Dorothy's family, friends, and acquaintances who so graciously complied with my request for an interview;

- Joann Kessler, O.S.U., and M. Bartholomew McCaffrey, O.S.U., archivists of my Cleveland Ursuline Congregation, for their quick, efficient response to my requests for information and materials;

- Grace Krieger, M.M., archivist of the Maryknoll Sisters, for her cooperation;

- Julie Fekete, Cleveland Diocesan Mission Office, for her invaluable assistance;

- M. Denis Maher, C.S.A., for her knowledgeable suggestions, particularly those regarding book publication;

- Ann Trivisonno and Celeste Wiggins, my friends in the Ursuline College English Department, Cleveland, Ohio, for their interest and encouragement;

- Ursuline College, for the financial support it has given me during the past four years;

- Marie Powers, Ursuline College Bookstore, Judith Berzinsky and Myra Fortlage, Ralph M. Besse Library, Ursuline College, and Eva Hendricks, Office Services, Ursuline College, for their efficient, knowledgeable assistance;

- Joanne Gross, O.S.U., for carefully editing the final draft of my manuscript and for helping to compile the index;

- Teresa Sullivan, Elaine Langlais, Christine Schwartz, and Amy Krzywicki for their help in preparing my manuscript for publication;

- Thomas P. Coffey, President of Dimension Books, Inc., for his openness and flexibility;

- Cleveland Ursuline congregational leadership, both present and past, for their support: Virginia DeVinne, Ritamary Welsh, Jean Iffarth, Angelita Zawada, Ann Kelly, Maureen McCarthy, Dorothy Bondi, Carolyn Clines, Rose Angela Johnson, Eileen Collins, and Julianne McCauley;

- Sisters of my Cleveland Ursuline Congregation whose encouragement, interest, and prayers sustained me through long hours of research and writing;

- Alice Philbin, Ellen E. Berry, Philip G. Terry, Allan Emery, and Christopher Morris, members of my dissertation committee at Bowling Green State University, who supported me in this project from its beginnings seven years ago;

- my family and friends for their concern, interest, and patience.

INDEX